Buried New England

A Pilgrimage Connecting Past and Present

CASEY FREDETTE

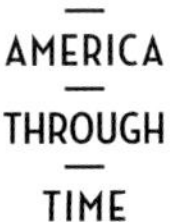

America Through Time®
An imprint of Sutton Publishing Inc.
www.through-time.com

First published 2025

ISBN 978-1-63499-538-2

Typeset in 10pt on13pt Sabon
Printed and bound in England

Contents

INTRODUCTION

The history of New England is one that is known, to some extent, far and wide. This area of the American Northeast has been the backdrop to pivotal historic moments. The region has seen some of the country's best and worst moments played out in front of the world, from the Boston Massacre to the Boston Marathon Bombing. New England is an area that has produced the people who have helped shape and shift the world, and it has acted as the cradle to a nation that would grow to be a leading superpower. A journey inside the graveyards and cemeteries of the region allows one to witness the monuments of those who were, those who did, and those whose names are now synonymous with history. Inside the gates of the grand cemeteries of New England, you can see masterpieces of art and sculpture used to commemorate not only those who made so many ideas come to life but those who built a history strong enough that it was able to stand as a bridge to the future. Across these states, those of humble and noble backgrounds lay beside the poor and rich. In the shadows of grandiosity, those buried in the rocky New England soil, eventually, are all equalized by time.

Looking beyond the cemetery walls, a seemingly never-ending supply of family graveyards rises from the landscape. What once were backyard, farm, or private graveyards now stand alongside highways, byways, streets, and in the shadows of massive multistory buildings and even behind shopping malls. Those burial grounds and the people and memories held within them are constantly at war with the new modern New England; many lost to time and many more likely to meet the same fate. As these small monuments to families that were strong enough to prevail against diseases, wars, and, possibly worst of all, New England weather sit alongside one another, a broader and more significant theme emerges. Inside these six states that come together to make New England, with their shared history, experiences, and impact on the world, emerges a unique people among a multicultural country: New Englanders. These people who identify by their region before their home state or town, those who boast of comfort in the extreme temperatures of the region, those who take to the waters on New Year's Day to swim in single-digit temperatures, and those who gave all they had to guarantee a future for a country not yet fully imagined come together. While the cohesion of the states since European colonization has held together for centuries, there does remain one of many unknowns: can the dead, and perhaps more importantly the memory of those dead, continue to survive and be represented in an increasingly crowded region?

Looking back across its history, New England has produced many successful and notable people since it was colonized. These states have been home to presidents, senators, actors, farmers, industrialists, and enslaved peoples. It has watched as native people have been decimated and their lands minimized or destroyed. But this region, that so many are proud to be affiliated with, has also produced medical, technological, and geopolitical successes that have positively impacted not only its own region but the world over. An exploration into some of the more than 19,000 formal burial grounds and countless smaller plots shows the true story of New England. Away from the Freedom Trail in Boston, far off from Mystic and its legendary pizza, away from the skiing hills of New Hampshire and Vermont, and even the lobster shacks along Maine. This is a region that was difficult to inhabit and continues to subject those who call it home to dangerous weather, beautiful but frequently deadly waters, and the endlessly parodied accents of those from Boston, with their inability to use "R" in a word, and New Englanders whose people take names like "Emma" and relay them as "Emmer." In an ever-expanding world, these burial grounds, used for centuries as gathering areas for the bereaved, as arboretums and green spaces for those who live against a cityscape, and, above all else, a place for New Englanders to be laid to their final rest, have fought to protect their interred residents.

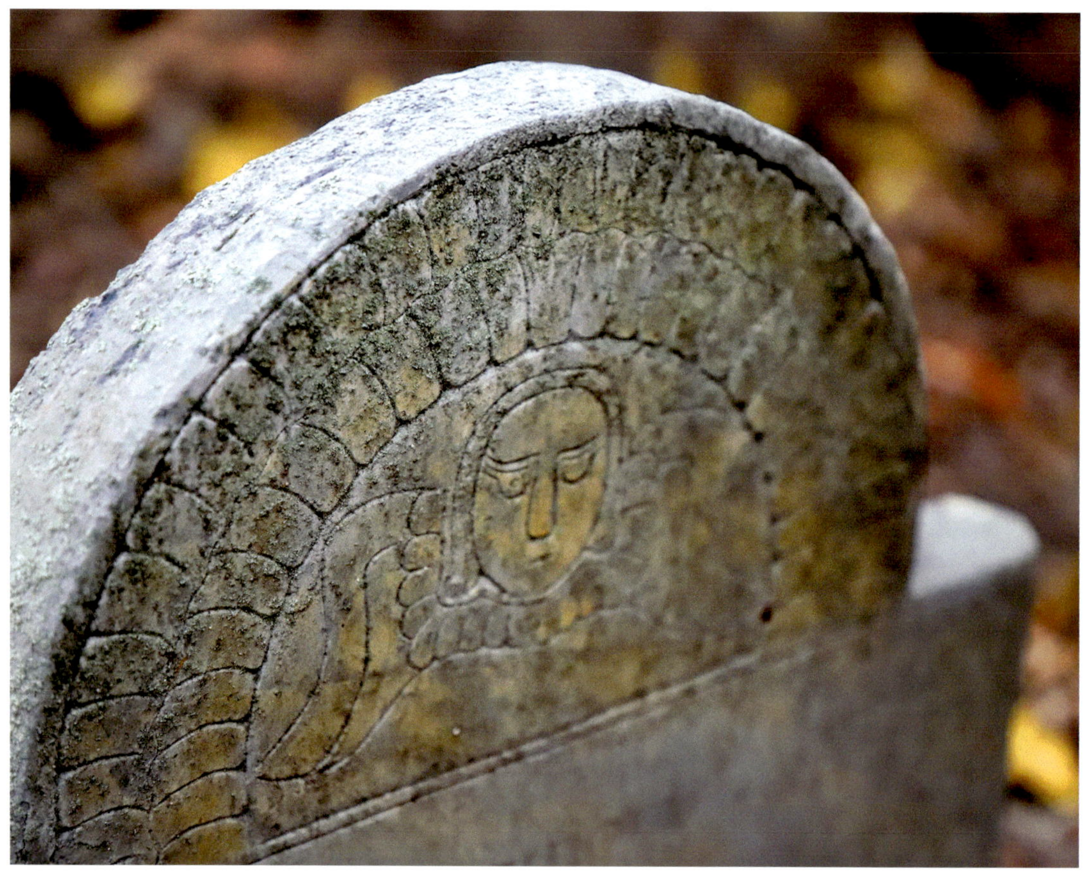

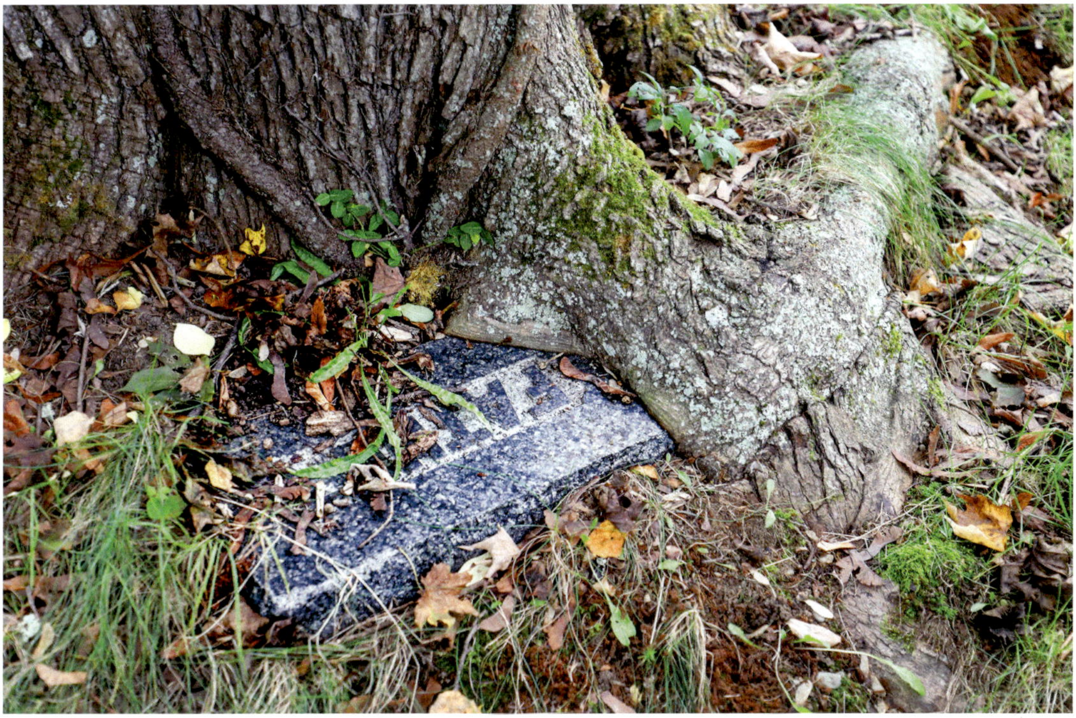

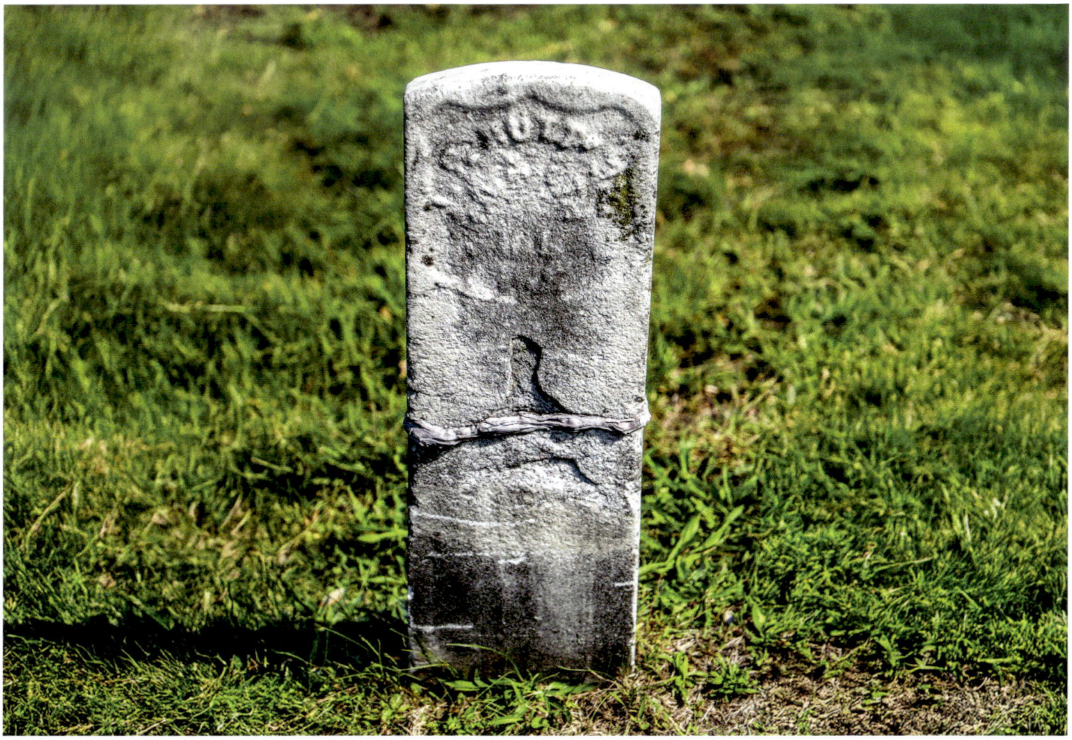

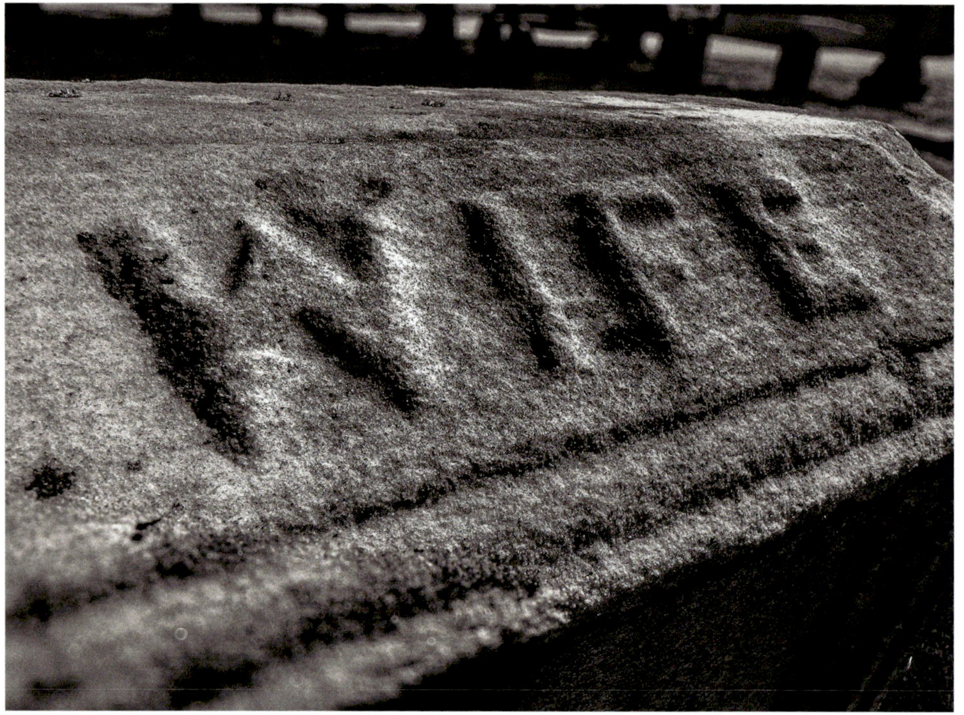

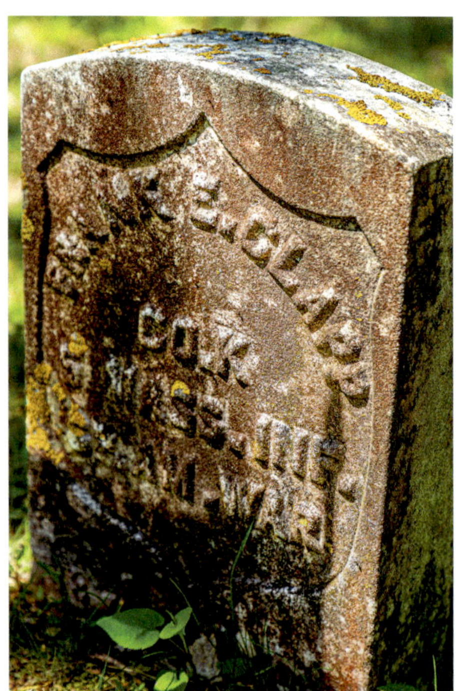

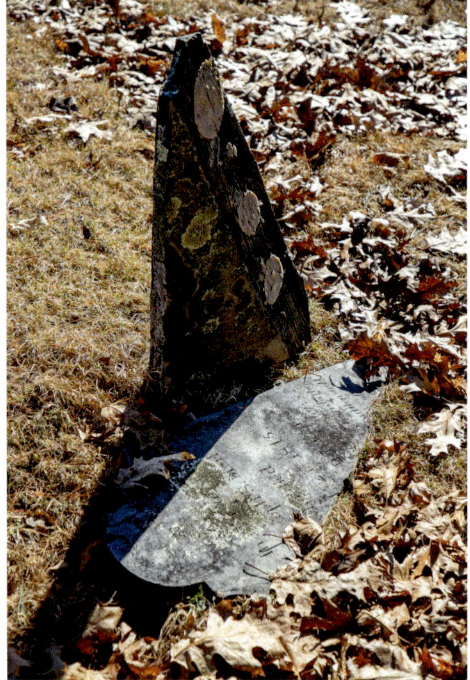

Above right: An attempt using an adhesive to reunify this grave has failed.

1
CONNECTICUT

The River Colony, Colony of Connecticut, The Constitution State, and the Nutmeg State

The fifth state admitted to the Union was also the first New England colony to join the new states. Having long been the home to indigenous peoples, the Great Atlantic Migration from Europe was a launching point for indigenous lands being lost to the new inhabitants. Initially, the Dutch established a trading post, capitalizing on the Connecticut River Valley. Beginning with less than a handful of villages making up the Colony of Connecticut, this state would eventually comprise 169 towns and nineteen cities. Hartford, Springfield, Wethersfield, and Windsor—the original settlements—became home to European settlers, who made their march south from the Massachusetts Bay Colony. The pastors were joined by their wives, children, and congregation as they set out for their newest home, thanks to a commission issued by the Massachusetts Bay Colony Courts.

With the ruling class in the eighteenth century practicing varieties of evolving Puritanism, this state saw significant changes. Having left behind Europe for the promise of this new world, so many risked it all to come to the shores of New England. Well into the 1700s, slavery was still being actively practiced. The practice, having begun at the end of the Pequot War, carried on across the first century. In a time where nearly half of all children born were lost quickly or did not reach adulthood, death was an active participant in the communities of the region. As the state of Connecticut pushed through the nineteenth century, the Civil War between the north and south was having a transformative impact on life across the young country. With many soldiers from Connecticut, both white and black, being shipped off to this war, the losses were unmatched in the state's history. What had long been a private family affair was no longer an option for the ever-growing dead of Connecticut in the second half of this century. In what likely seemed like an instant, the private grieving that had long been the norm in this society was shattered. Train after train arrived with dead fathers, husbands, sons, uncles, and neighbors. Their families were forced to endure their grief quite literally in the public square.

The nineteenth century expanded on the changes of the previous one. Small, crowded churchyard burying grounds could no longer provide for the growing society. Colonial burials, while monuments to the era in which they were erected, the peace and serenity those buried inside craved, were being encroached on. Rural cemeteries, burying grounds based outside of the busiest areas of the state, overtook the previous burial tradition, largely. The practice of embalming, having grown since its introduction during the war between the states, became a more common practice. Coffins, previously simple and plain boxes, became more varied. While practices from the previous centuries carried on, practical changes were happening, and then came the wars. World War I and II would drastically change funerals in New England. What were once small at home, intimate gatherings transitioned into more public episodes due to the overwhelming losses being returned home on the trains.

In modern times, Connecticut has seen a massive population growth; what were once small spaced-out settlements are today sprawling cities and towns. With the proximity to New York City, Connecticut has seen itself become something of a suburb. Today there are an estimated 5,000 graveyards and cemeteries across the state. Journeying across those spaces gives you access to the active history of Connecticut, its people, and its past. From the pilgrims of their day to the professors of Yale, these burial grounds offer an unparalleled opportunity to see the history of this state laid bare.

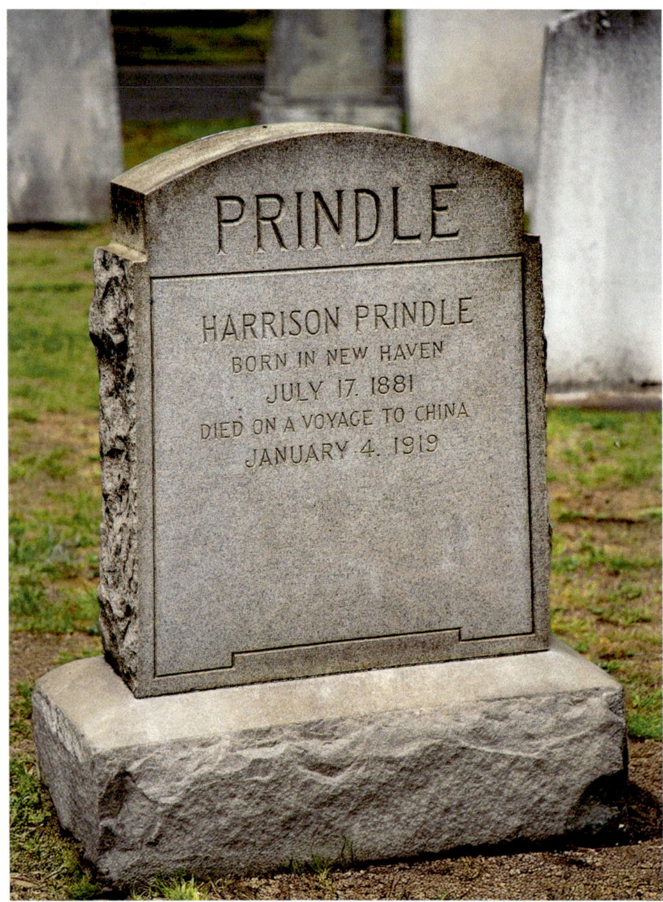

Harrison Prindle of New Haven, Connecticut, as his headstone states, died on a voyage to China. It is reported that he died close to Japan at thirty-seven years old.

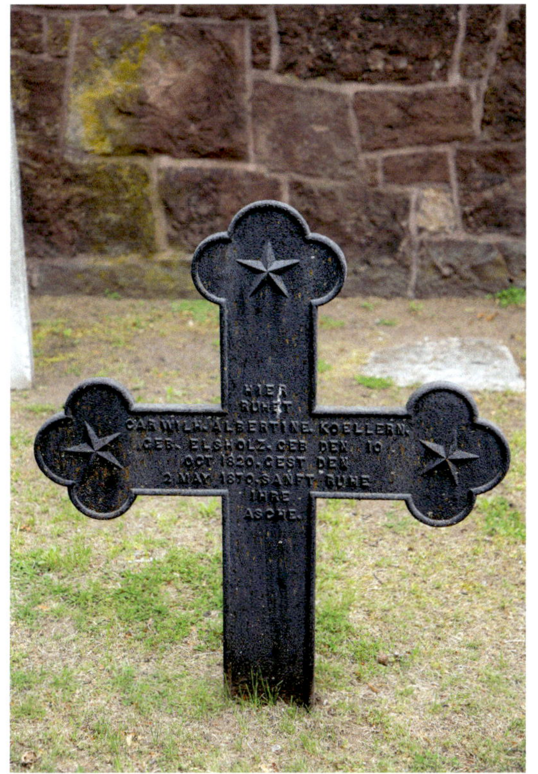

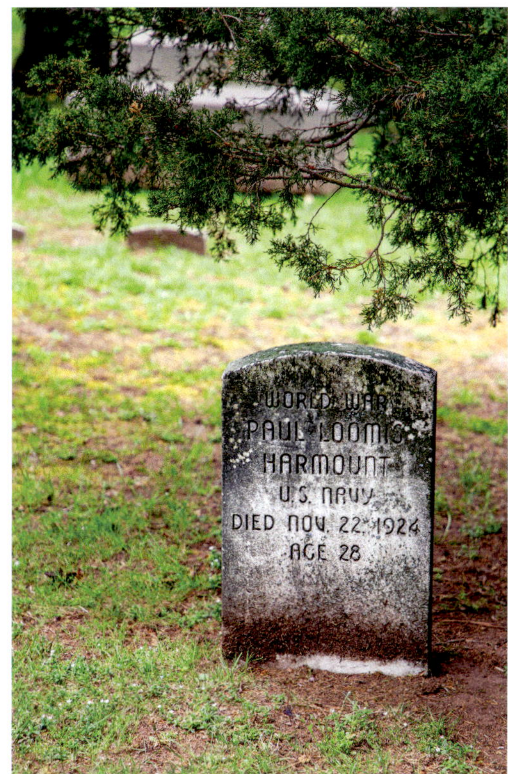

Above right: United States Navy veteran of the world war.

Right: The headstone seen here is a replacement for the original one that rests beneath.

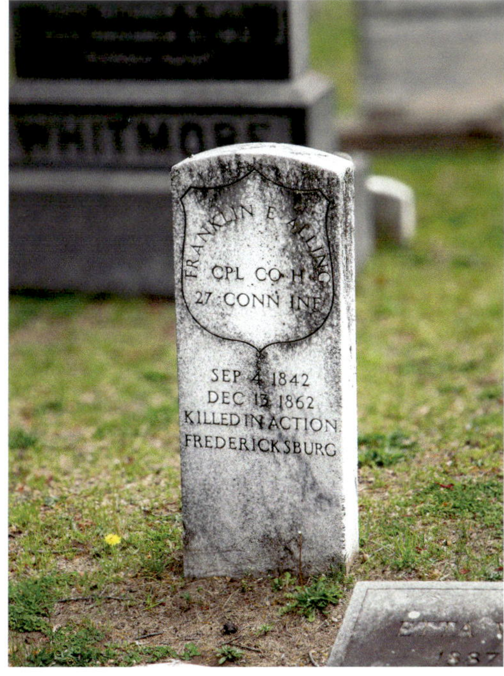

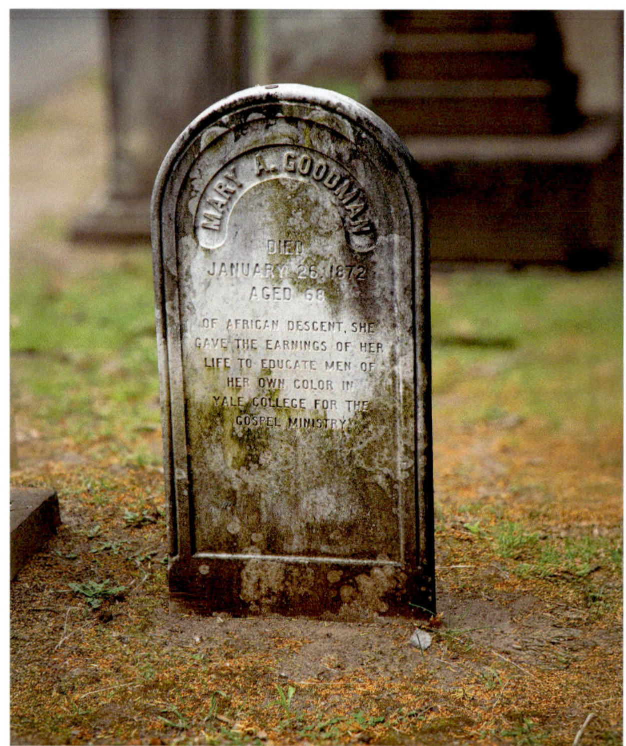

Left: Of African descent, this woman gave her life's earnings to educate men of her own color in Yale College for the gospel ministry.

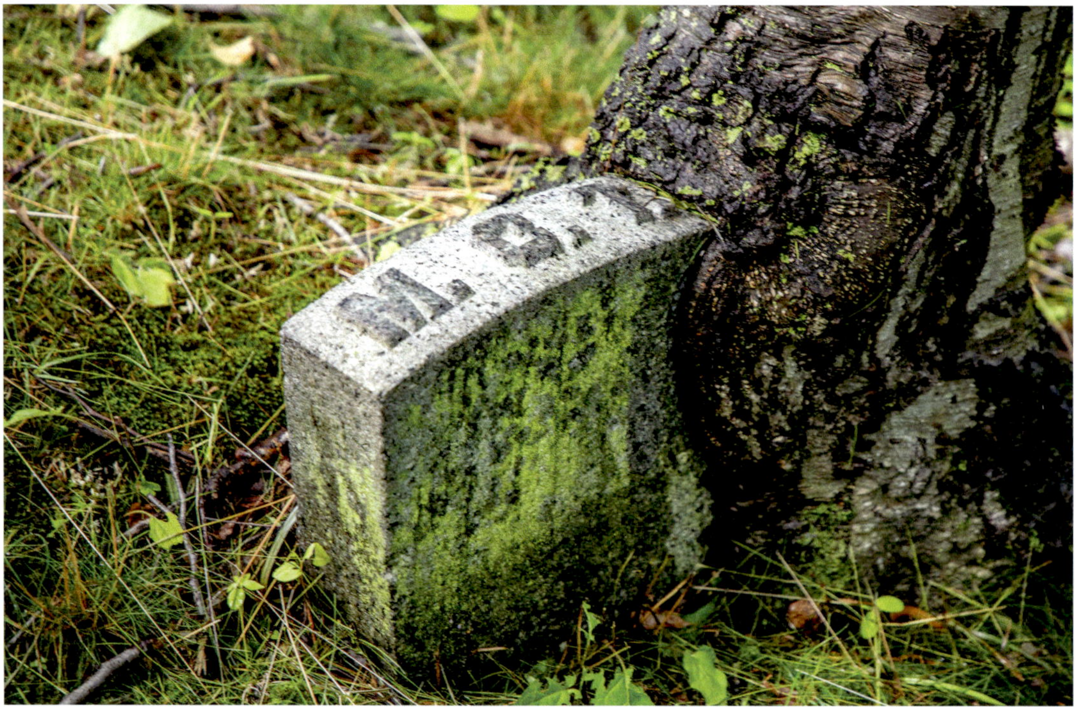

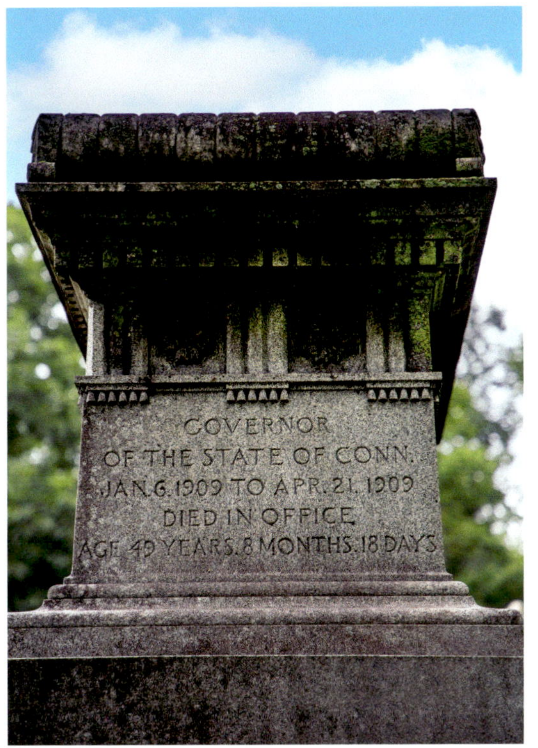

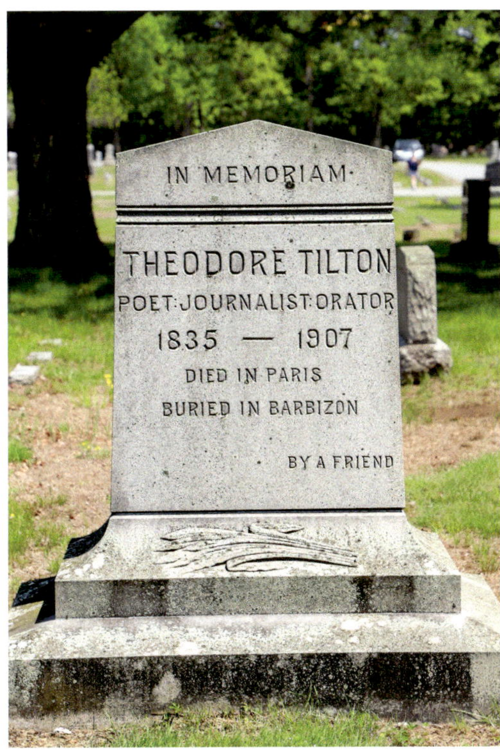

Above left: Governor George Leavens Lilley. In office from January 1909 until his death in April of the same year.

Above right: The poet, journalist, and orator died and was buried in France. Someone, "A Friend," nevertheless saw fit to stand up a memorial stone in Danielson, Connecticut.

Right: Rare poet and author Elizabeth Akers is remembered today thanks to her personal friend, Gilbert A. Tracey.

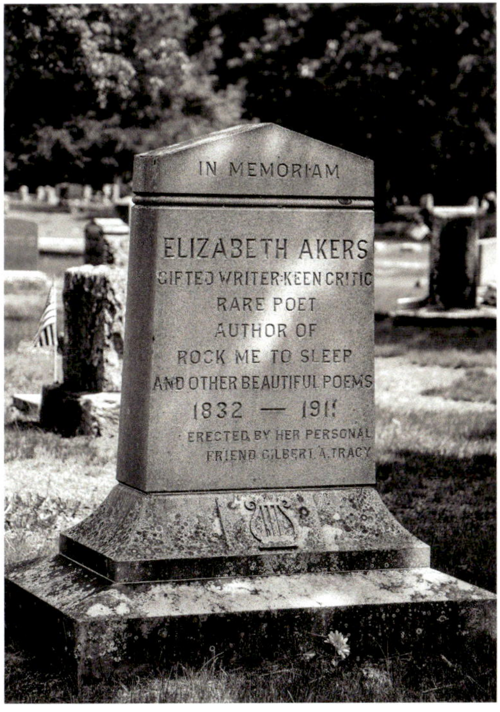

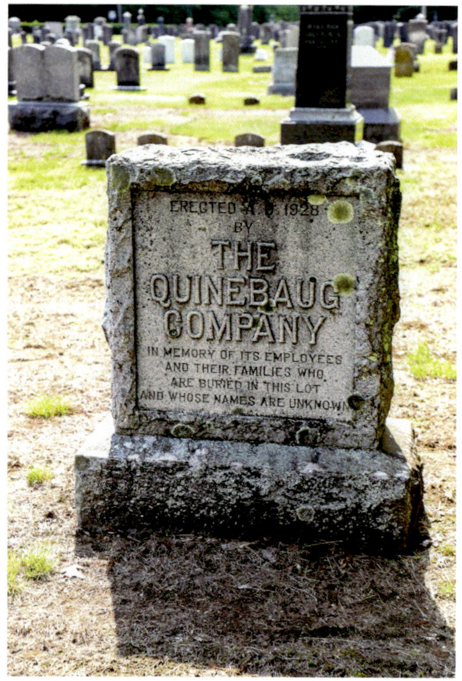

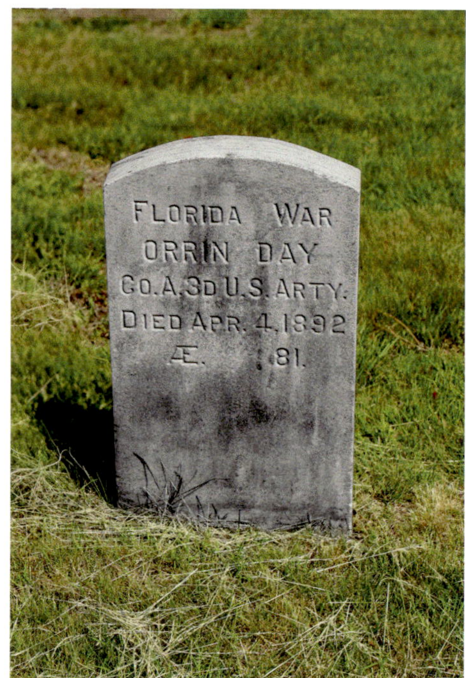

Above right: Veteran of the Florida War.

Below: "We Defend the Country"

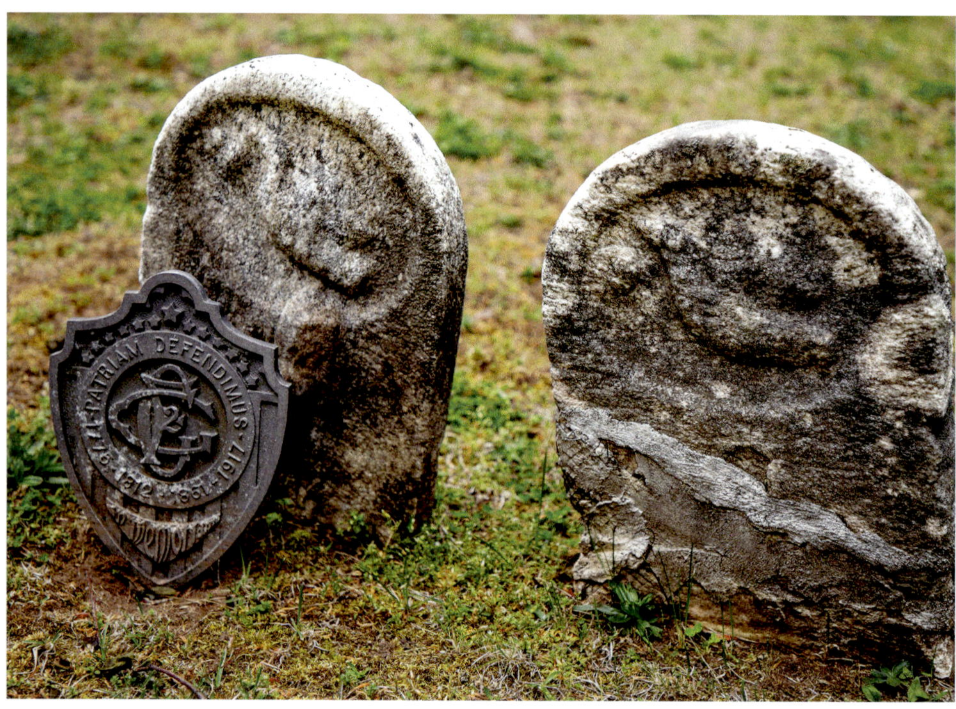

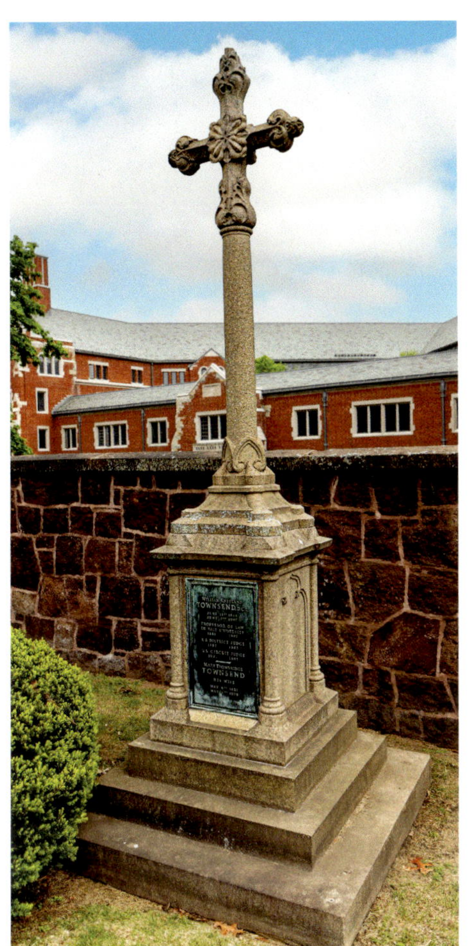

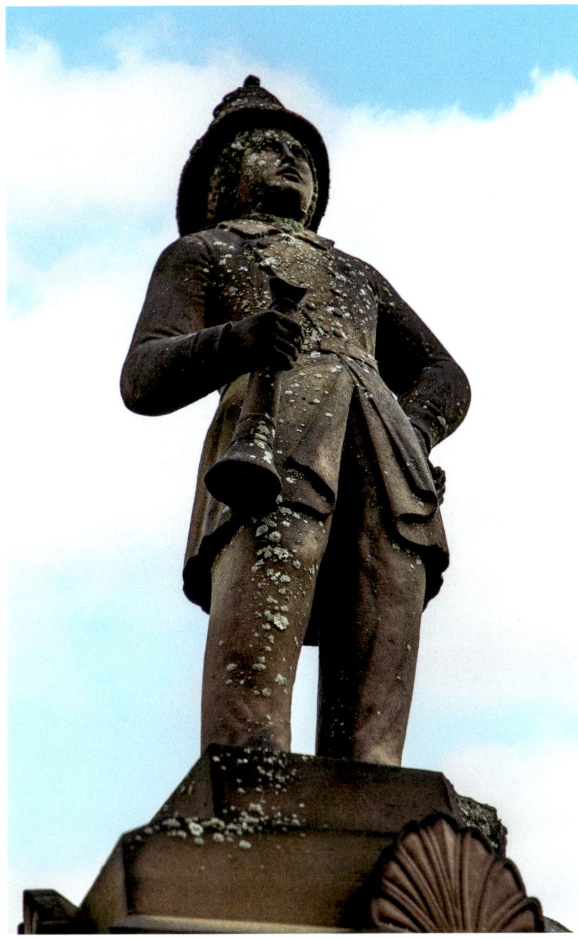

Above left: W. K. Townsend, professor of law in Yale, U.S. district judge, and U.S. circuit judge. M. T. Townsend, his wife.

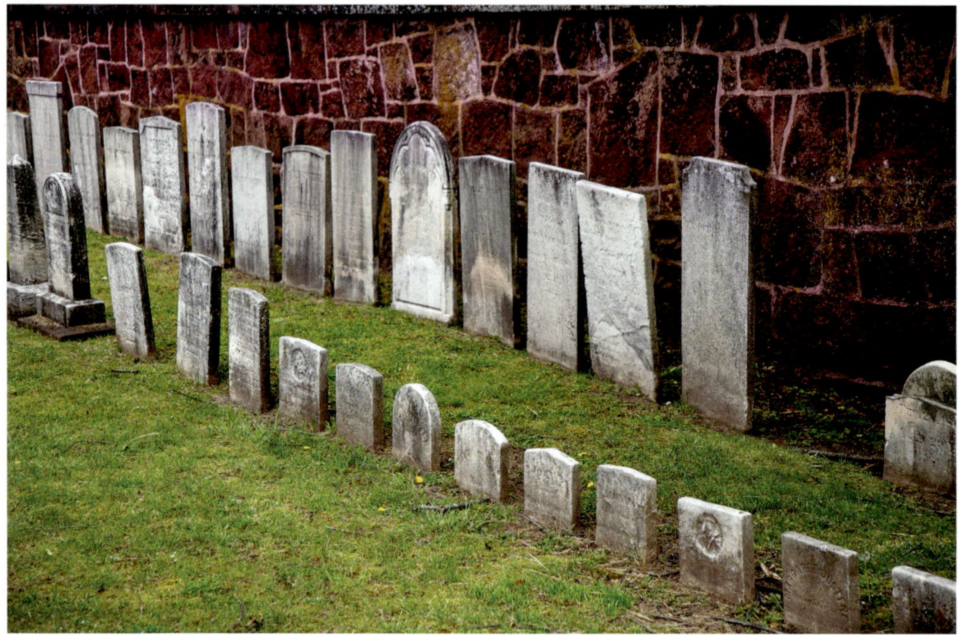

In the shadows of Yale University, Grove Street Cemetery in New Haven, Connecticut, is unsurprisingly a stunningly, beautiful space. In this cemetery, even the border walls are pretty.

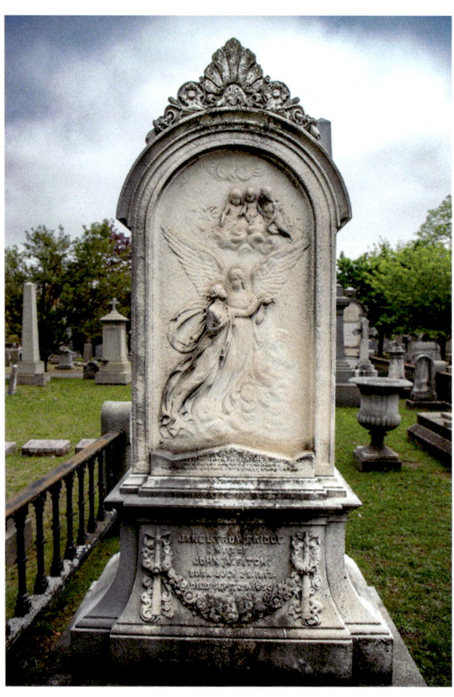

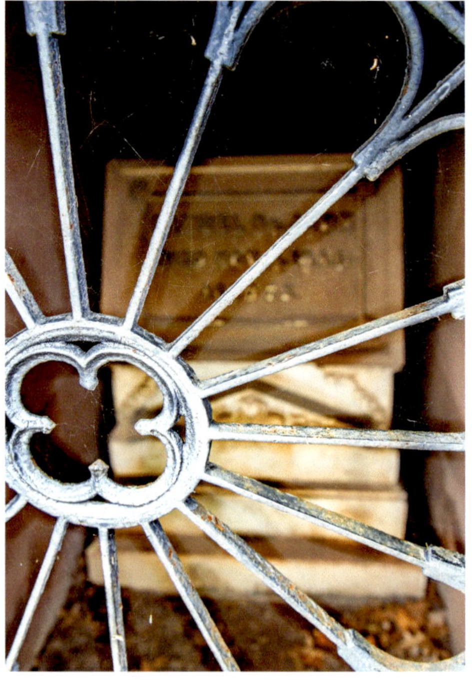

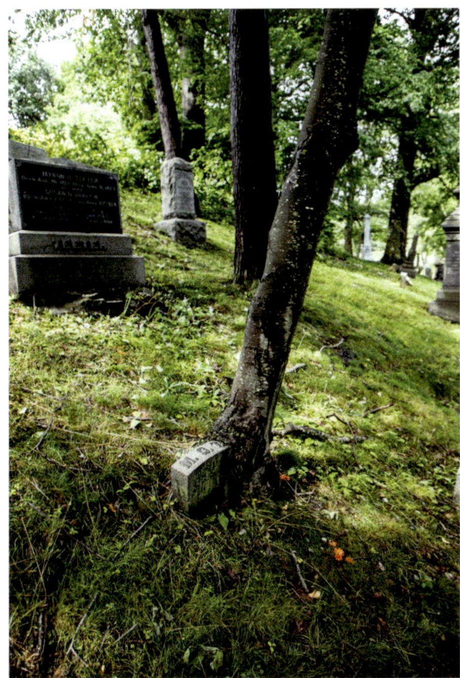

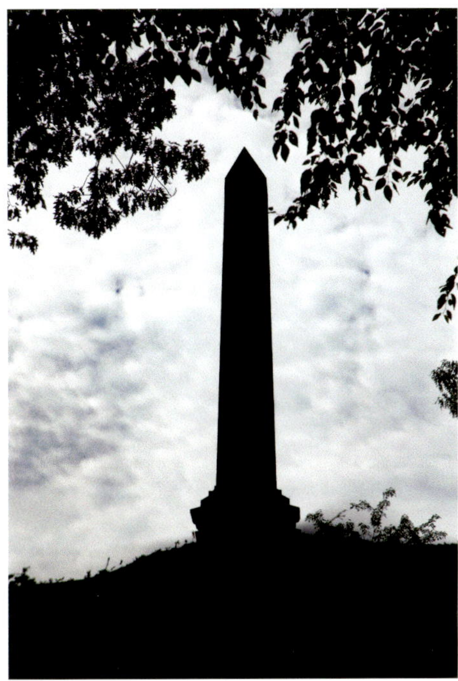

Above left: During the nineteenth century, New England burial spaces began designing cemeteries into arboretums. Started in Mount Auburn Cemetery and Arboretum in Cambridge, MA, it was a brilliant idea and fantastic way to revitalize open spaces into a garden feel. Obviously, having that many trees and graves leads to something of a competition.

Above right: Wisdom.

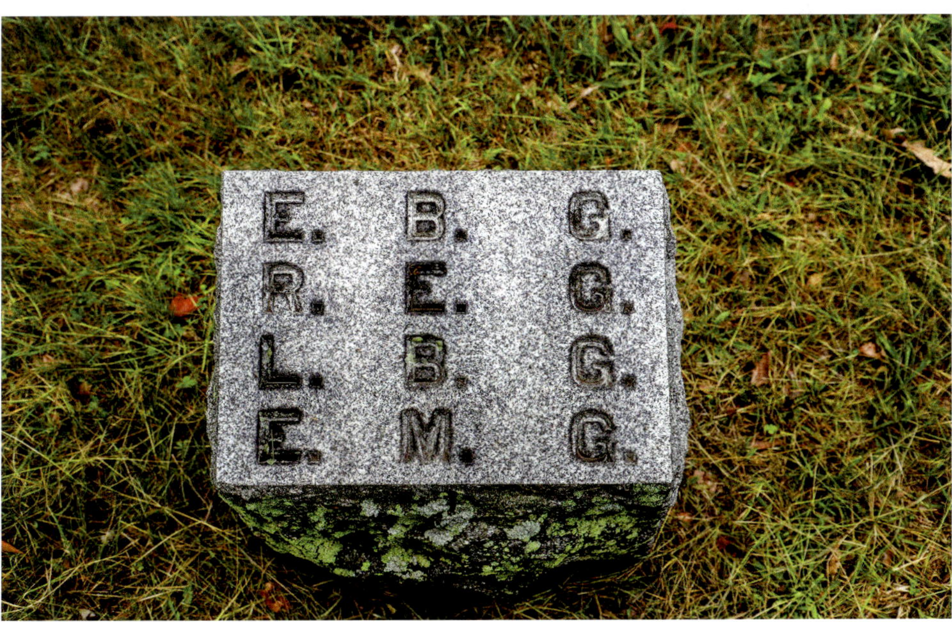

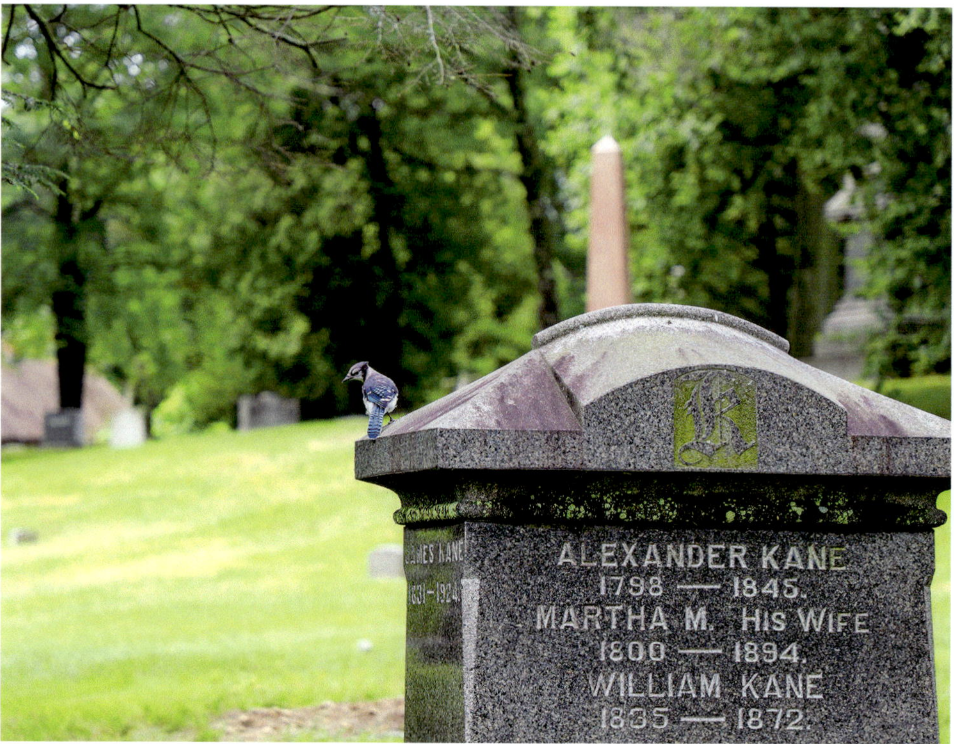

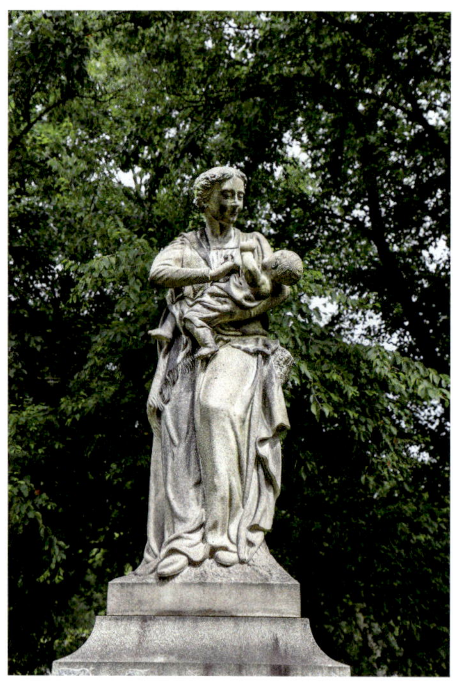

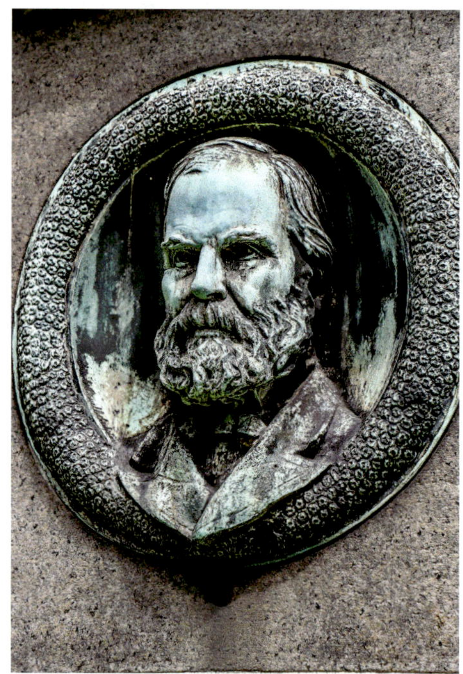

Above right: Hair parted and dearly departed.

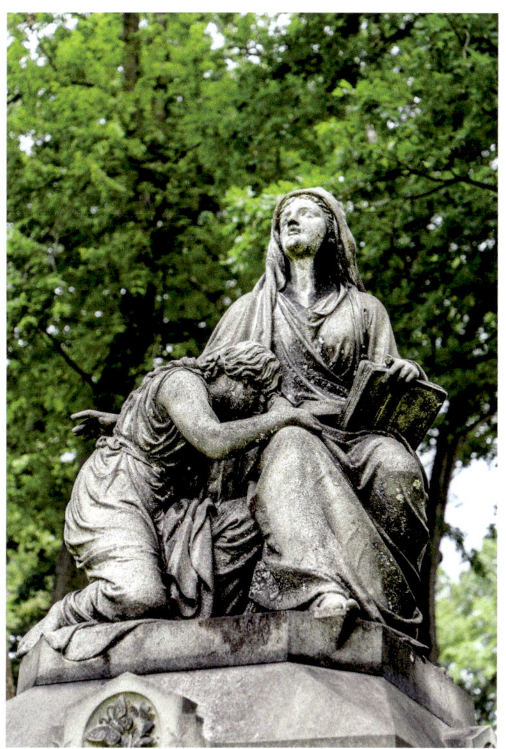

Below: Grave on high.

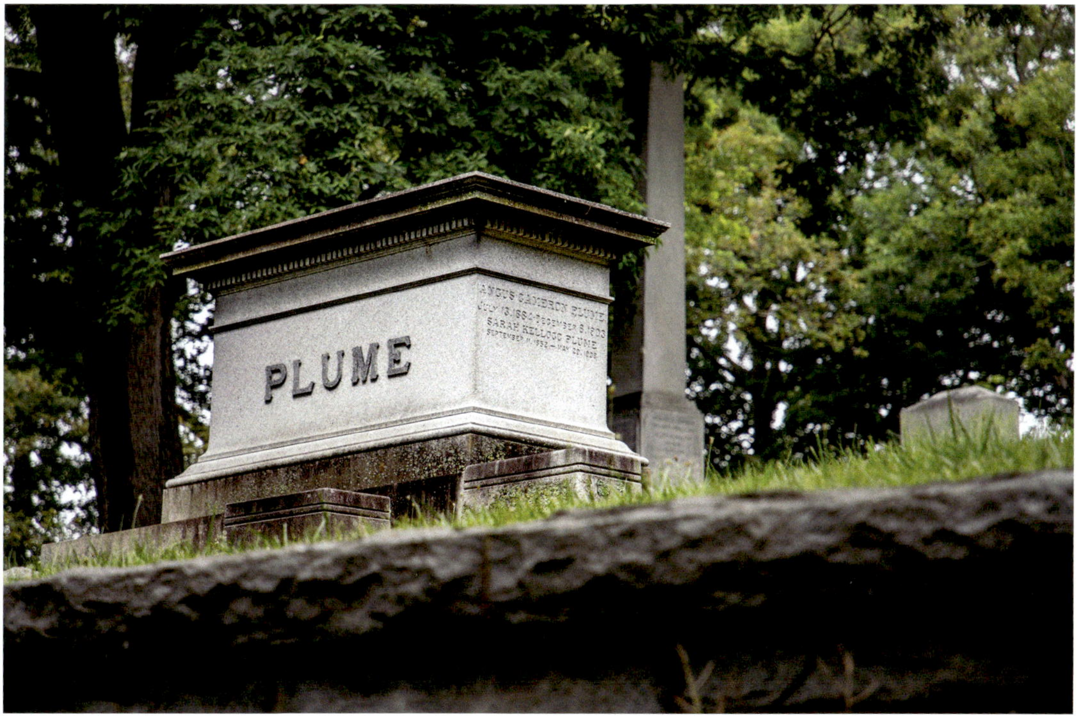

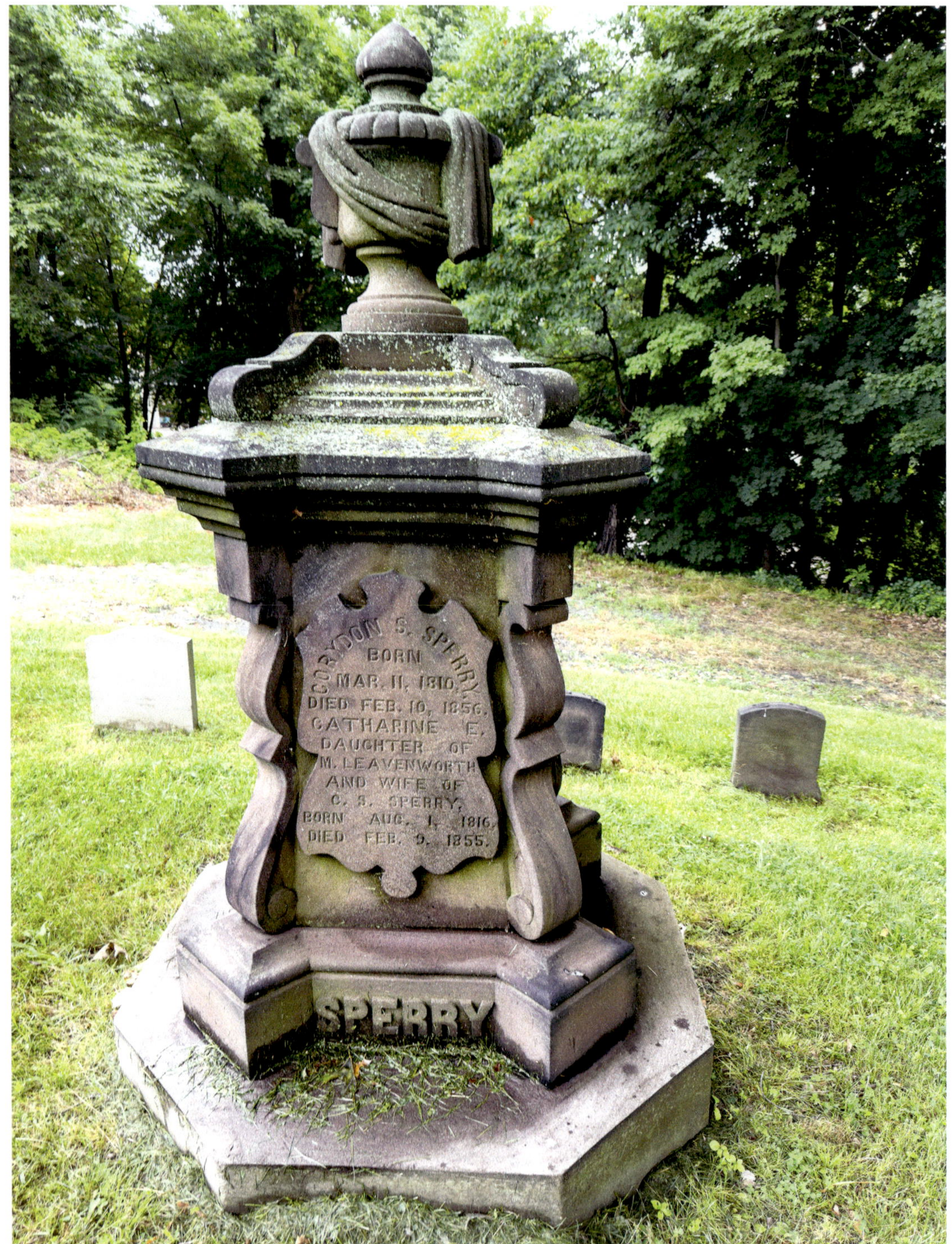
CORYDON S. SPERRY
BORN
MAR. 11, 1810.
DIED FEB. 10, 1856.
CATHARINE E.
DAUGHTER OF
M. LEAVENWORTH
AND WIFE OF
C. S. SPERRY,
BORN AUG. 1. 1816.
DIED FEB. 9. 1855.
SPERRY

2
Massachusetts

Massa-adchu-es-et, The Plymouth Colony, Massachusetts Bay Colony, The Bay State

Touring the burial grounds of this ancient section of the United States provides a unique perspective for its sister states. Across the 351 towns and cities that make up the Bay State, burying grounds are, to be technical, everywhere. Today, those named dead can be found dating back to the early 1600s. Those early natives, enslaved peoples, and socioeconomically challenged men, women, and children are, if lucky, relegated to mass graves. Generally, these rare monuments dedicated to those lost to time appear with markers giving an estimate of the people buried below. Even today, traveling across the Commonwealth of Massachusetts is no easy feat with the state running from the tip of Cape Cod all the way to the border of New York. However, an exploration of these burying grounds offers an amazing voyage into the region's colonial past, through its industrial age, and into the buzzing city of finance and opulence that stands today.

In the cemeteries, graveyards, churchyards, and burial mounds lie the graves and markers of those who truly inhabited this area first: the indigenous peoples, those who sailed aboard the *Mayflower*, those who helped shape and form a new country, those who helped lead it, and those who made history. New England's weather is extreme; hurricanes, nor'easters, and extreme temperatures are just a few of the challenges grave markers must overcome. Massachusetts showcases tombstones, both old and new, in various states of destruction. Graves made of slate, sandstone, marble, and granite sit alongside one another showing the flaws of their design. Burial grounds who are attentive and have the capital to fund it fight against time and nature, using the leading binding agents of the time to reattach broken pieces back together. Creatively using frames to keep ancient stones from falling to literal pieces. Replacing old markers that have been lost fully to time with brand-new markers. These efforts can be found across most of these grounds.

In Cambridge, a majestic burial ground sits inside the busy city; Mount Auburn with its never-ending pieces of grim art and impeccably maintained grounds will wow most. Children, parents, soldiers, governors, and celebrated people face an exceptionally uncertain future in their afterlife. Inside Hingham's St. Paul's cemetery, graves that once rose out of the ground as actual monuments to the memory of lost loved ones are now submerged and making their way back into the earth. In Salem, a myriad of monuments mark the memory of the lives of those who caused, suffered from, and lost their lives in the service of the Salem "Witch Trials." Inside what would go on to be known as The Burying Point, the less than 1.5-acre spat of land has renewed its commitment to preserving the space. While the attempt is in earnest and sorely needed, what has been lost, defaced, or destroyed is gone irrevocably. The burial ground, now flanked by homes and businesses, was the first land set aside for the burial of its residents beginning in 1637. In the centuries that have passed since its opening, only about 700 are reported to have been buried inside. Those residents inside have markers that span the centuries back to the 1600s, stunning and simple memorials sit near one another.

Across the burying grounds of Salem, the memories and final remains of many historically important people include judges, governors, explorers, and married couples like the Franklins—mother and father to Benjamin Franklin. Salem's Halloween allure for people near and far has negatively impacted spaces such as this burial ground. Tourists coming in massive numbers have trampled across all of Salem to take part in the ongoing Halloween events across the town. Where the home of one of history's most notorious judges, John Hathorn, once stood, today hosts a statue of the lead character of one of America's most beloved television series, *Bewitched*. As the interest in Salem's history continues to remain intriguing to outsiders, spaces like The Burying Point have had to adjust to preserve the nearly 400-year-old space and the monuments that grow up from its ground.

Moving to the southern coast of the Commonwealth, the graves of the State Farm Cemetery in Bridgewater bear only numbers. The numbers indicate those who passed while in the custody of the Commonwealth of Massachusetts; from the prison, state hospital, and the almshouse, primarily. A small area sits adjacent, dedicated to victims of Smallpox. In Quincy, south of Boston, tucked into a small area arrested in time within the bustling city sits Hancock Cemetery, so named for the father of Founding Father John Hancock, Reverend John Hancock Jr. Inside this cemetery, the 2nd and 6th presidents of the United States are buried along with their first ladies. While John, John Quincy, Abigail, and Louisa Adams would be relocated later, the cemetery still holds many of the Adams family. To the north in Brookline, the parents of nine children, Ambassador Joseph and Mrs. Rose Kennedy, are buried. This dynastic family included Rose's father, John F. Fitzgerald, or Honey Fitz, who served as a congressman, mayor of Boston, and state senator, and who is also buried in Brookline. Patrick Kennedy, father of Joe Kennedy, served in both the Massachusetts Senate and House of Representatives and was buried in Malden. Joe and Rose's children all have gone on to play their parts in history.

The oldest, Joseph Jr., was lost with his co-pilot and the plane they were aboard during a flight mission in World War II. With no remains to bury, a number of monuments have been erected in Joseph Kennedy II's honor, including a marker in Arlington National Cemetery. John F. Kennedy, the 35th president of the United States, and before that, senator and congressman, was buried inside Arlington National Cemetery after his assassination. The oldest sister, Rosemary, would in due time die from natural causes and be buried by her parents. Kathleen or "Kick" Cavendish, marchioness of Harrington, would go on to die in a plane accident like her eldest brother and be buried in England.

Eunice Kennedy Shriver, founder of the Special Olympics, died at eighty-eight years of age and put to rest inside of a Cape Cod cemetery. Patricia Kennedy Lawford would die from pneumonia in her eighties and be buried in New York. Robert F. Kennedy, a senator, attorney general, and candidate for president, was assassinated and buried near his brothers in Arlington National Cemetery. Youngest sister, Ambassador Jean Kennedy Smith, died at home in New York at ninety-two years old and was buried inside a Catholic cemetery in New York. The last child of Rose and Joe was Senator Edward "Ted" Kennedy. After surviving a plane crash and enduring a long recovery, Ted stayed in his senate position until his death forty-seven years after he began; Ted joined his brothers inside Arlington National Cemetery. Former First Lady Jacqueline Kennedy and two of President and Mrs. Kennedy's children were also laid to rest in Virginia.

Atop a peek inside a Fall River cemetery, the infamous Lizzie Borden is buried alongside her sister Emma. Lizzie and Emma were the daughters of Sarah and Andrew Borden. About three years after Lizzie's birth, her mother, Sarah, died. Three years later, her father, Andrew, remarried Abby Durfee Gray. Their marriage would last, in life, until they were seventy and sixty-four, respectively. After the death of the Bordens in 1892, the younger Bordens lived on until 1927. By 1927, the sisters were living in different states. Emma, the older sister, took up residence in New Hampshire while the younger Lizzie stayed in Fall River. Though separated geographically, both sisters died within the first two weeks of June 1927. All five of the Andrew Borden family went on to be buried in the same section of the cemetery.

Without Massachusetts, American history would likely have looked different, from the *Mayflower* in Plymouth, the Adams and Kennedy family, as well as President Bush the first. History is rich across New England but nowhere else is the history so rich and piled upon itself as it is in Boston. Boston has been the canvas upon which historic moments have been painted since European settlers landed in the region. History books act as a carbon copy receipt for those events. Revolution sprang from the streets of Boston, genius has been cultivated in the halls of the state's great universities, and medical history has forever been changed on the battlefields and in the surgical theaters of the city. The issue, as with all the American Northeast, is preservation of the past. How much longer can these monuments of centuries gone by be maintained?

Exploring the cemeteries and graveyards of Massachusetts shows you a fascinating history of the Bay State, but it also shows you the failings and attempts of preservation. Graves, markers, tombstones, and crypts lost and reclaimed to the ground. Loved ones, survivors, and others commit the dead back to the earth after they have died, in doing so there is a hope that the life and experiences of that person will live on, never to be forgotten, and would tell the story of the person in perpetuity. Having entered a sixth century of individual burials in the Commonwealth of Massachusetts, the concept of never forgotten is a hope and not an actual guarantee. These issues are the great unifier as evident in the poshest burying sites from the ocean to the mountains as it is in the Shaker and Friend's cemeteries. The burial sites of yesterday may have already been lost to become the streets, homes, and parking lots of today. Those not displaced or built over are wholly dependent on the whims and considerations of those today and tomorrow to care and preserve their final resting spots.

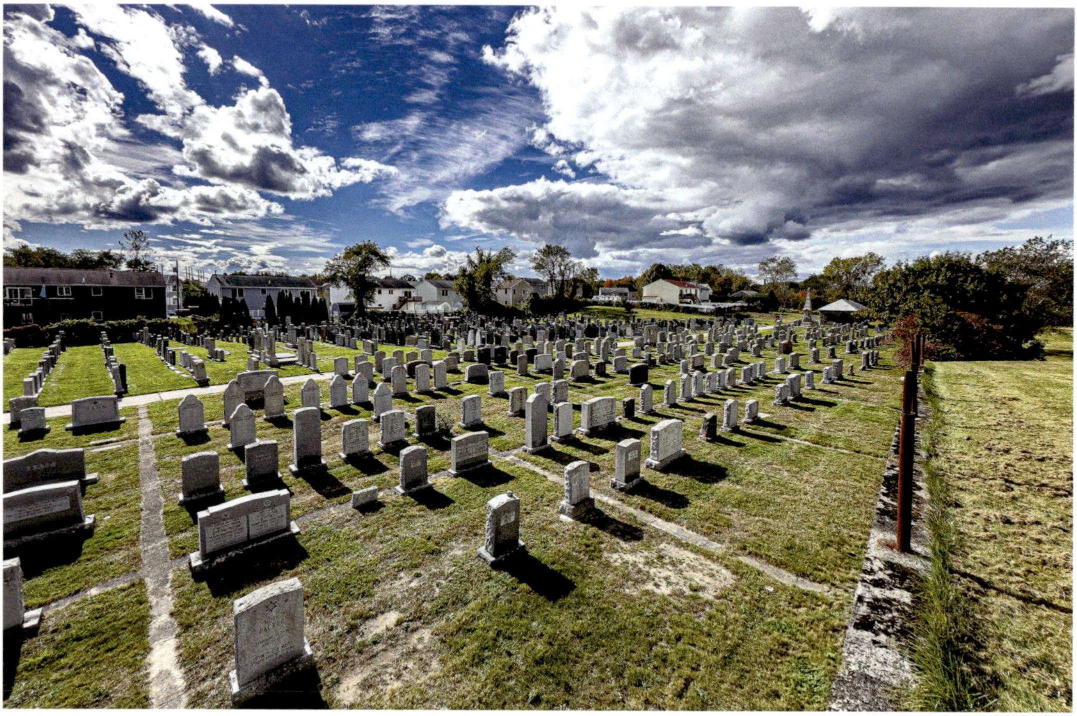

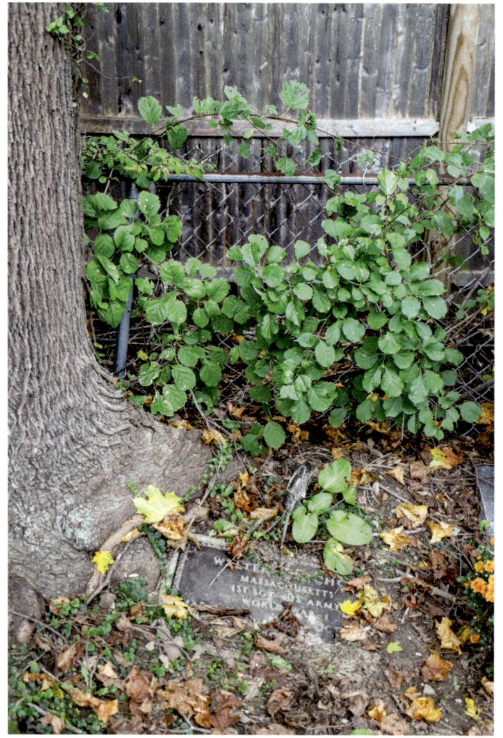

Above: The Hebrew Cemetery from above.

Left: W. Nichols, first sergeant U.S. Army, fought in World War I. Today, he is fighting not to be swallowed into a tree that has been slowly marching toward him.

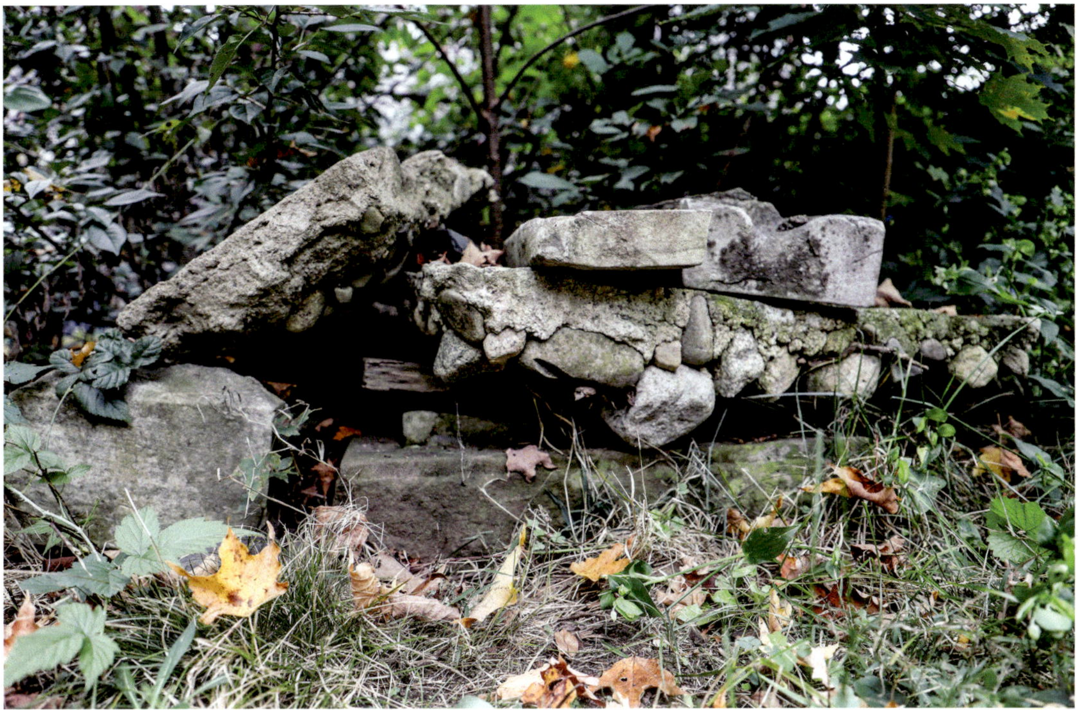

This small cemetery, at less than 2.5 acres, dates back to the first half of the 1700s. Three centuries later, piles of grave parts like this one have become common inside Liberty Plain Cemetery.

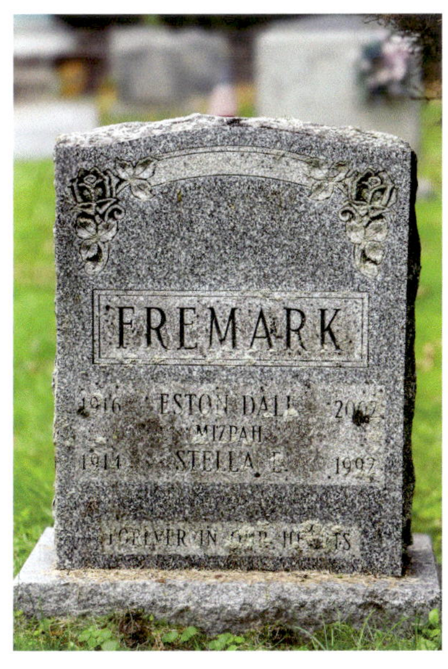

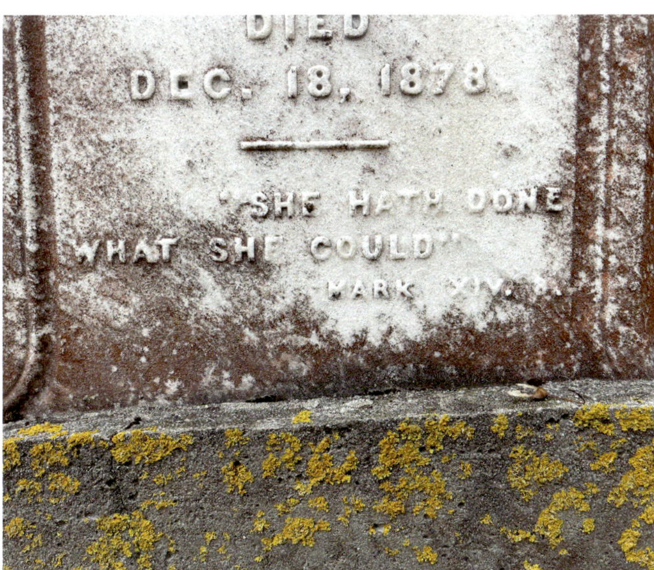

Above left: Mizpah!

Above right: She hath done what she could.

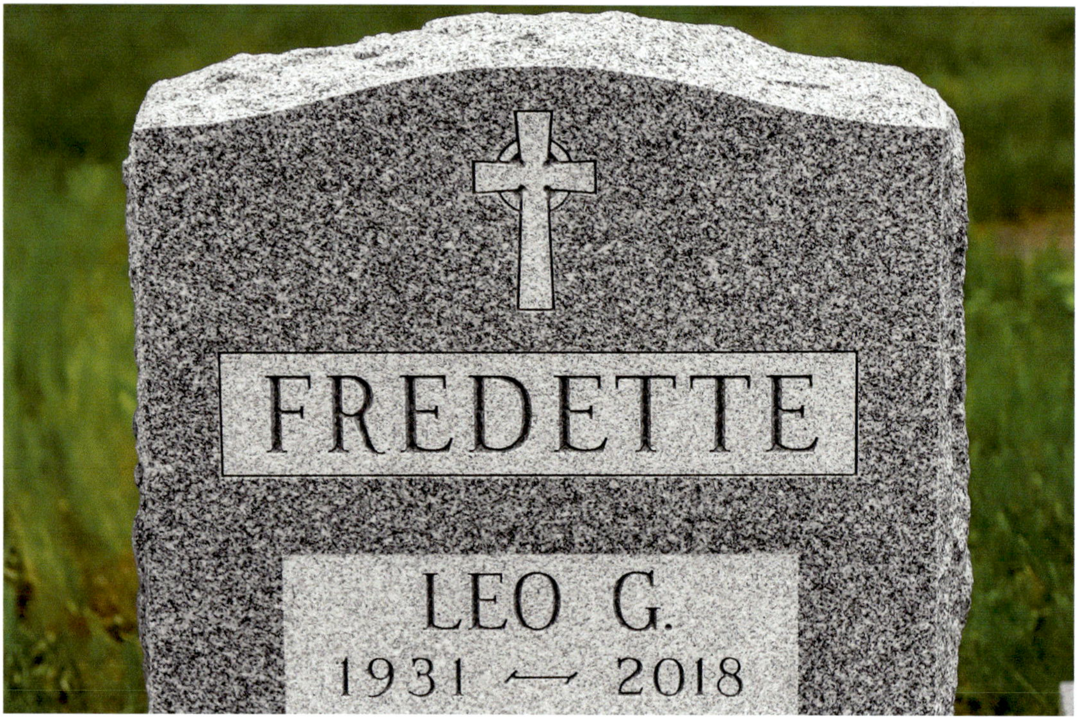

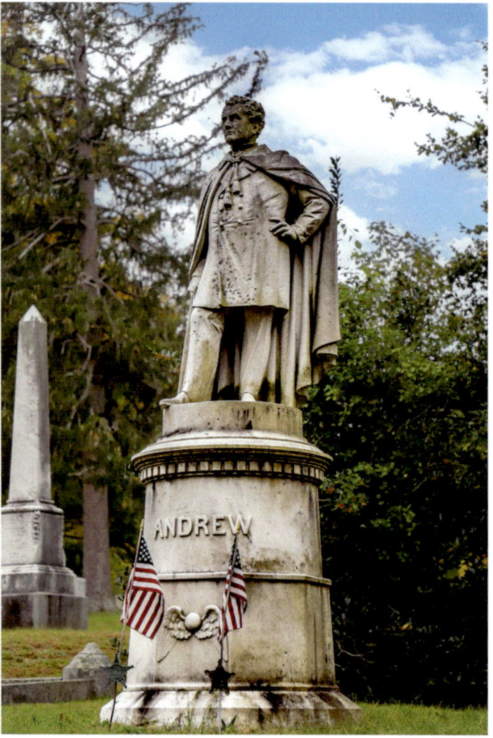

Above: In New England, where 40 percent of people identify as Catholic, it is very common to see a variety of crosses across the region's burial grounds.

Left: John Albion Andrew forever standing high, looking over Hingham and the Commonwealth of Massachusetts. The twenty-fifth governor and member of the Massachusetts House was born in 1818.

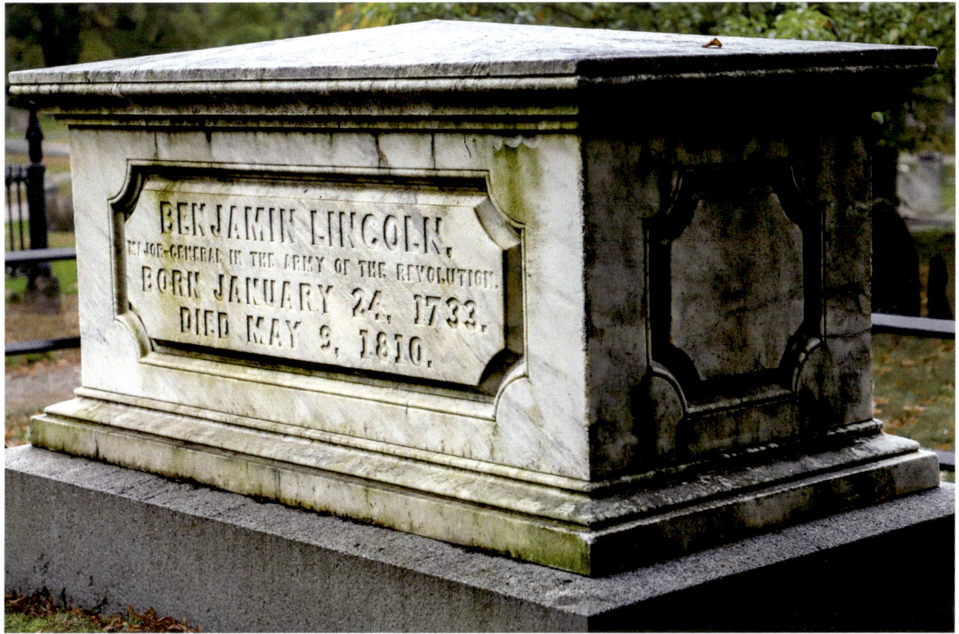

Federalist Benjamin Lincoln, an indirect cousin of President Abraham Lincoln, has an impressive story of his own. As the second lieutenant governor of the Bay State, under Governor John Hancock, the first collector of the port of Boston, Lincoln was persuaded to stay in his post by President Thomas Jefferson. He also served as the first U.S. secretary at war, holding the office until President Washington moved Henry Knox into the role. Lincoln, among his many titles, was also a veteran of the American Revolutionary War, as well as the French and Indian War.

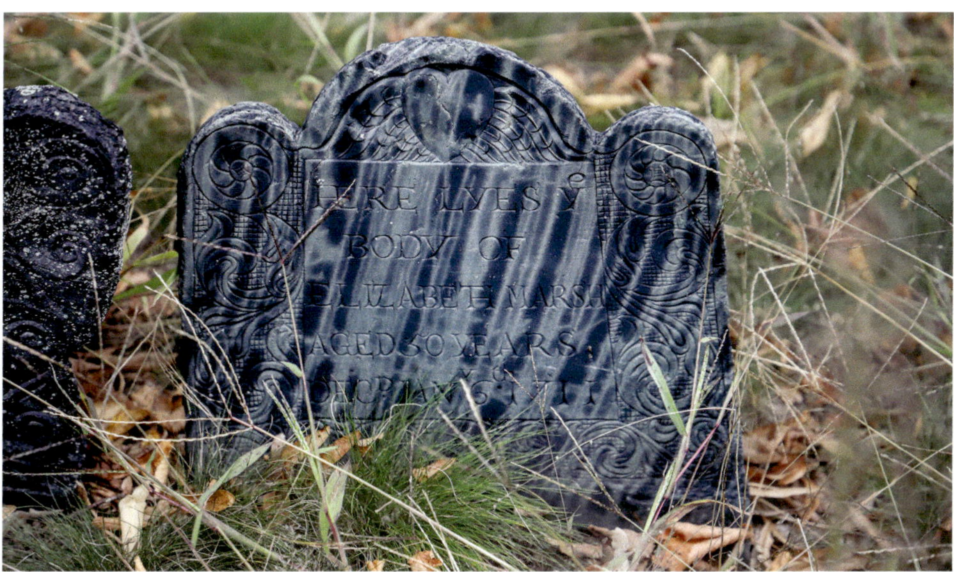

Elizabeth Marsh, dead at fifty years. December 1711.

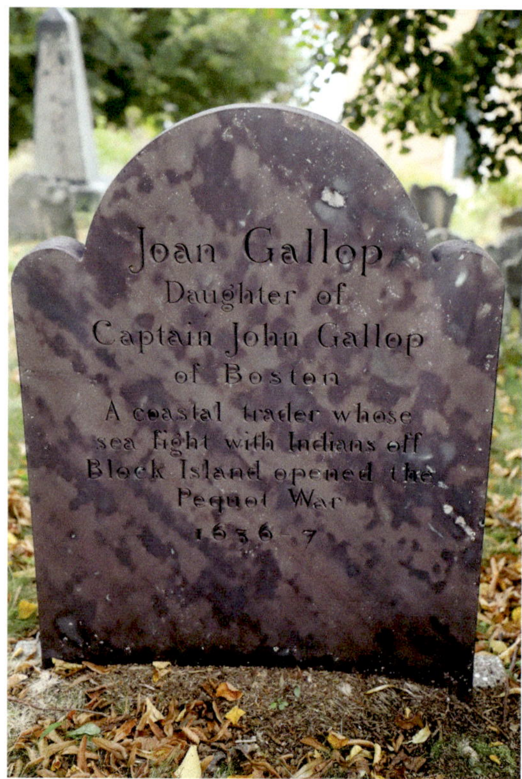

Left: Joan, daughter of Captain John Gallop, was also the wife of Thomas Joy.

Below: Sarah Hawke died March 1693/4.

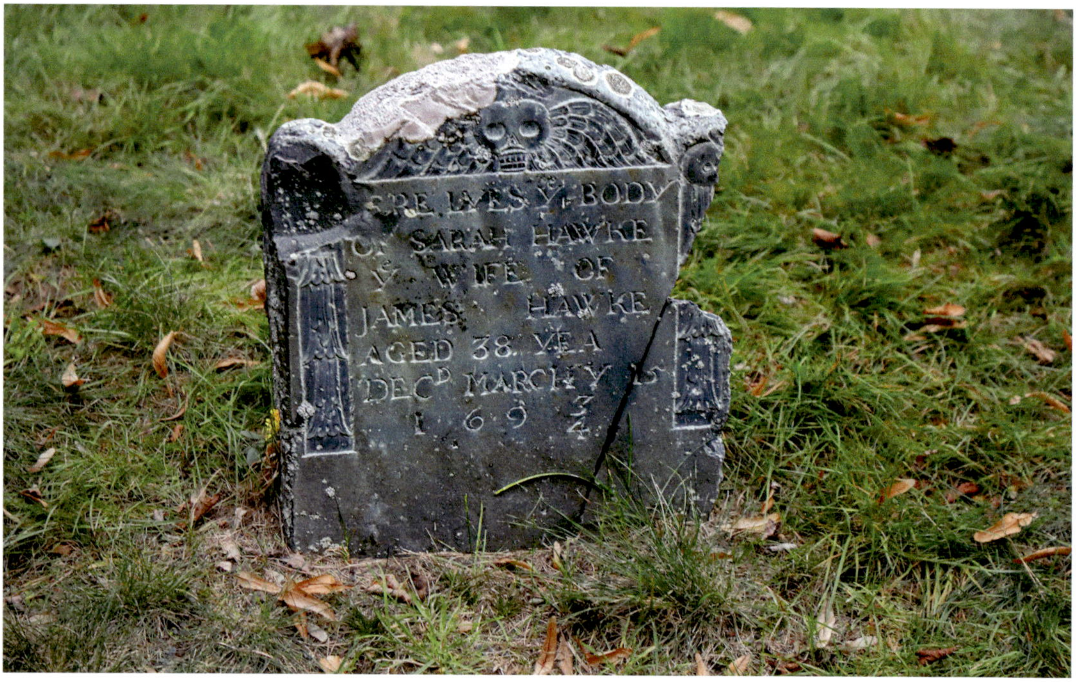

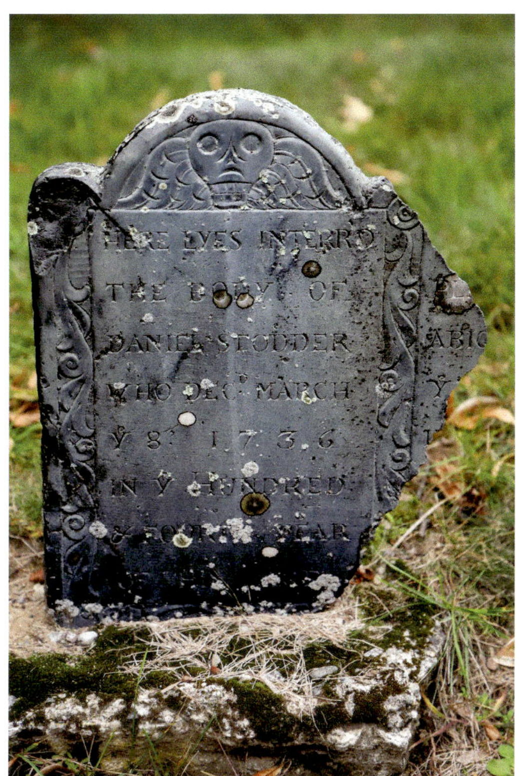

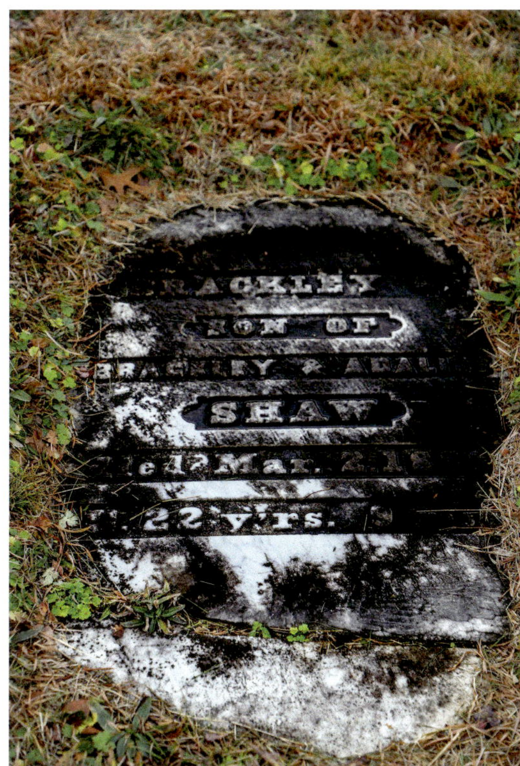

Above left: 104-year-old Daniel Stodder died in 1736 and was buried in the Hingham Cemetery. Notably half of his grave marker, that of his wife Abigail has been broken away and lost to time. The Stodder family left England in the early 1600s, settling in Hingham. The name Stodder would go on to be spelled as such as well as another version of the name, Stoddard. The latter version is a surname that is still prevalent in this area, nearly 400 years later.

Above right: As memorials are sucked down to the ground, frequently a war for their preservation begins. Brackley's grave has been a target of the grass his grave marker now lays upon. In the fight for preservation, you can see the attempts that have been made to save this marker.

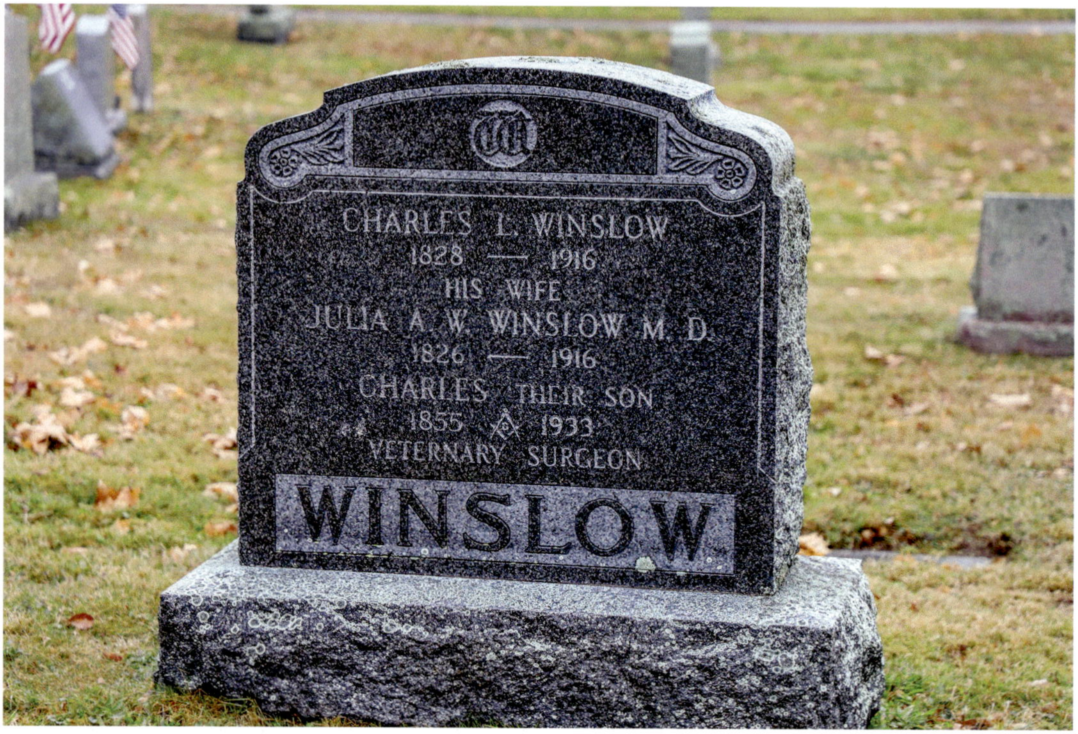

Doctor and Mister Winslow and their son, veterinary surgeon, Charles.

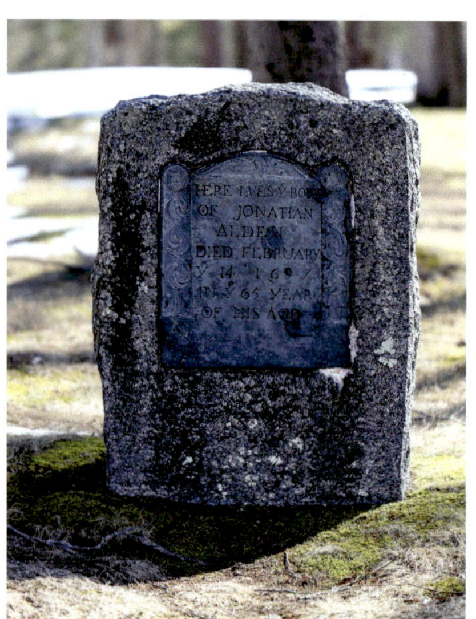

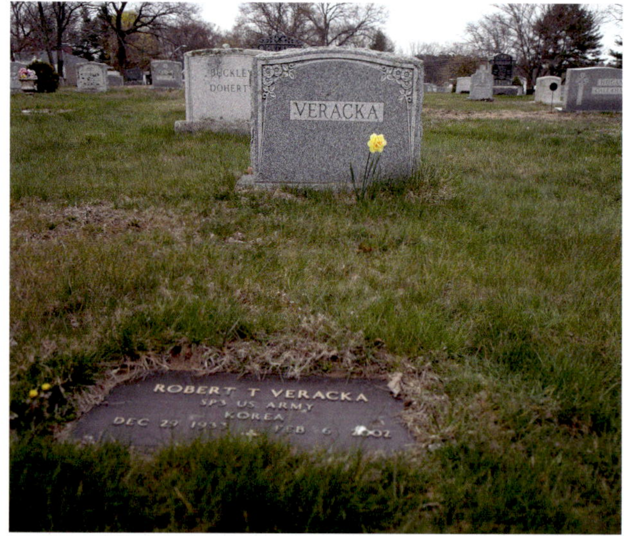

Above left: Born in 1632 and dead sixty-five years later in 1697, the grave of the eventual Captain has been preserved well enough that it is still in one piece and legible 328 years later.

Above right: This one lone flower stands sentry above the grave of this veteran.

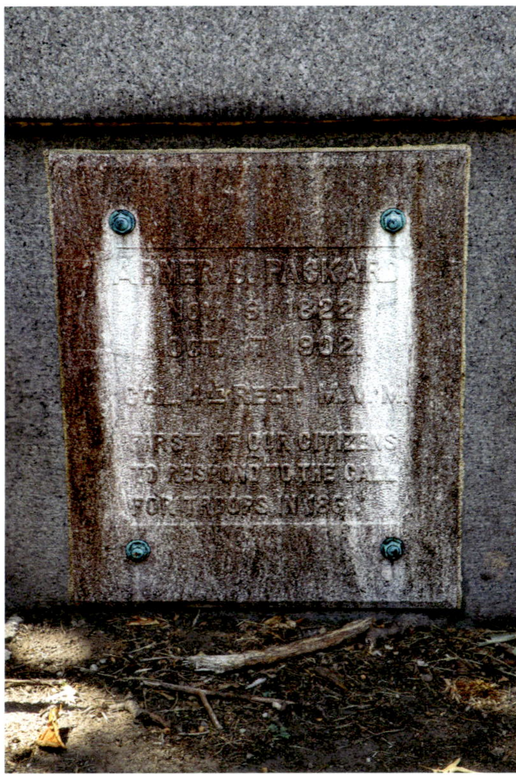

Right: A cacophony of colors across this grave marker.

Below: Ellsworth Murah Harding

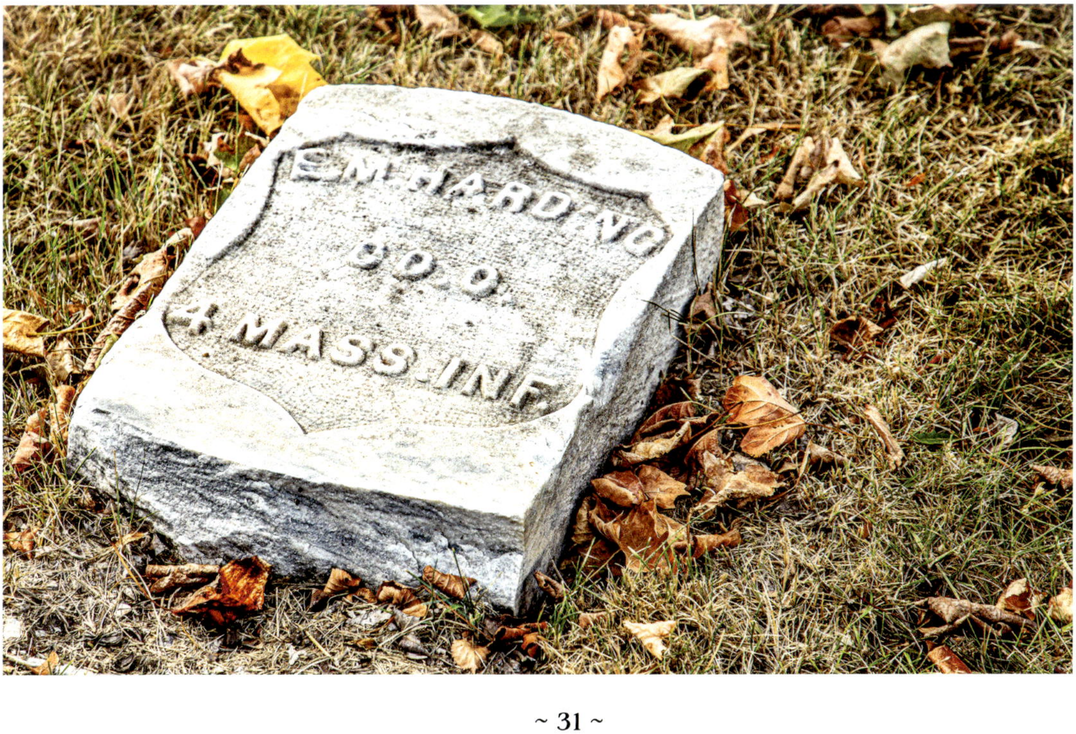

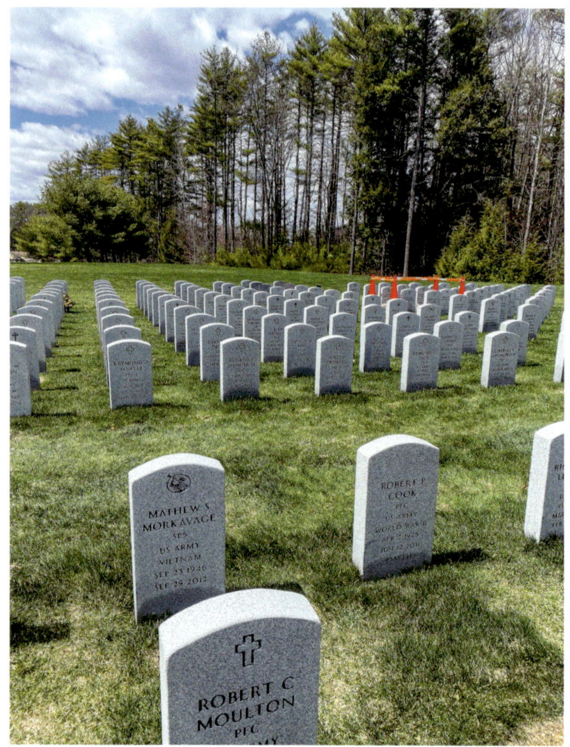

Left: In the small town of Winchendon, Massachusetts, this cemetery for veterans sit unassumingly on a slight incline. This burial ground is one of three in the Commonwealth, the others being located in Bourne and Agawam.

Below: Joshua James is remembered as a savior to many shipwrecked off the coast of the peninsular town of Hull, Massachusetts.

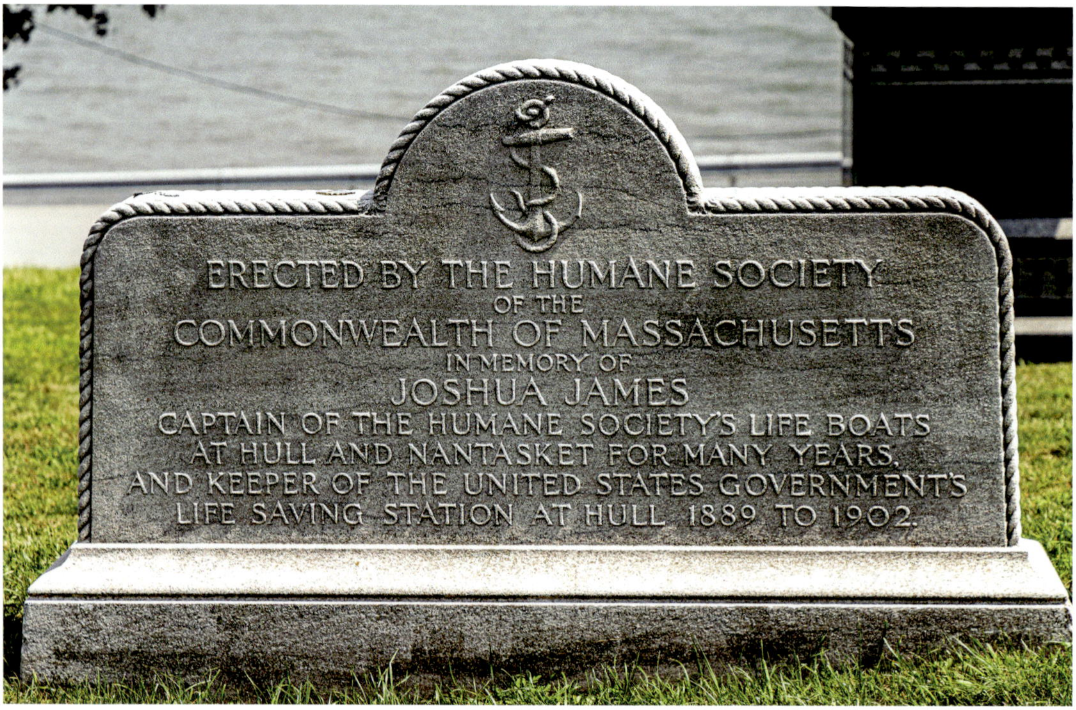

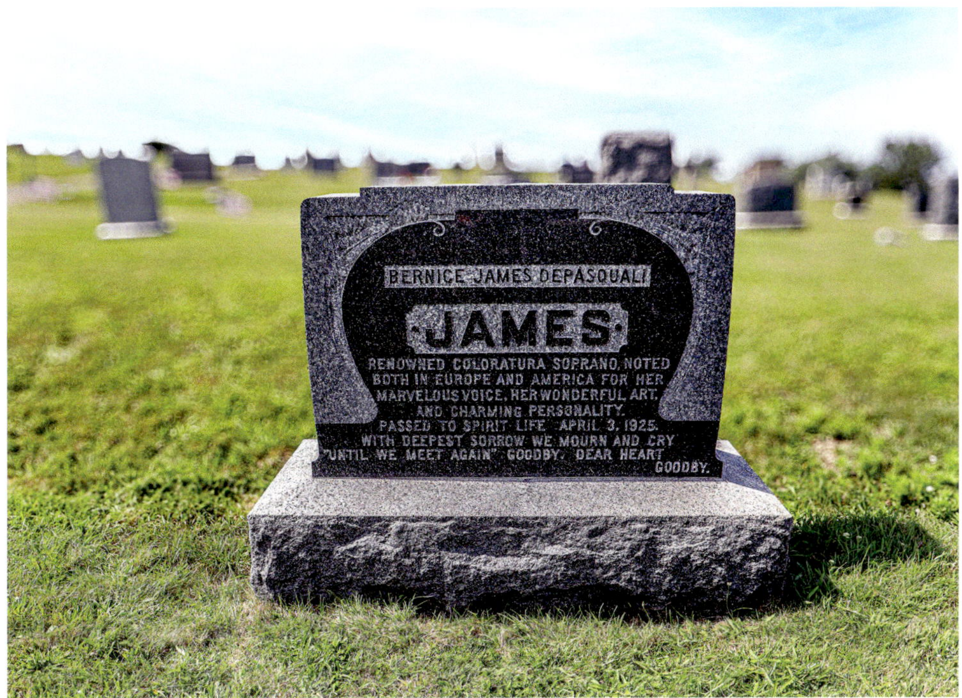

Bernice James Depasquali.

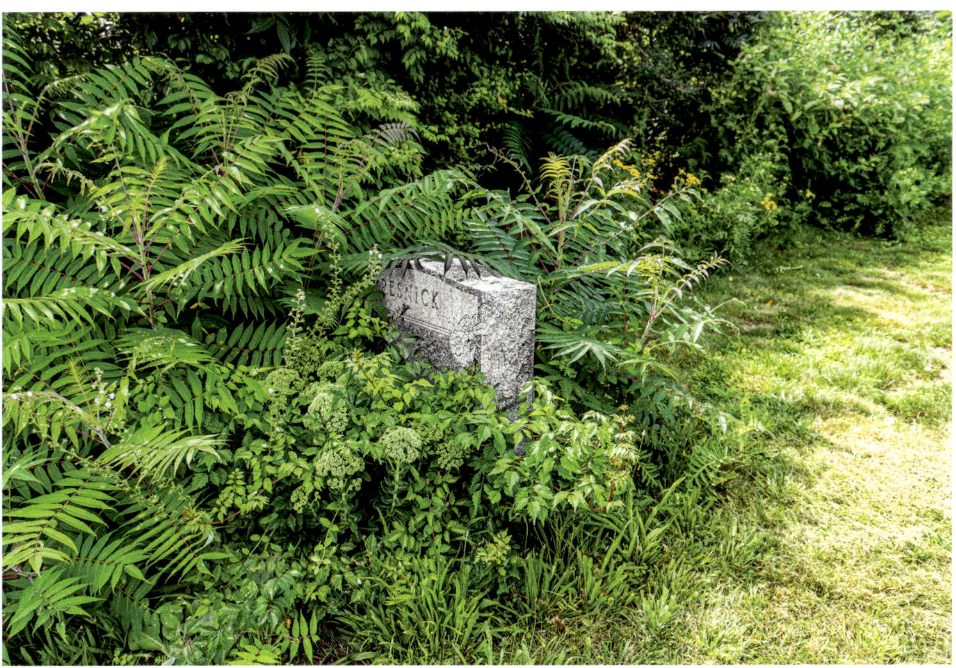

Loss of gravestones comes in many shapes and sizes.

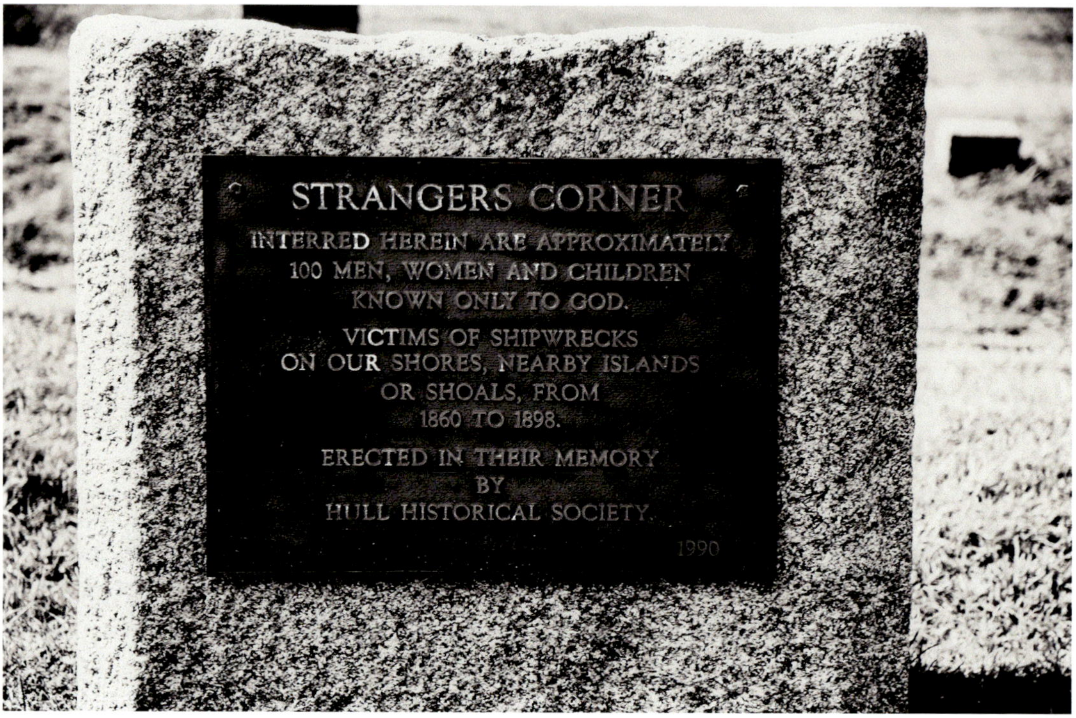

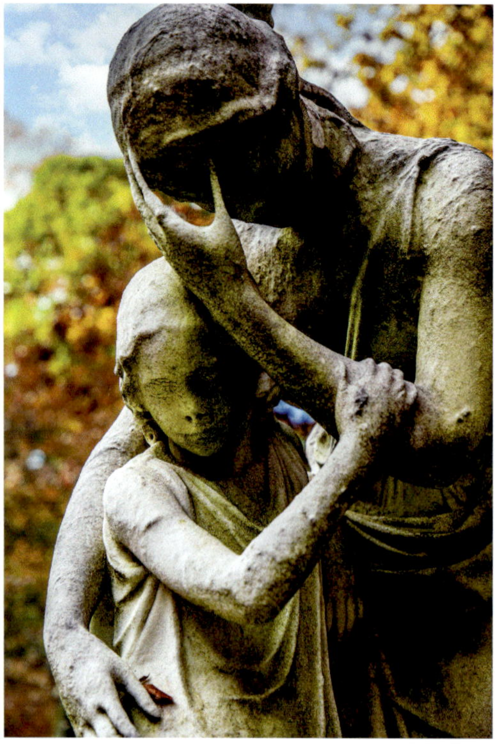

Left: Weather and time have worked in tandem to remove the faces of those featured on this statue.

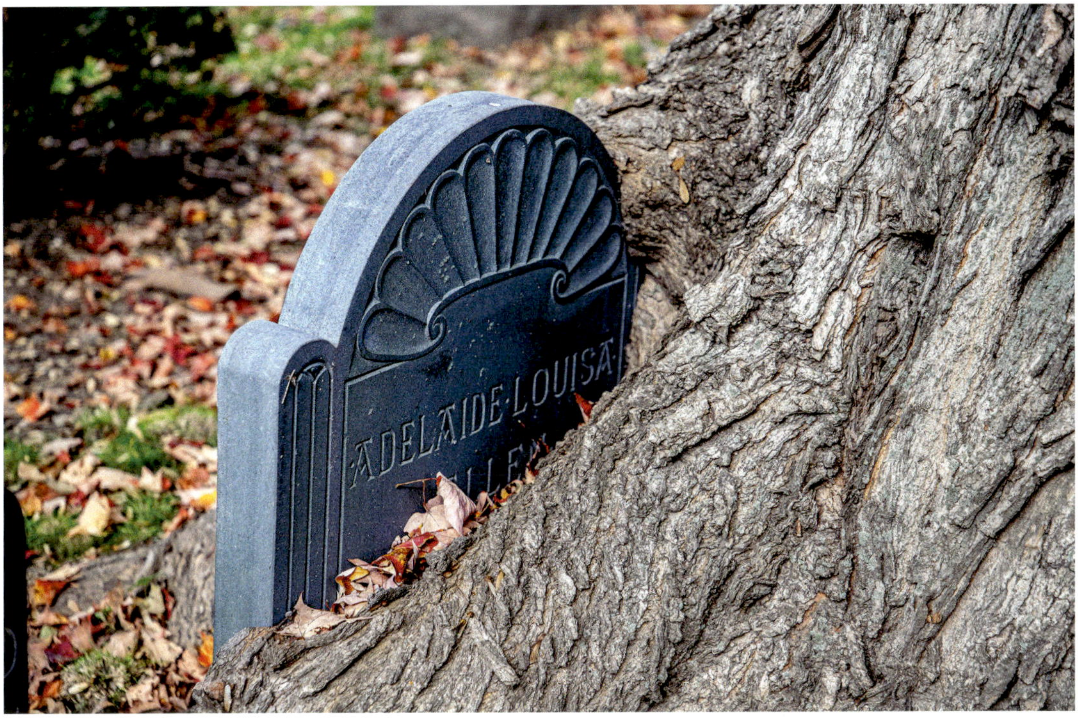

Right: A one-winged statue looks down from its washed away face.

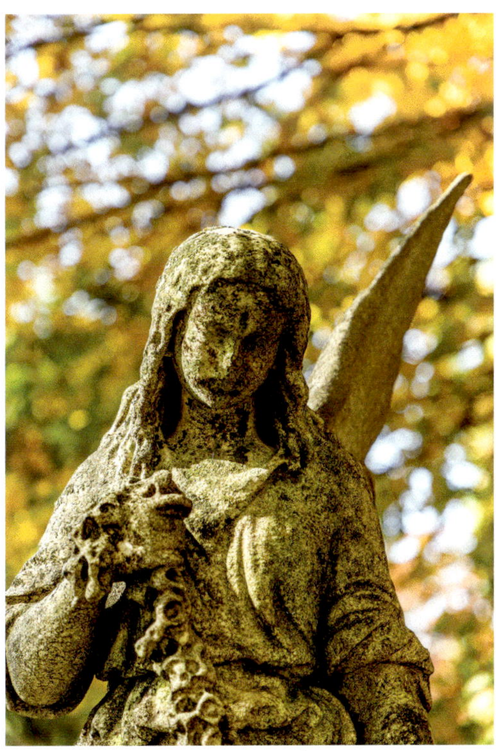

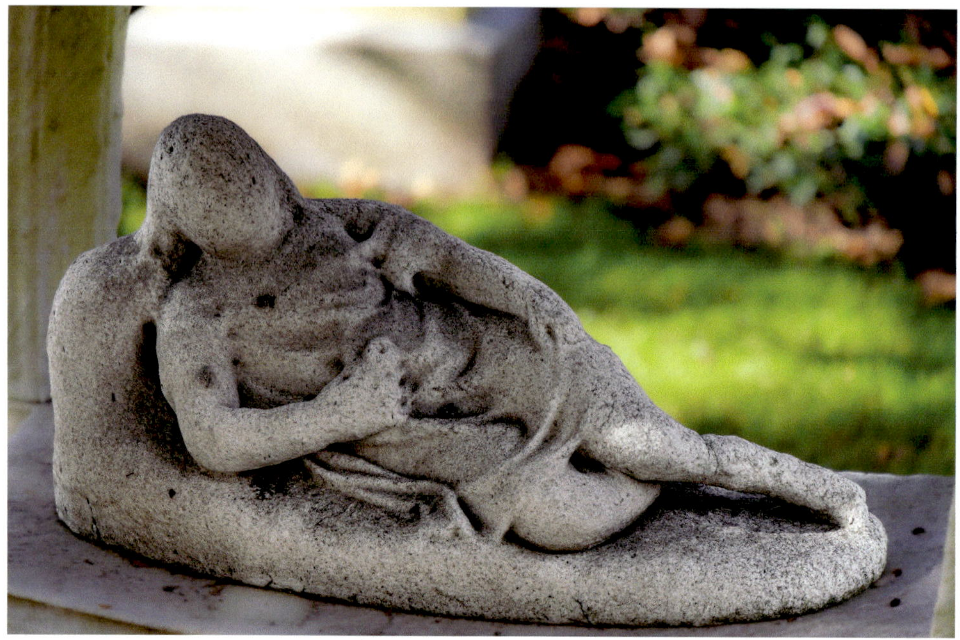

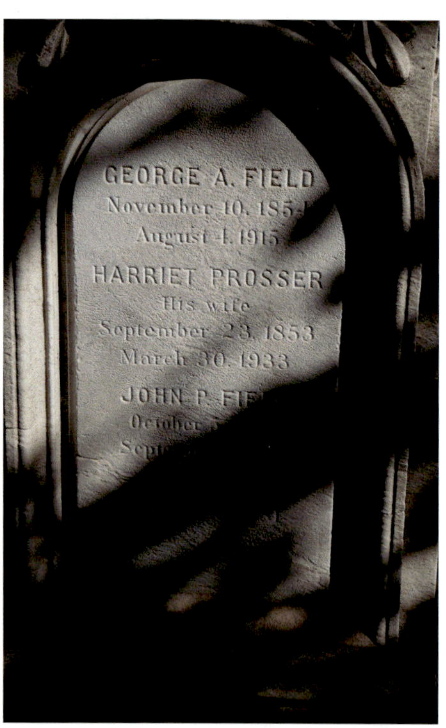

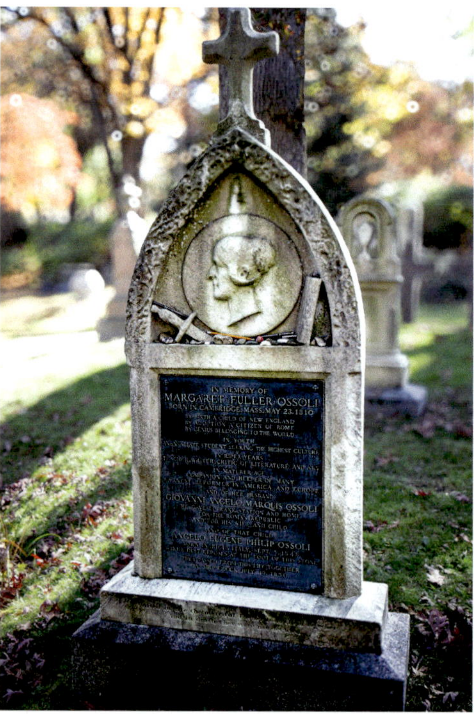

Above right: The accomplished woman, Margaret Fuller Ossoli, died alongside her one-year-old due to a shipwreck in July 1850.

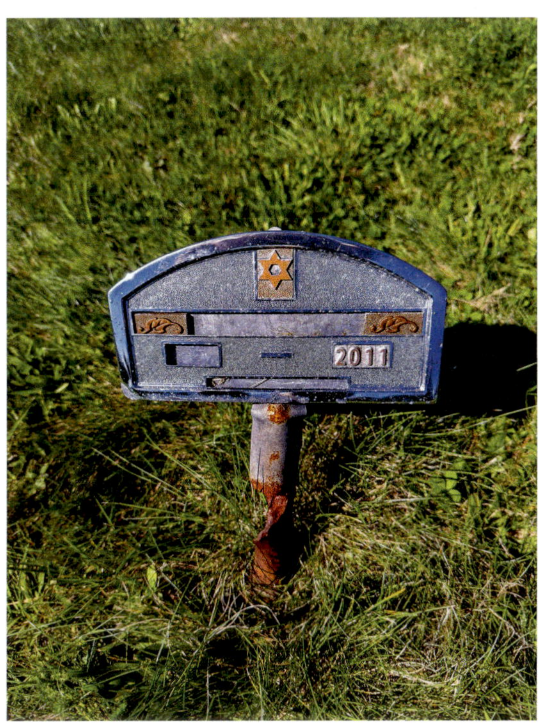

Right: Fourteen years after being erected inside the Hebrew Cemetery in Fall River, Massachusetts, this now nameless memorial plaque sits only with the year of death.

Below: This burying ground is marked predominantly by numbered markers. With the dead considered to be patients of the hospitals and some poverty stricken, the grounds today are allowed to grow up in an unruly manner.

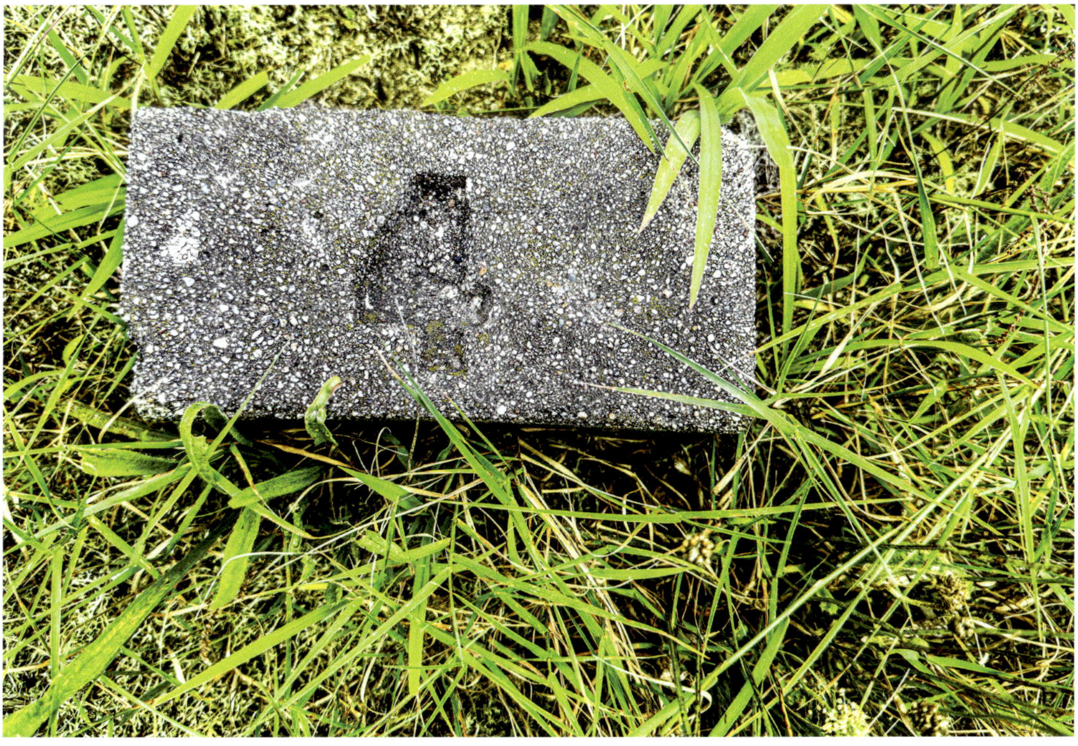

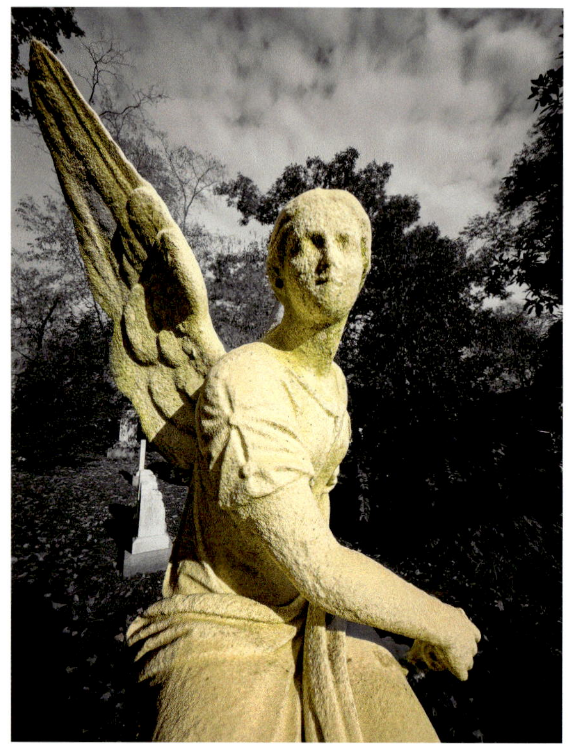

Below: Myles Standish.

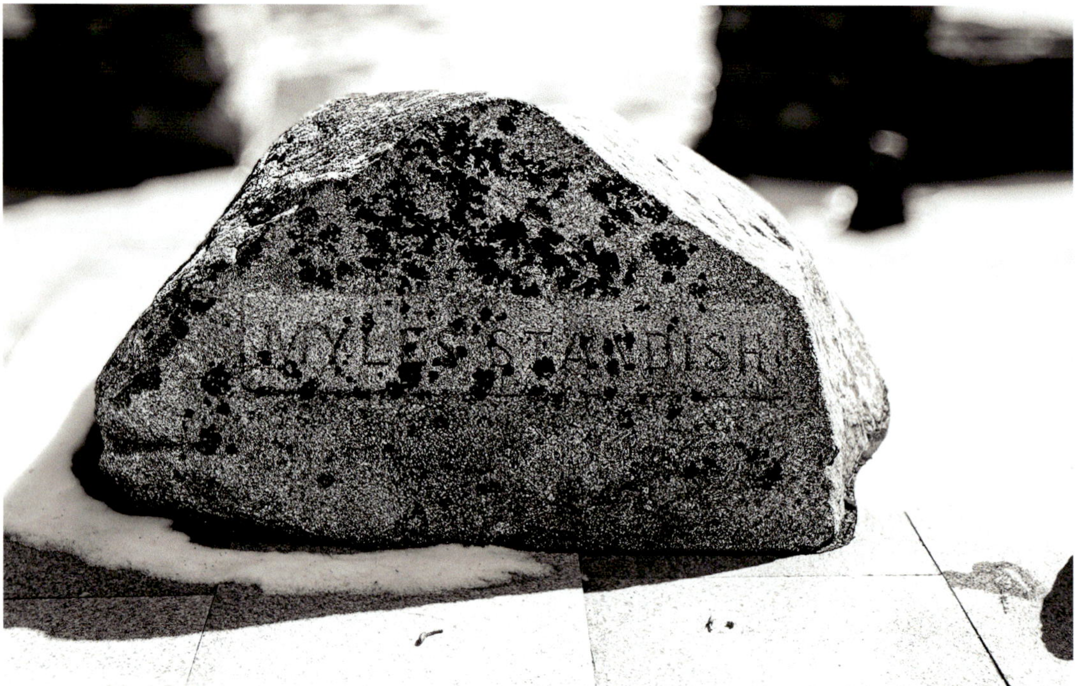

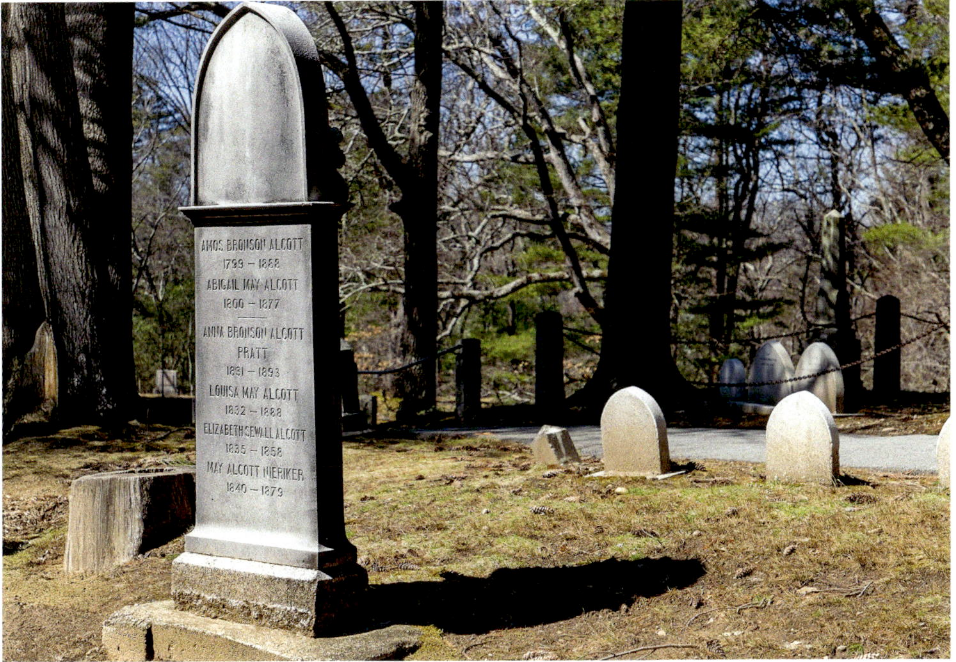

The Alcotts, including Louisa May, famous for her writing, are buried together on what is now known as Authors' Ridge.

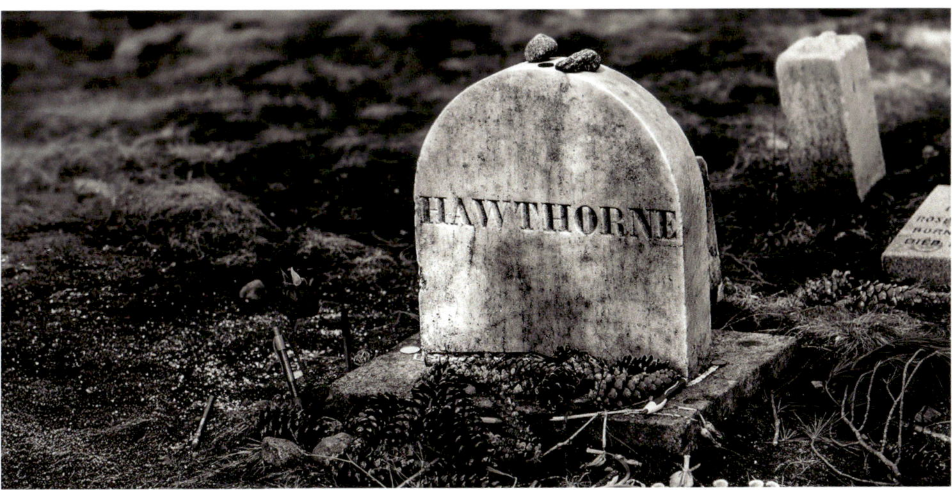

The true New England experience can be characterized in Hawthorne. Hawthorne, originally Hathorne, was the grandson several times removed to William Hathorne, a judge known for his harsh penalties. William's son, John Hawthorne's great-great-grandfather, would go on to be a central figure in the Salem trials. Through his time in college, he would become close friends with the future President Franklin Pierce, as well as Henry Wadsworth Longfellow. Later in life, he would become friends with the family of Louisa May Alcott, Ralph Waldo Emerson, and Henry David Thoreau. This author of *The Scarlet Letter* and many other literally works would go on to be buried among the other literary giants of the day on Authors' Ridge.

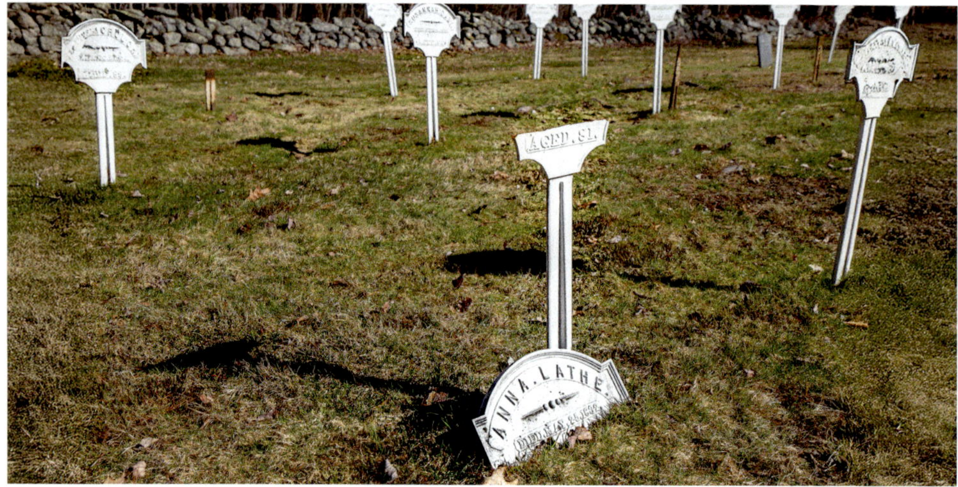

The Shaker Burying Ground, otherwise known as Lollipop Cemetery, is in Harvard, Massachusetts. Quakerism began in the eighteenth century in England and eventually moved across the sea to New York, New England, and locations. Shakers, originally The United Society of Believers in Christ's Second Appearing. The relatively small group of believers stuck to certain tenets that separated them from the cultural and societal norms of the day. The core beliefs among others include equality, an opposition to violence, and living together as brothers and sisters and elders and eldresses.

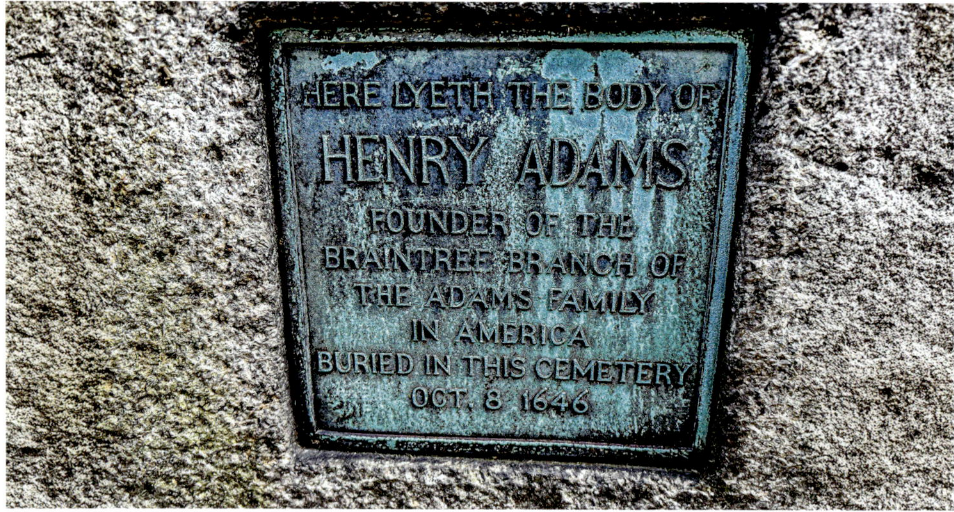

Henry Adams, a farmer who left Braintree, Essex for Braintree, Massachusetts. His descendants, as it is told, include President John Adams, President John Quincy Adams, President Calvin Coolidge, Founding Father and Patron Saint of Boston Beer, Samuel Adams, future governors, members of the U.S. House of Representatives, teachers, doctors, ambassadors, and First Lady Mamie Eisenhower. Additionally, there are poets and authors and chemists, John Steinbeck, Dickinson, supreme court justices, royalty, and perhaps most notably the inventor of self-adhesive labels.

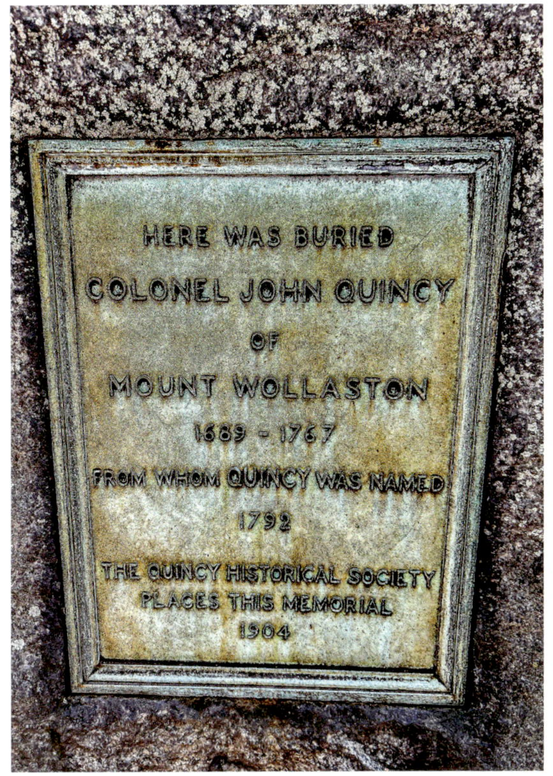

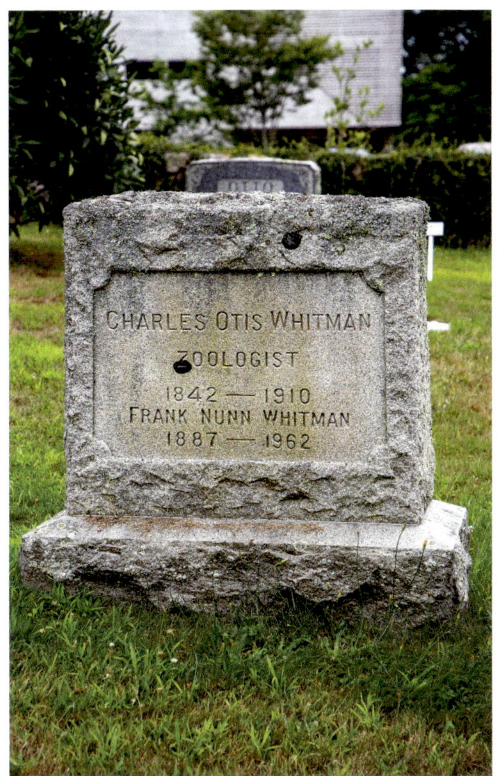

Above right: Zoologist.

Right: 1748.

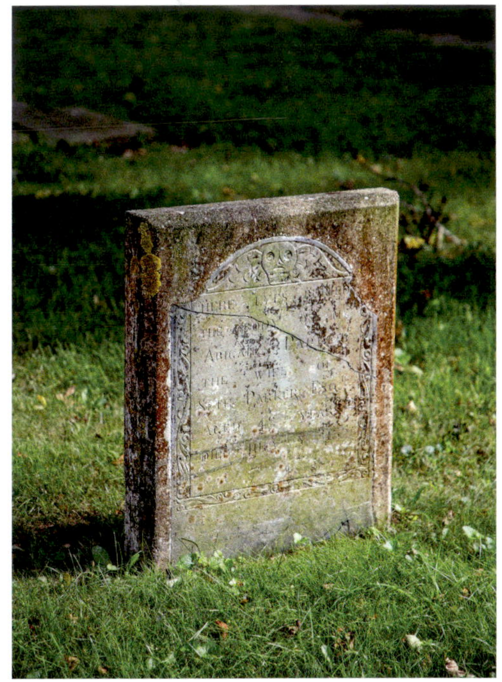

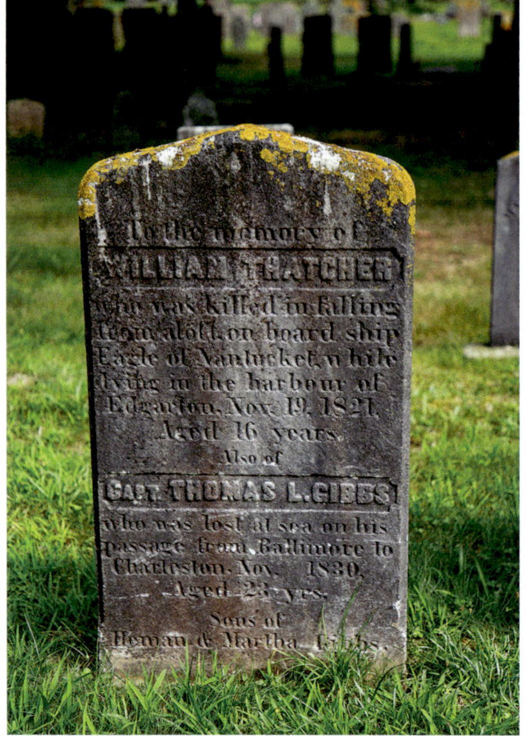

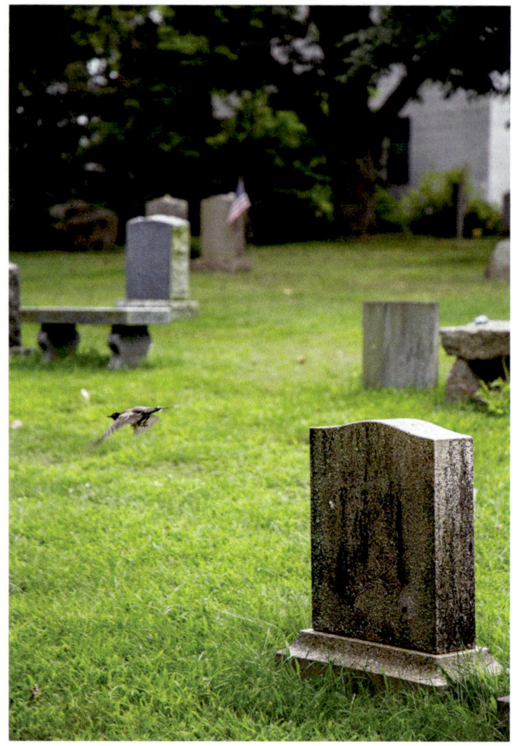

Above left: The Gibbs' sons. Killed falling off the Eagle of Nantucket. Lost at sea travelling from Baltimore to Charleston.

Above right: Preservation under attack by lichen.

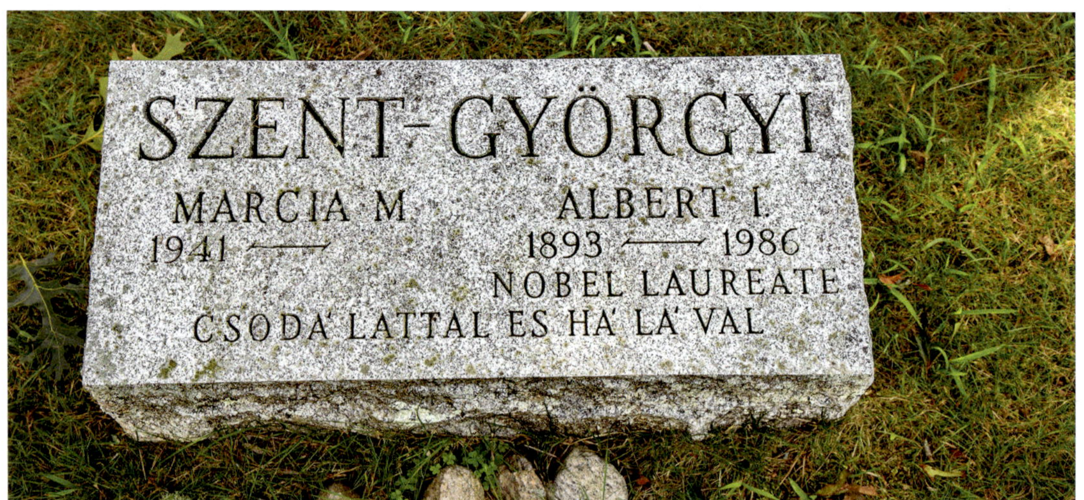

The Hungarian-born Nobel laureate was a veteran of World War I who taught and learned across Europe and is credited for discovering vitamin C.

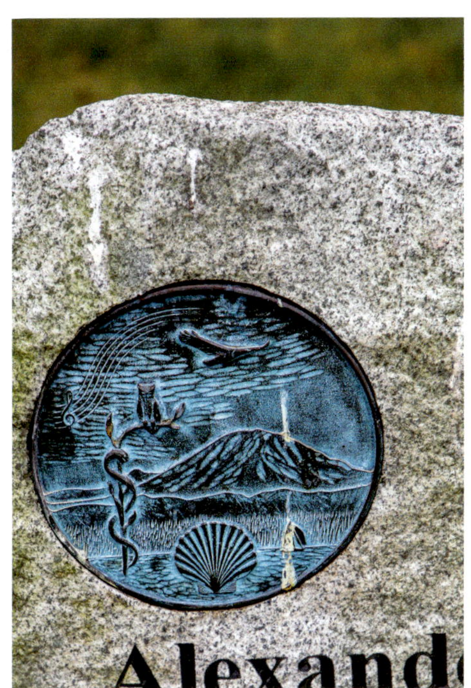

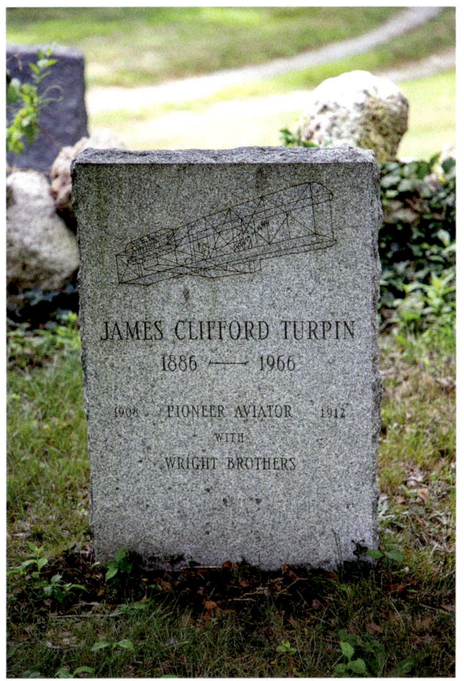
JAMES CLIFFORD TURPIN
1886 —— 1966
1908 PIONEER AVIATOR 1912
WITH
WRIGHT BROTHERS

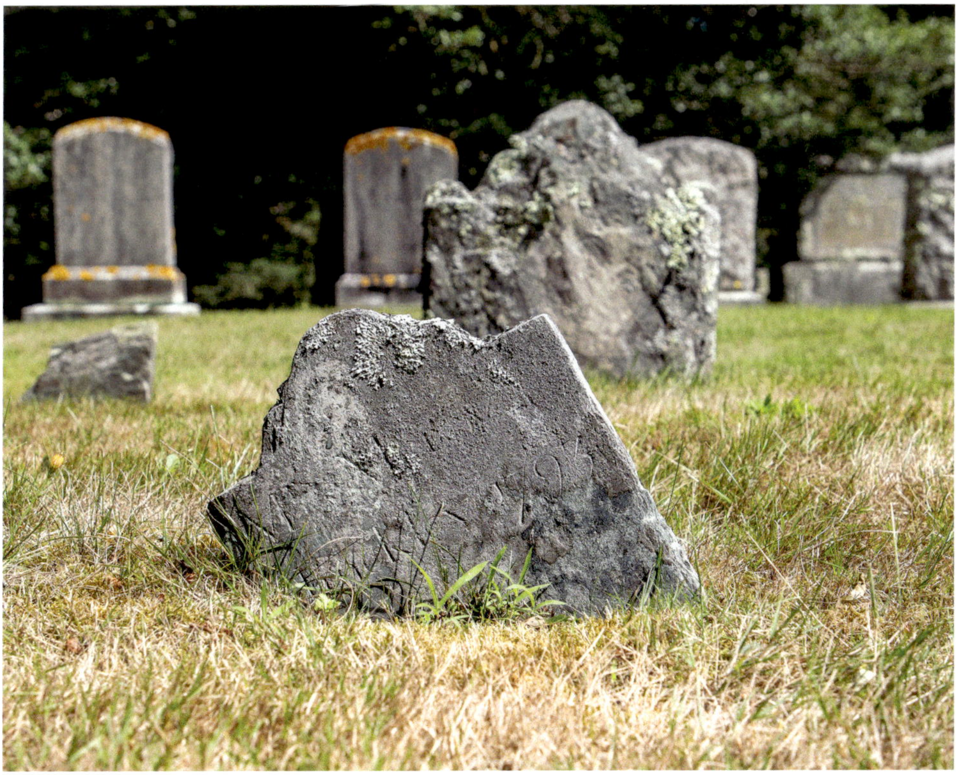

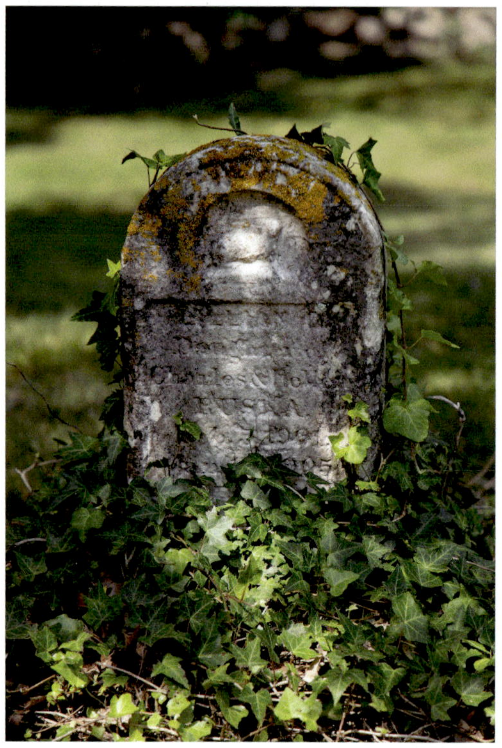

Left: A small stone for a massive loss.

Below: Lighting designer for dozens of musicals and operas.

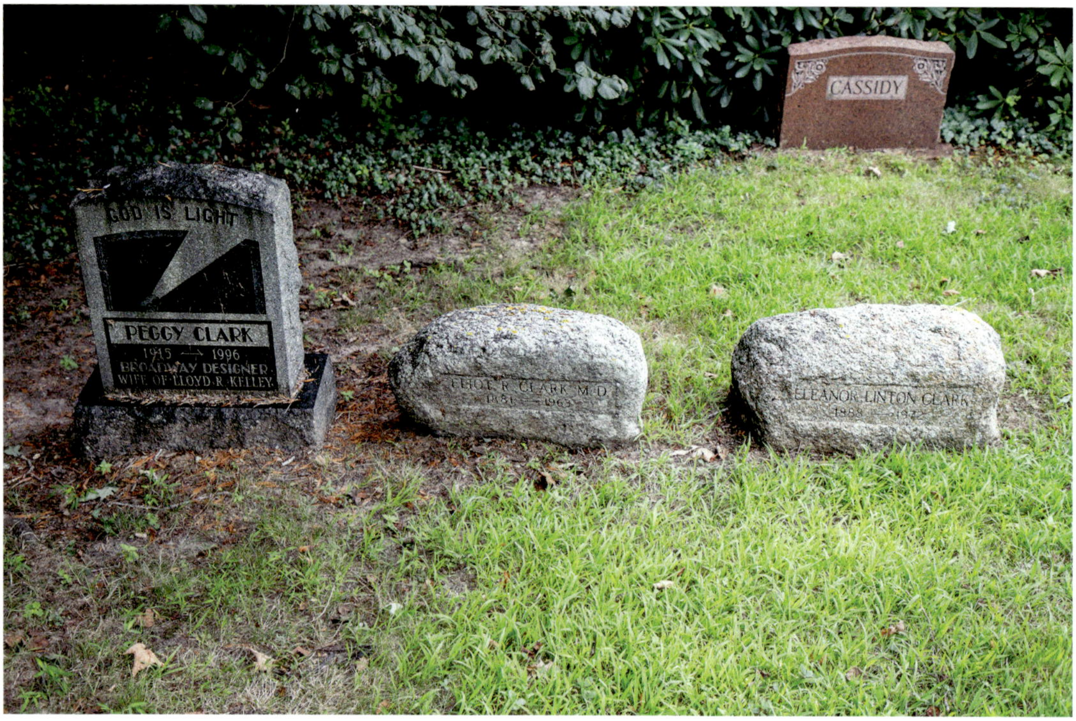

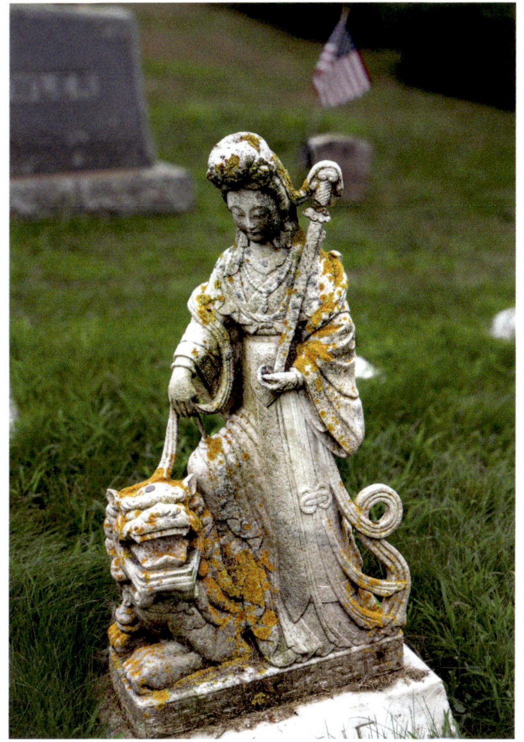

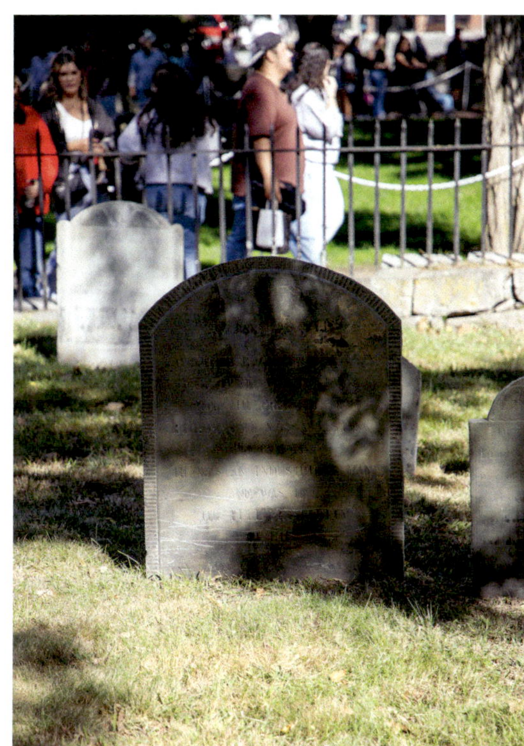

Above right: Droves of tourists can be seen swamping the open areas of Salem in late September.

Right: 1686.

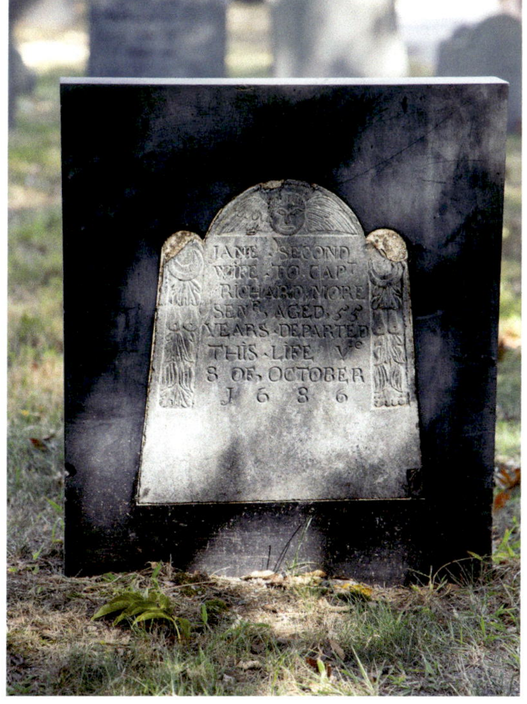

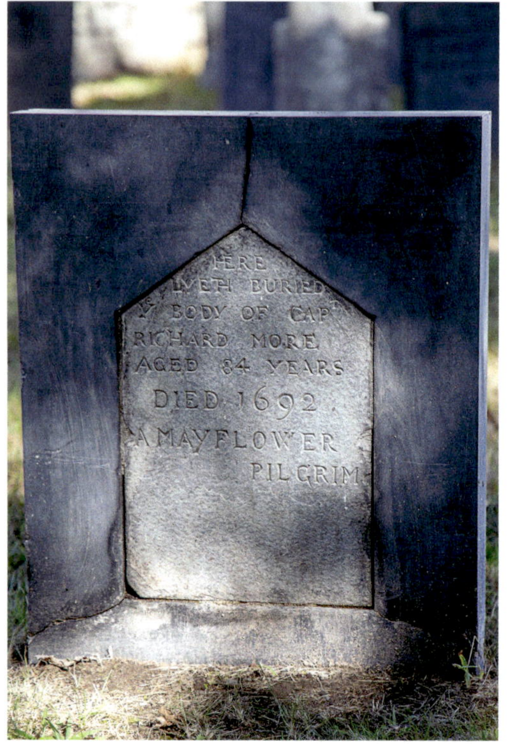

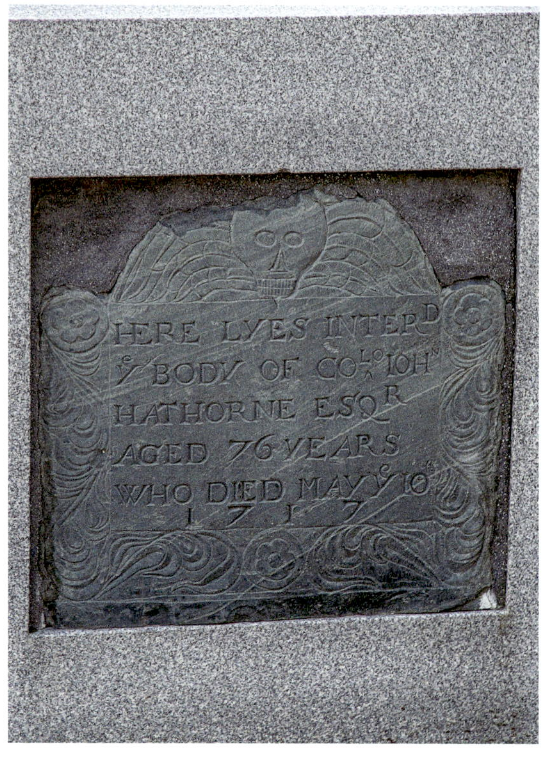

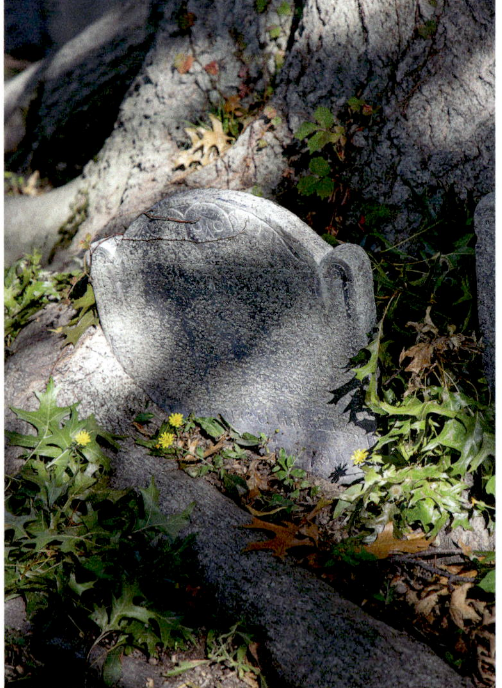

Above left: Preservation of Cap Richard More, a *Mayflower* Pilgrim dead at 1692.

Above right: Judge Hathorne, one of the more notorious residents of Salem, is remembered today as the judge from the Salem witch trials. Hathorne is less known as the great-great-grandfather of Nathaniel Hawthorne, buried at Authors' Ridge in Concord.

Right: Doraty Cromwell has the oldest memorial stone inside the Burying Ground in Salem. The year of her death, however, is reported to be a late addition. While the date 1673 is accurate, it is reported to have not been on the stone originally.

Below: The skull and crossbones are a favorite for use in burying grounds.

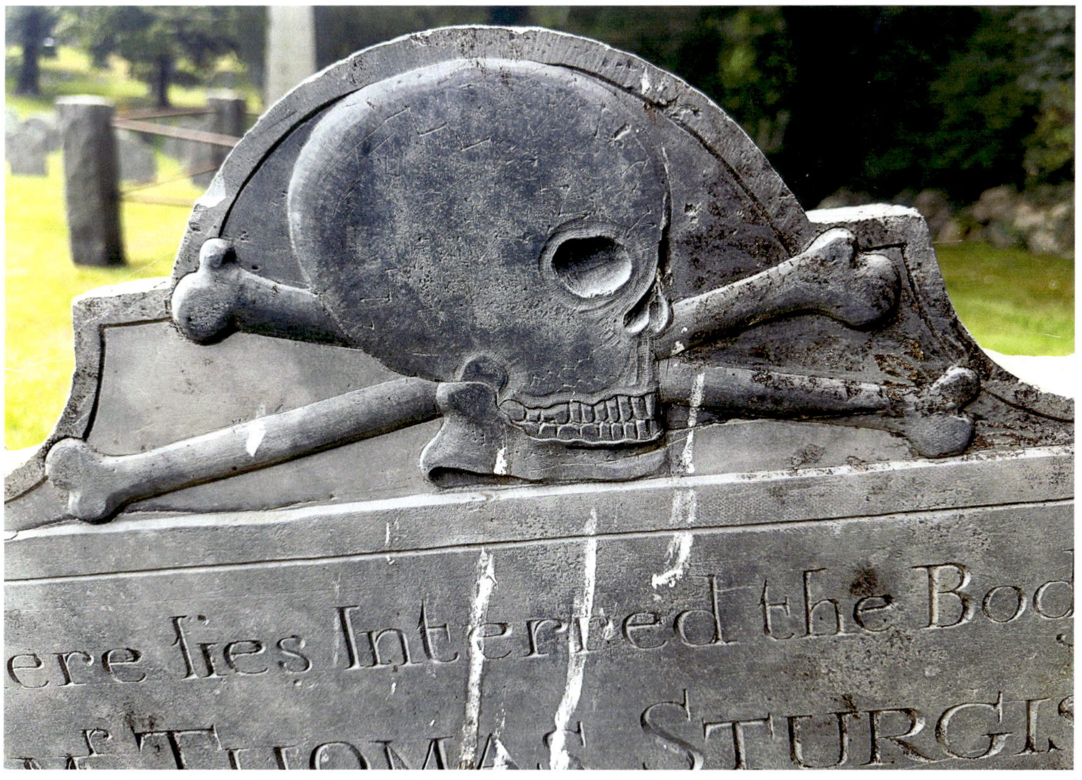

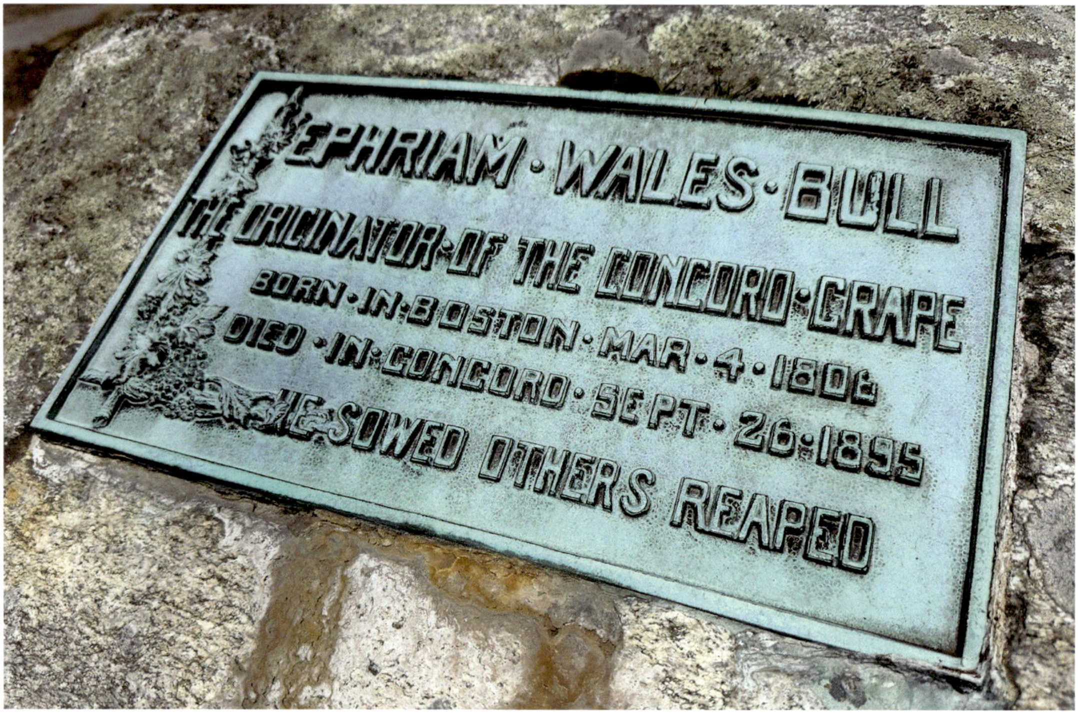

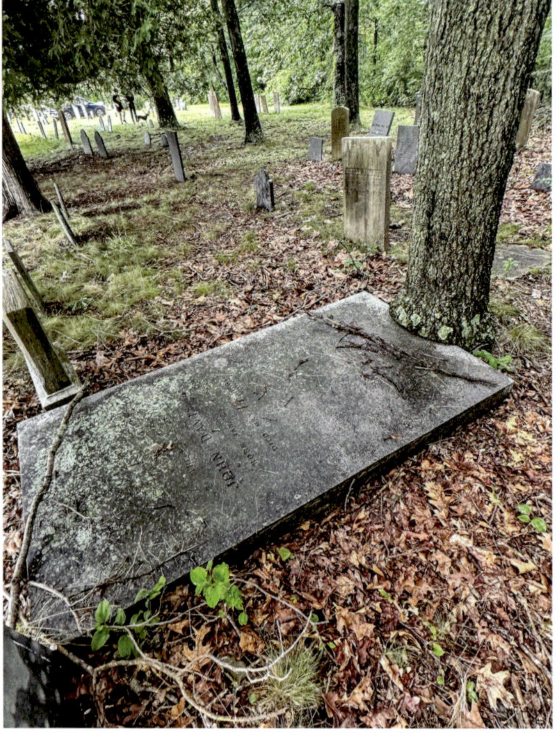

Left: Nature was here before us, and it will be here after us.

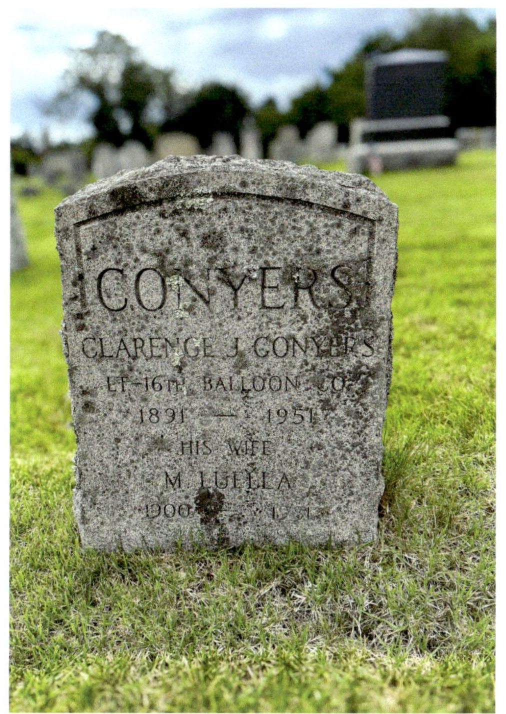

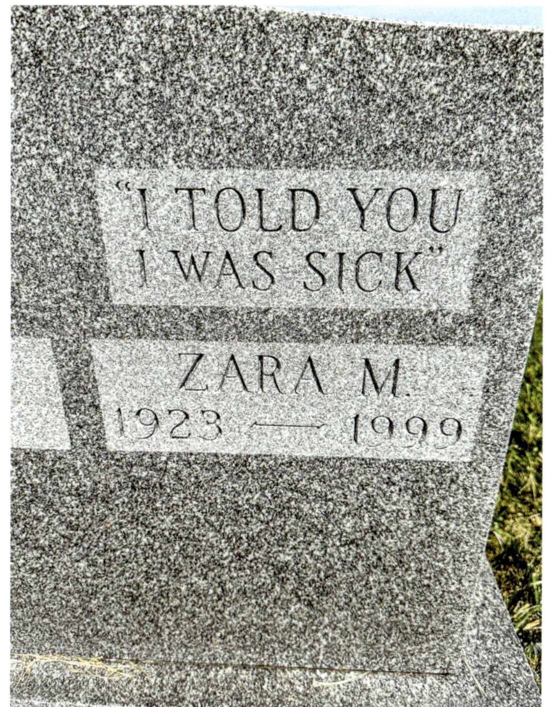

Above left: During World War I, the Balloon Company was part of the AEF, otherwise known as the American Expeditionary Forces.

Right: He would rather be fishing.

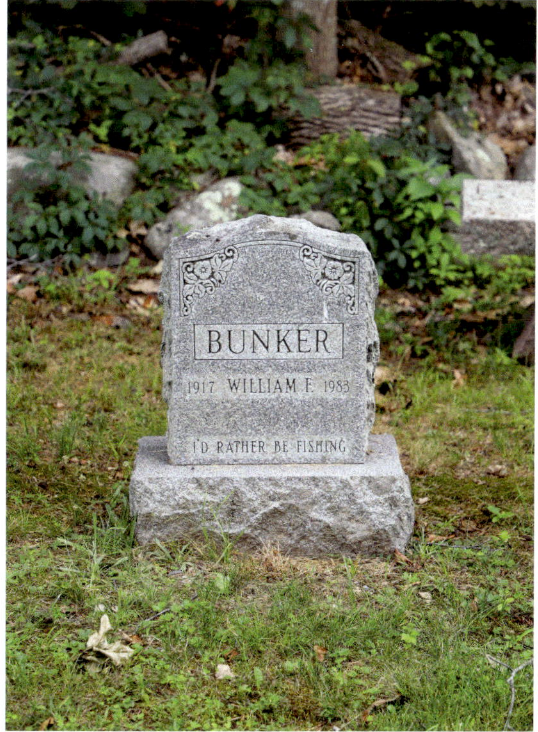

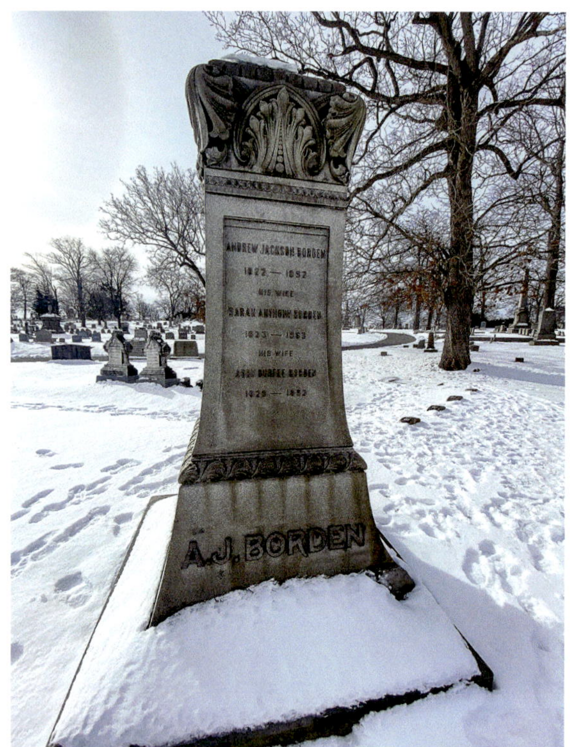

Left: Andrew, Sarah, and Abby Borden with daughters, Emma and Elizabeth, buried behind them.

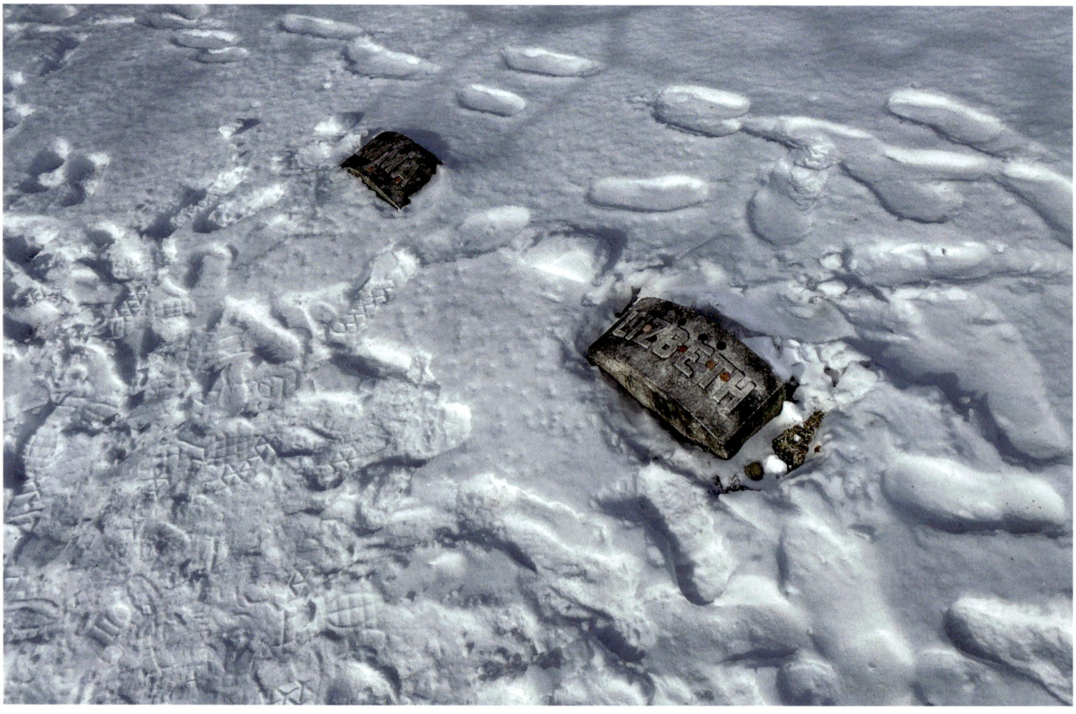

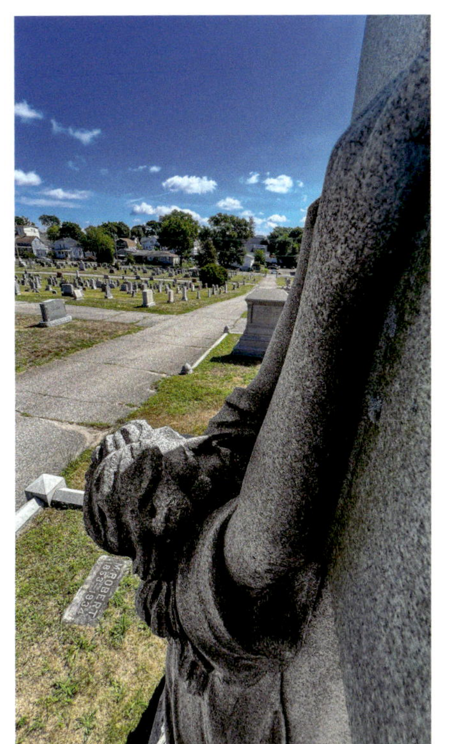

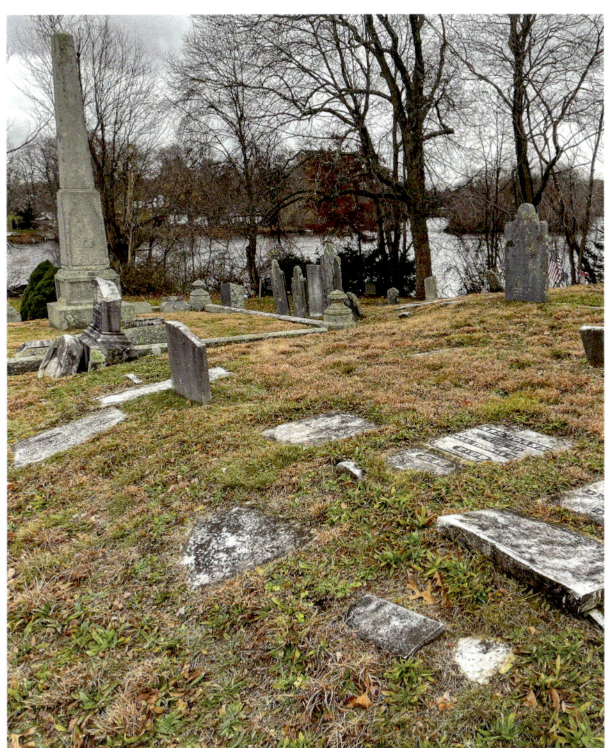

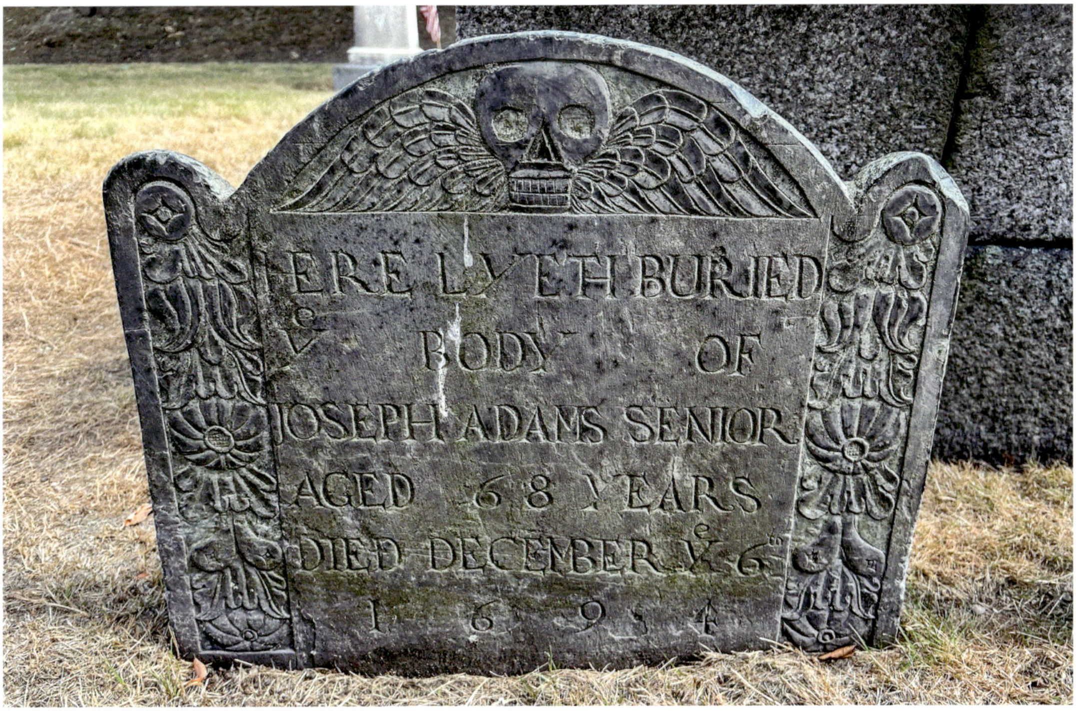

ERE LYETH BURIED
ye BODY OF
JOSEPH ADAMS SENIOR
AGED 68 YEARS
DIED DECEMBER ye 6th
1694

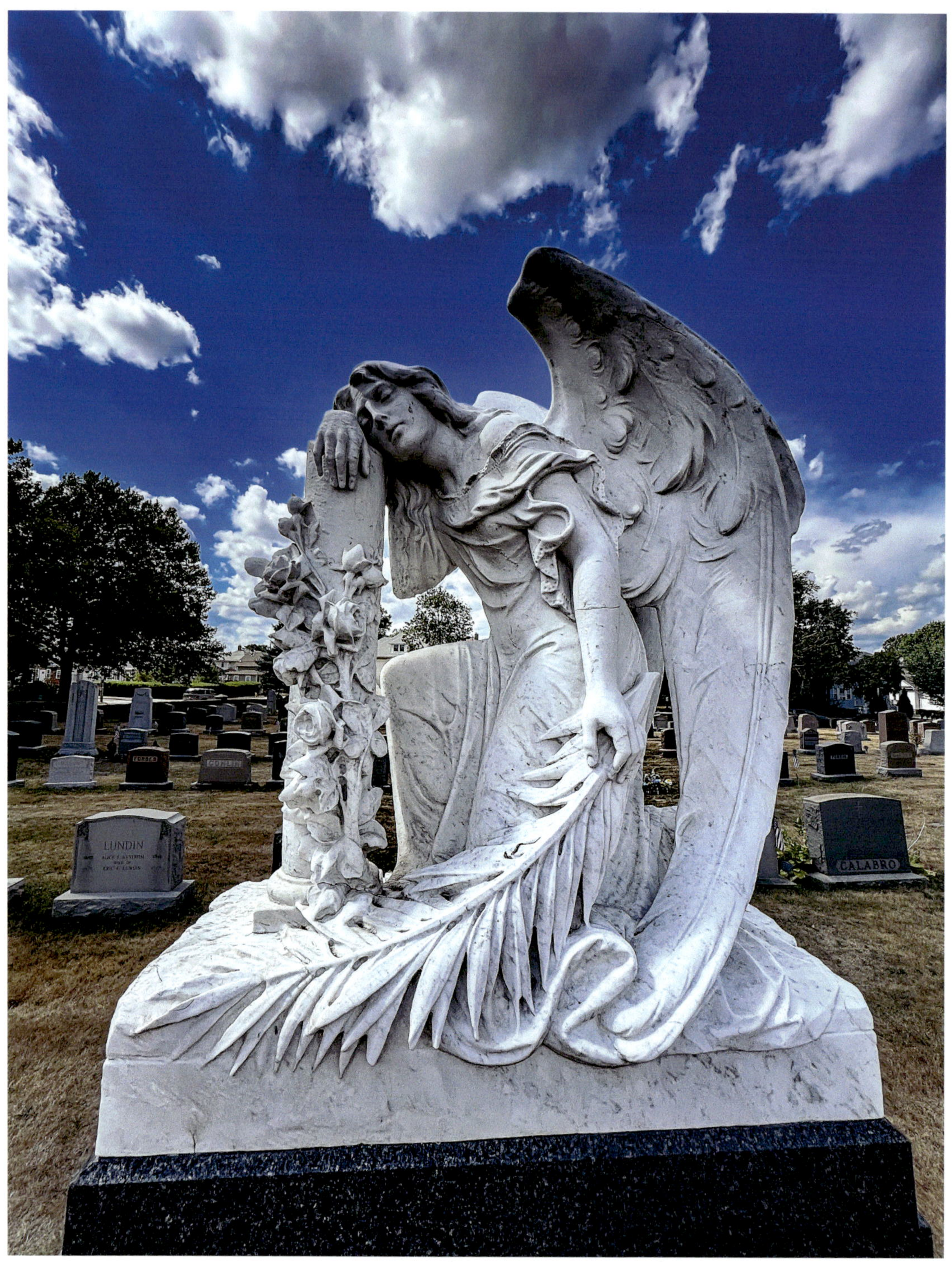
LUNDIN
CALABRO

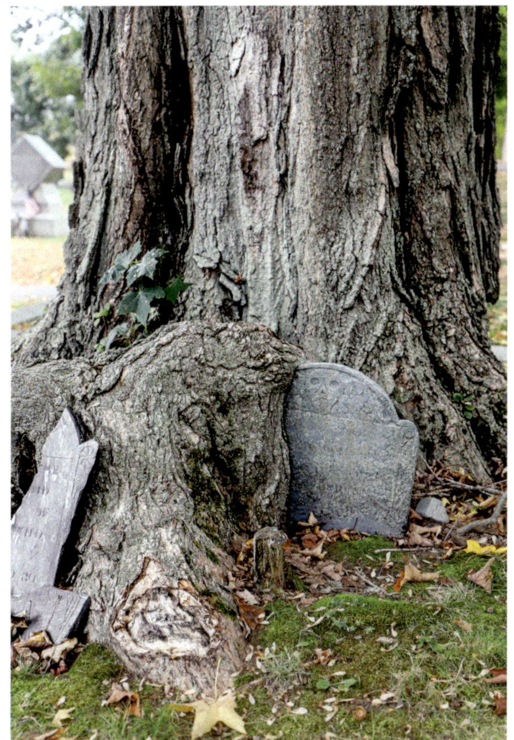

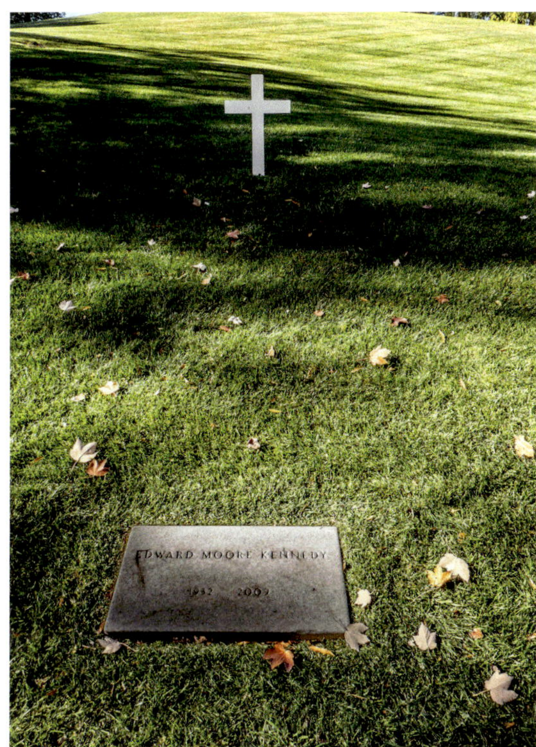

Above left: Some slate markers that have survived the centuries without giving into disintegrating through layer breakaways are generally exceptions in New England. For those who do survive, there is always a new challenge, like this tree absorbing them into it.

Above right: The youngest of Joe and Rose Kennedy's children, Senator Edward "Ted" Kennedy, a Massachusetts native, joined three of his brothers, his sister-in-law, and a niece and nephew in Arlington National Cemetery.

Right: Joseph P. Kennedy Jr., the eldest of the Kennedy children, born in Hull, Massachusetts, and died in Europe during a World War II mission.

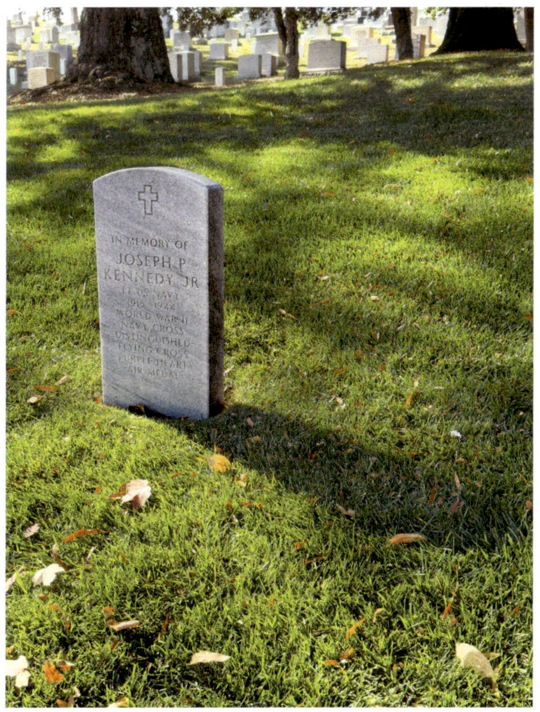

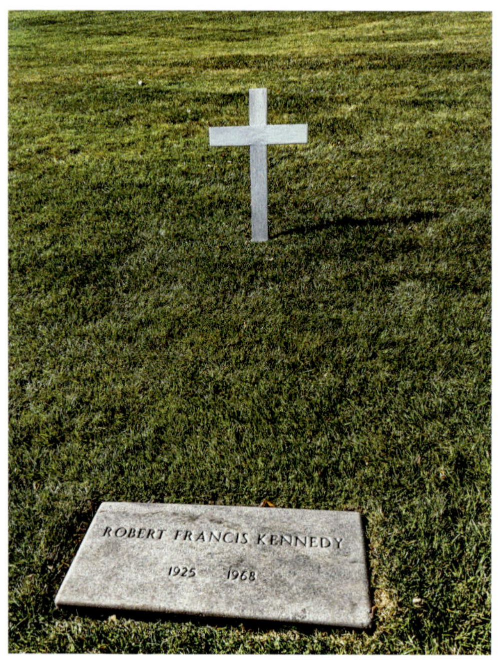

Left: The impact of New England on America has been carried across in many ways. One of the most predominant ways has been through politics. Robert Kennedy, senator from New York, attorney general of the United States, and presidential contender was assassinated in California.

Below: John F. Kennedy, 35th president of the United States, former congressman, senator from Massachusetts, and veteran of World War II, was buried in Arlington National Cemetery and has been joined by his widow, Jacqueline, their briefly lived son, Patrick, and their infant daughter.

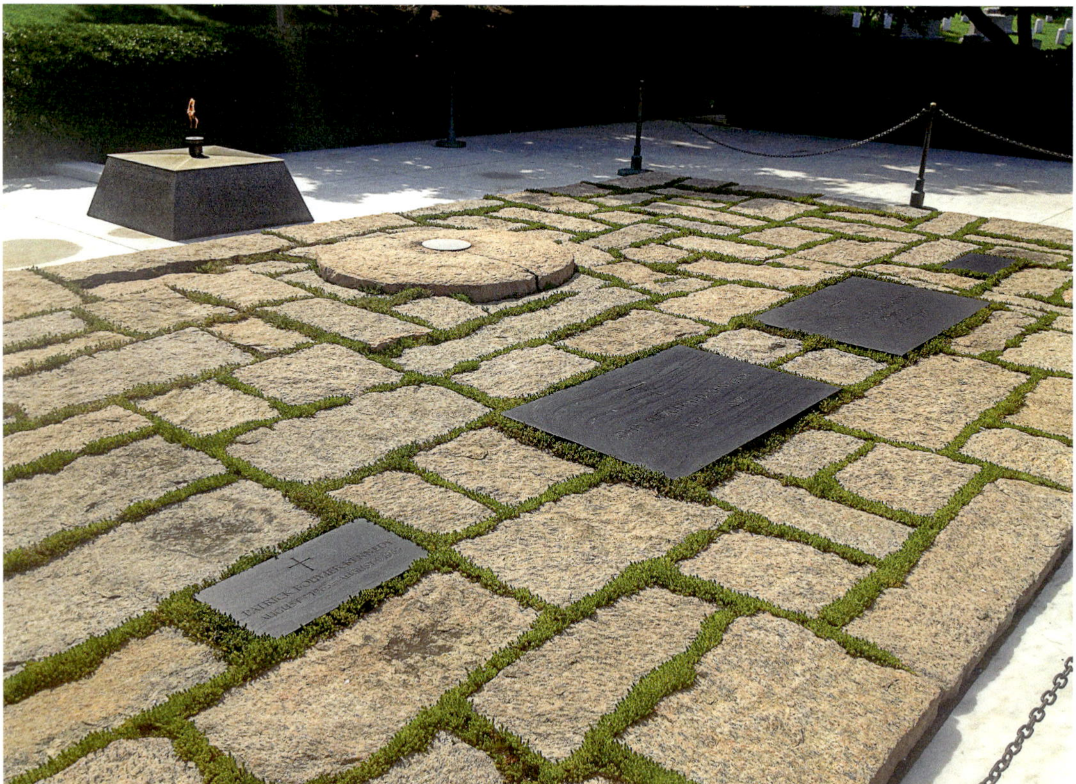

3
New Hampshire

The Granite State, North Virginia, New England, and the Live Free or Die State

New Hampshire, like many of the New England States, began under British direction and funds. European settlement began to capitalize on the fishing opportunities available. Those original villages eventually grew to be Dover and Rye, both chosen for their fishing advantages. Eventually this area was parceled out, under the direction of the British Crown. Prior to the arrival and establishment of European settlers, this area was home to a large number of indigenous peoples. They would utilize the areas for hunting and foraging, living, in many ways, in concert with the wilderness. Over time, New Hampshire would welcome settlers from Great Britain, Ireland, Scotland, and Canada. Today, one is welcomed along the highway to New Hampshire with signs that read "Bienvenue." The greeting is intertwined with the rich French heritage of so many French Canadians. To this day also lives the representation of the Scottish heritage found in many places, but especially in the Scottish Highland Games hosted annually in Lincoln.

New Hampshire has experienced much development and modernization over the 400 or so years of its colonization, but it still maintains its lush forests and natural beauty. The expansive wilderness that cared for and nurtured the Abenaki, a term used collectively for the native populations, as well as the lakes, mountains, and beautiful woodlands, still provides enjoyment for people today. Of course, further expansion of European villages and settlements resulted in less lands for the native peoples, resulting in their relocation or demise as they fought for their freedom in various wars. Many of the burial practices of New Hampshire's early settlers matched those of the surrounding colonies. Early burials feature many depictions of death on the tombstones. Skulls and crossbones, alone or with wings, adorn many of the oldest stones still standing today. The first burial ground of colonial New Hampshire was established in the early seventeenth century, in the Dover Colony.

Today it is easy to find those buried Granite Staters in the many burial spots across the state. Inside those spaces you are likely to find captains of ships used for trade, fishing, war, and exploration. Preachers and their flocks. Pioneering and notable women from across the decades. Children lost to frigid winters or outbreaks of disease. Men and women who contributed not only to New Hampshire, but many who contributed to America itself and even the world. Notably, the 14th president of the United States, Franklin Pierce, is buried in Concord. The only president to date to call New Hampshire home, Mr. Pierce's grave is exceptionally unremarkable. Sat inside a small, segregated area surrounded by fencing, the Pierce headstone includes the president, his wife, Jane, and their children. Mr. Pierce, a former U.S. congressman and senator, went on to serve one term inside the Oval Office. The grave of the Pierce family is indeed notable, in that it is dwarfed by monuments inside the same burying ground. The relatively simple grave marker sits with the names alone, no remnants of the presidency or other offices once held. President Pierce, apparently, approached death in a manner consistent with his fellow Granite State residents—simply.

Modern New Hampshire fights a fight that is not unfamiliar in the neighboring states —preservation *versus* prosperity. As corporate America continues to branch out ever further from Boston, so too do the workers. Farmlands have become cities; wooded areas are encroached upon regularly and often go to the highest bidder. Families continue to part and parcel off their land in order to survive financially. In roughly 120 years, the population has risen by more than a million people. Peering back to the founding of the state and its reported 500 European settlers, a modern population of more than 1.4 million people would have seemed impossible. While modern New Hampshire fights to blend its past and present, it is hard to see a clear path forward for both sides to make it to the future. The granite state of the 2020s is one that has seen its forests significantly reduced, its Man on the Mountain collapsed, and its historic cemeteries encroached upon. Once-desolate rivers are now the focal point of waterfront breweries, mountain tops now host skiers from the region and beyond, and the supple waters off the coast are now over-exploited commercial fishing grounds. Expansive centuries-old burying grounds are now reduced and squeezed between the many large buildings that stand around them. New Hampshire will continue, that seems certain, but how much of this unique and tangible history will go with it seems uncertain at best. For a state so proud of its history, so unwilling to remove the Man on the Mountain from its state symbols, it seems that its tangible history in the burial yards of the state may indeed be at risk of going extinct.

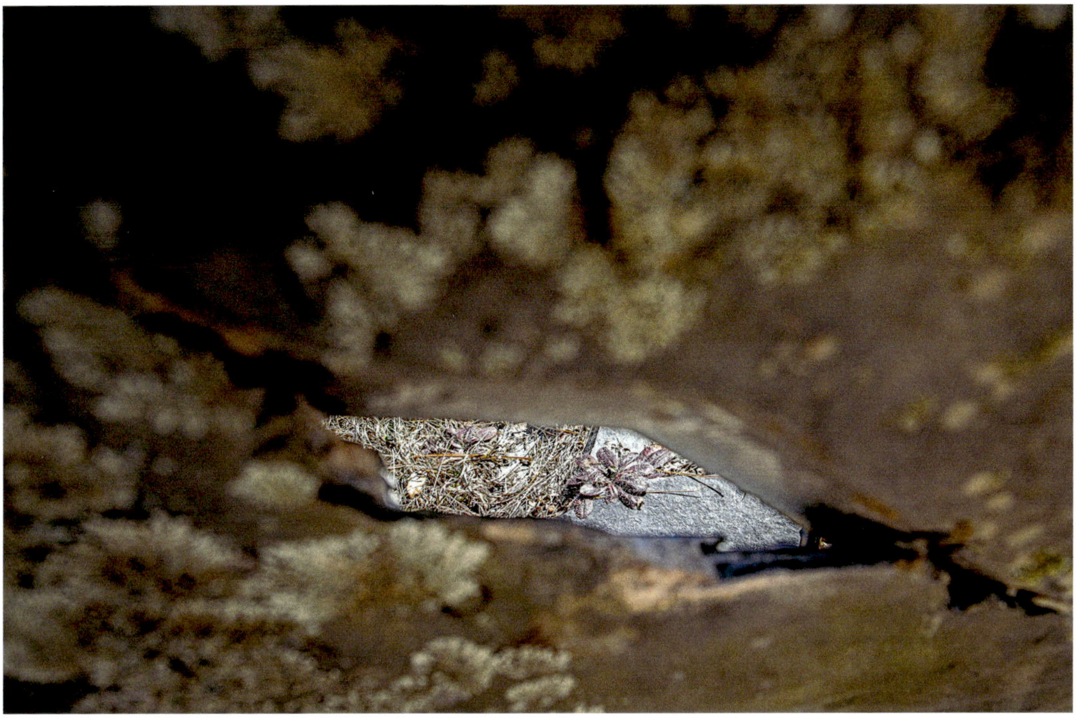

Above: A grave seen through a grave.

Right: Died at Brady's Bend, Pennsylvania, in 1853.

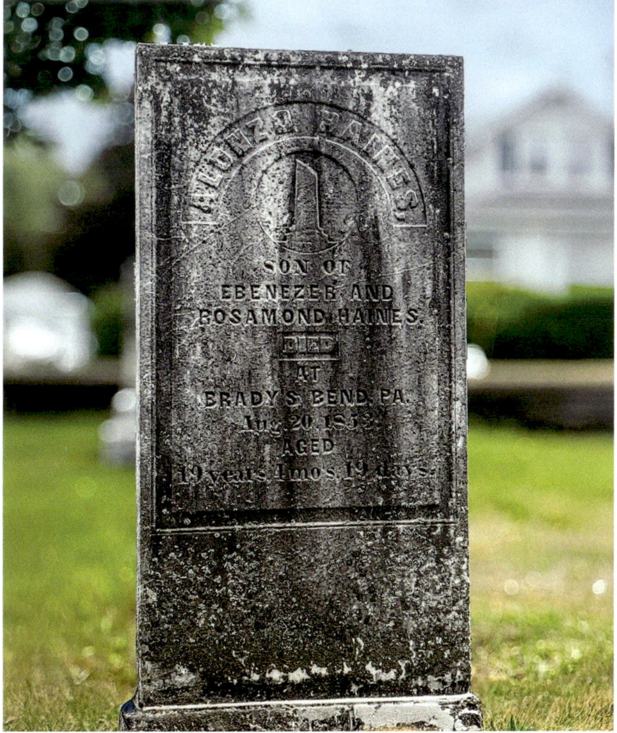

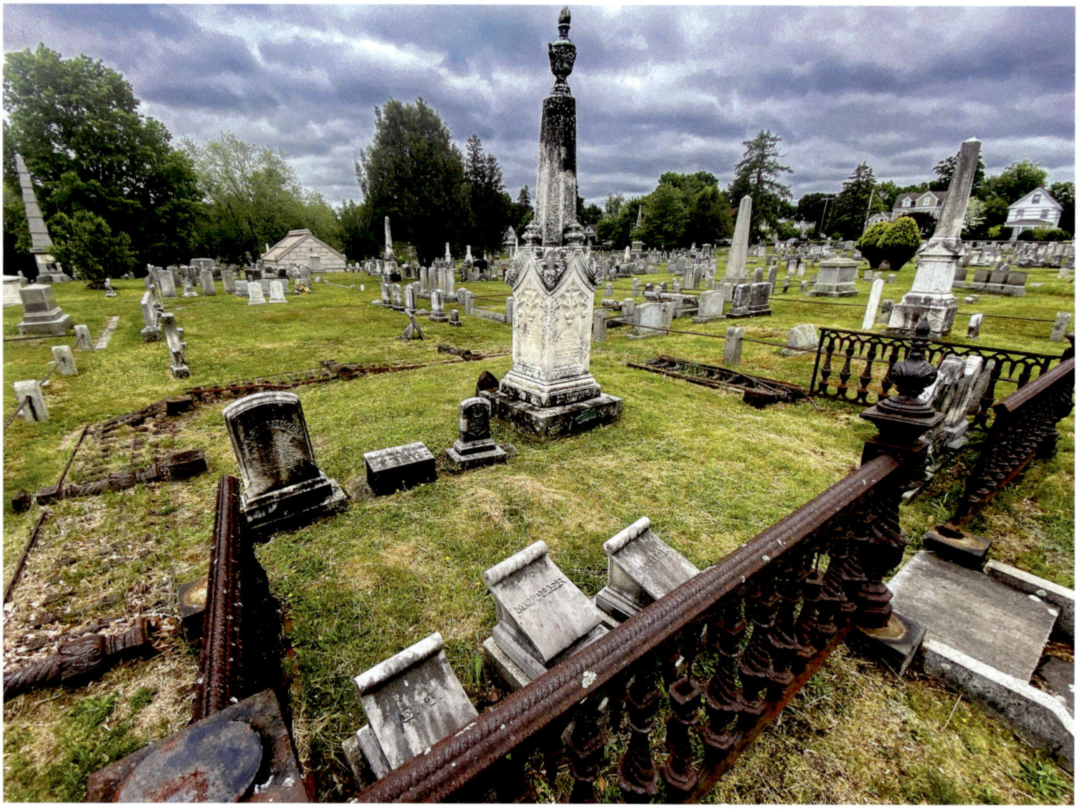

Above: Harmony Grove Cemetery in Portsmouth, New Hampshire, is reported to have opened in 1847. Nearly 180 years after opening, sections of the cemetery have begun their return to the earth. As seen in this image, an ornate family plot shows its age as it falls into the ground.

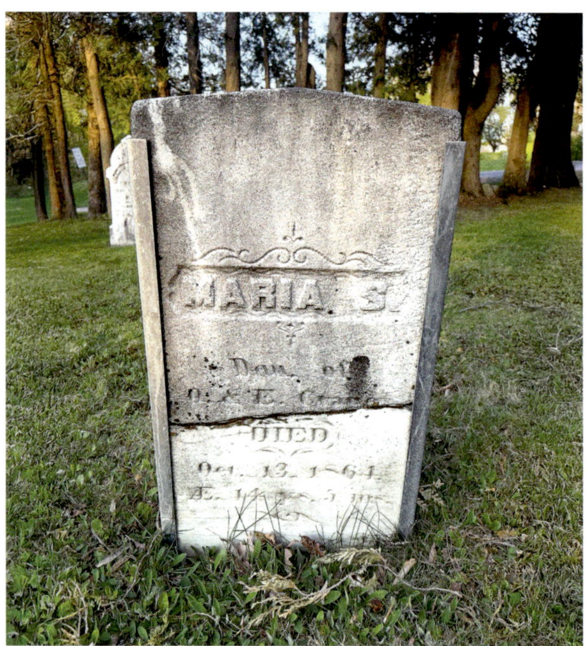

Left: In an attempt to maintain the stone memorial of Maria, two sides have been added after the stone broke in two.

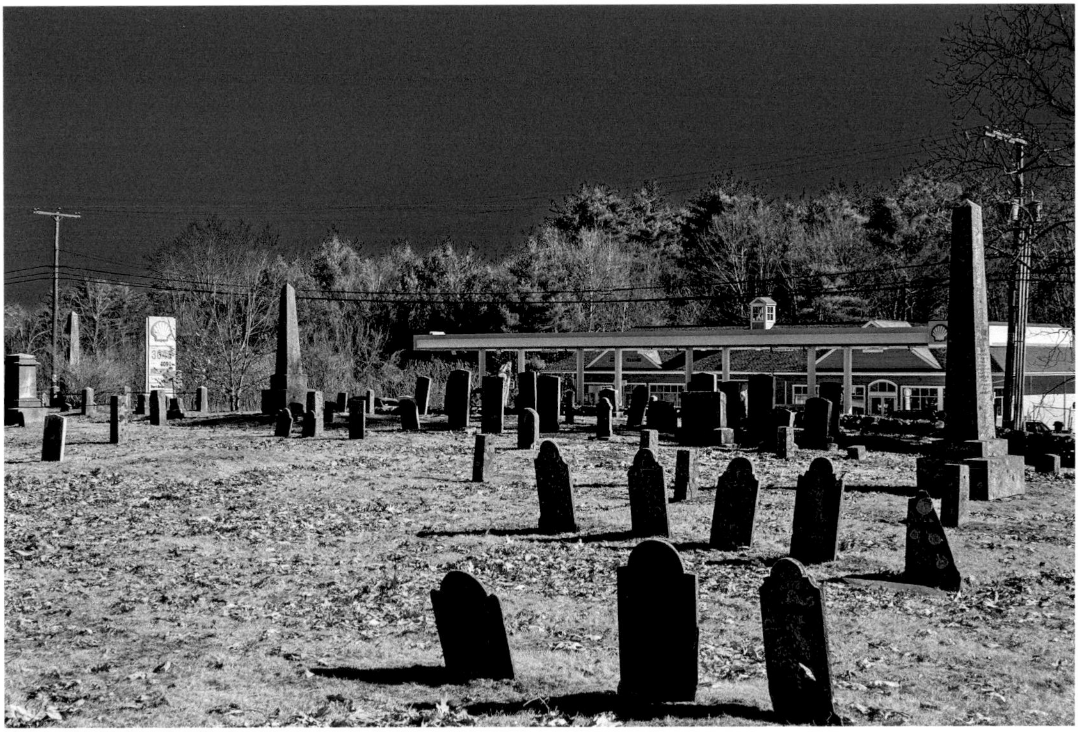

Once a quiet area of burial and memorialization, this cemetery today sits across a busy road from a gas station.

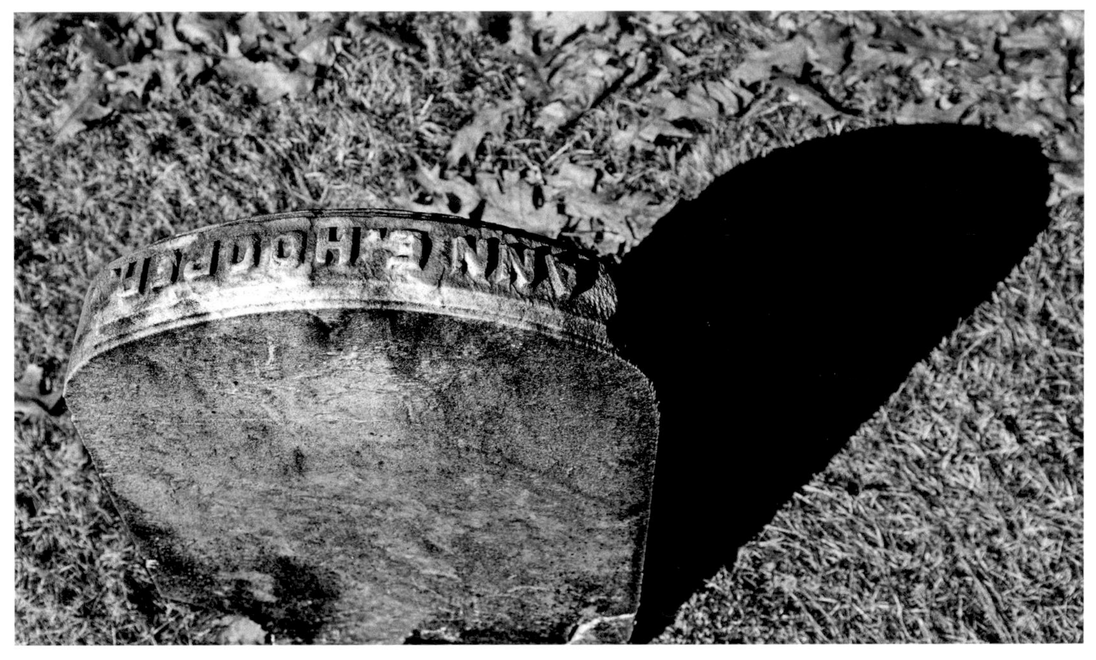

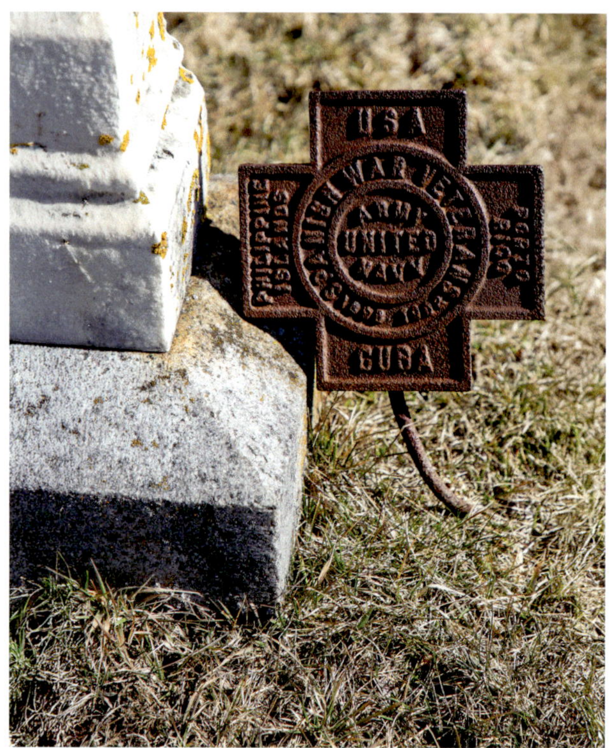

Left: Alongside a grave sits a medallion honoring the war veterans time in Cuba, Porto Rico, and the Philippine Islands.

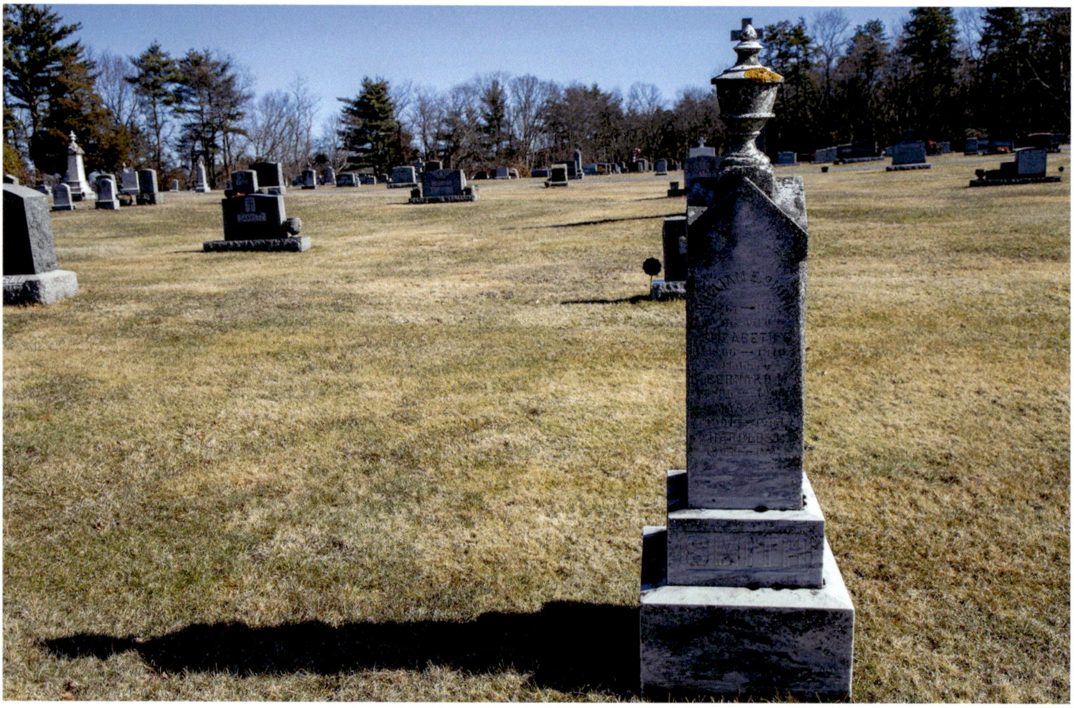

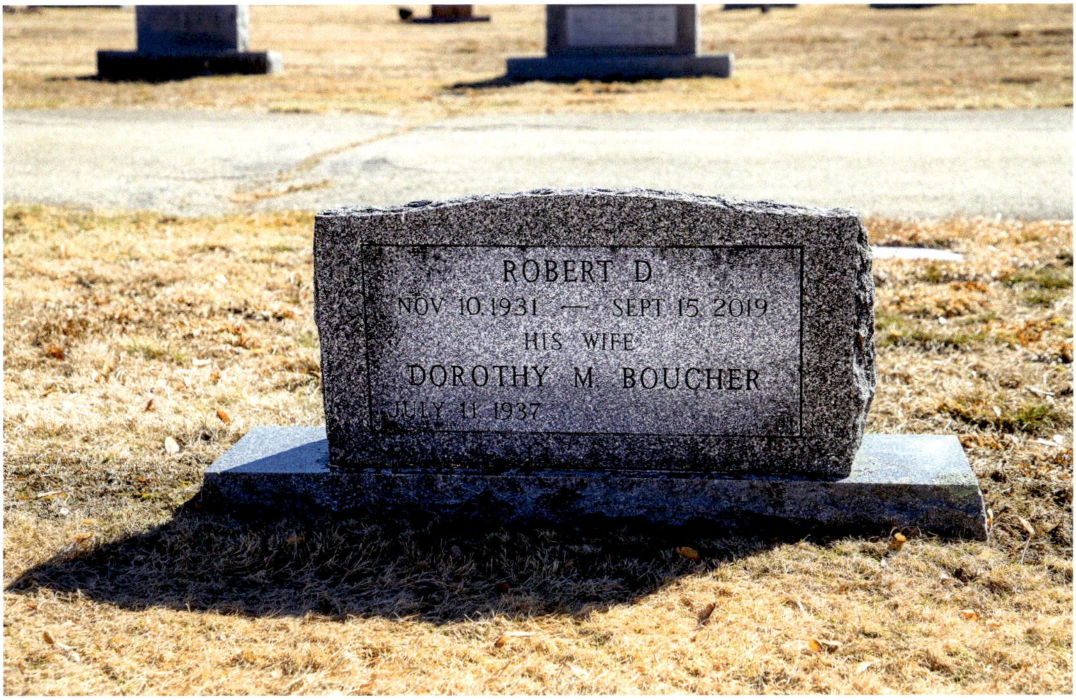

When death does us part, our reunion may begin.

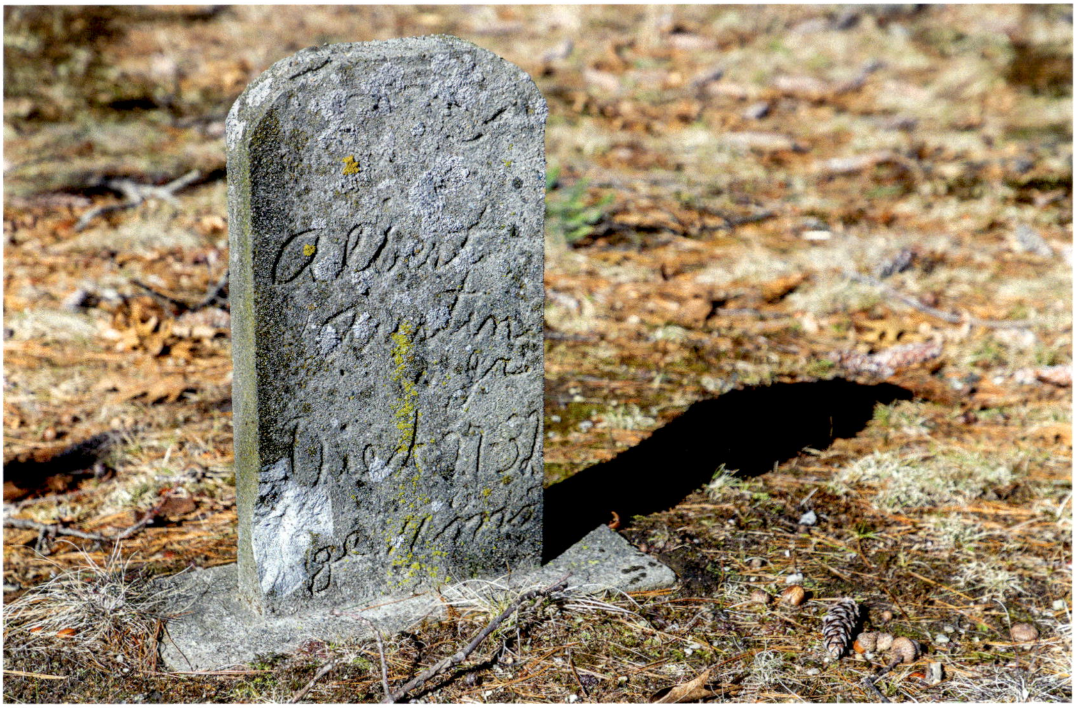

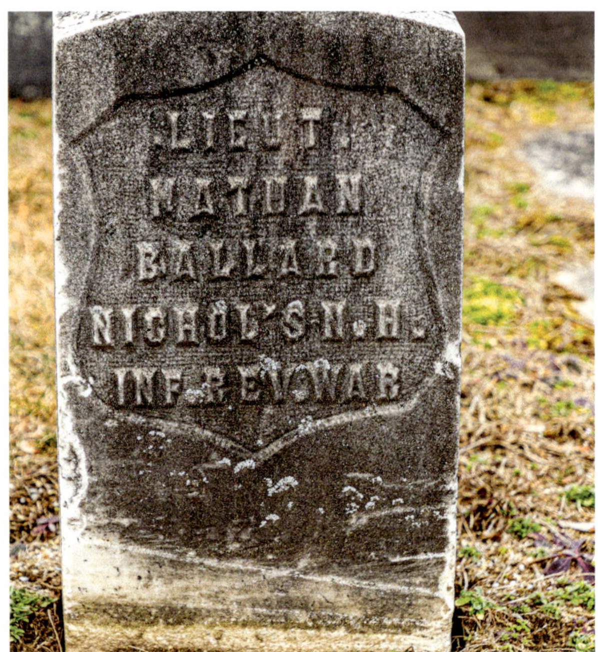

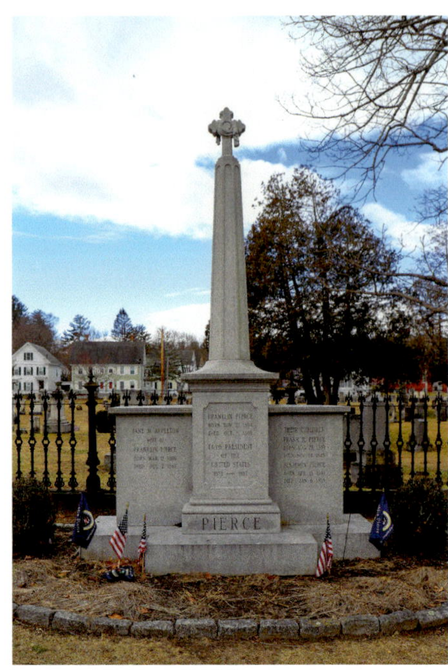

Above right: The 14th president of the United States and family.

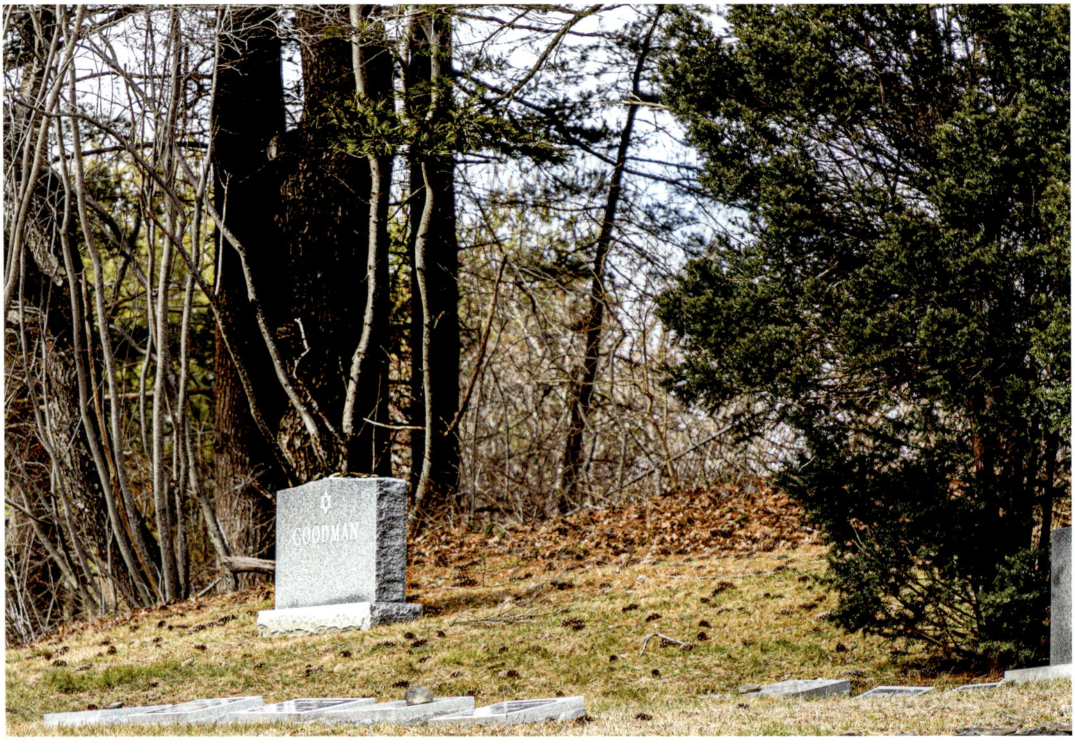

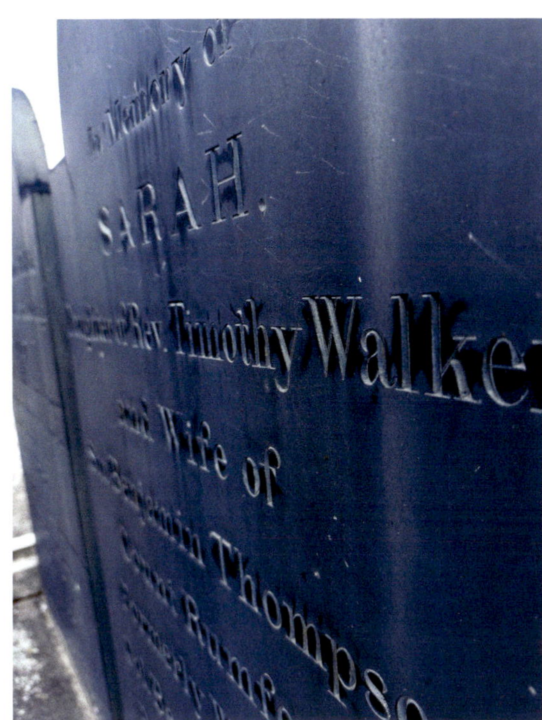

Below: A spoonbill bird appears to interact with its young.

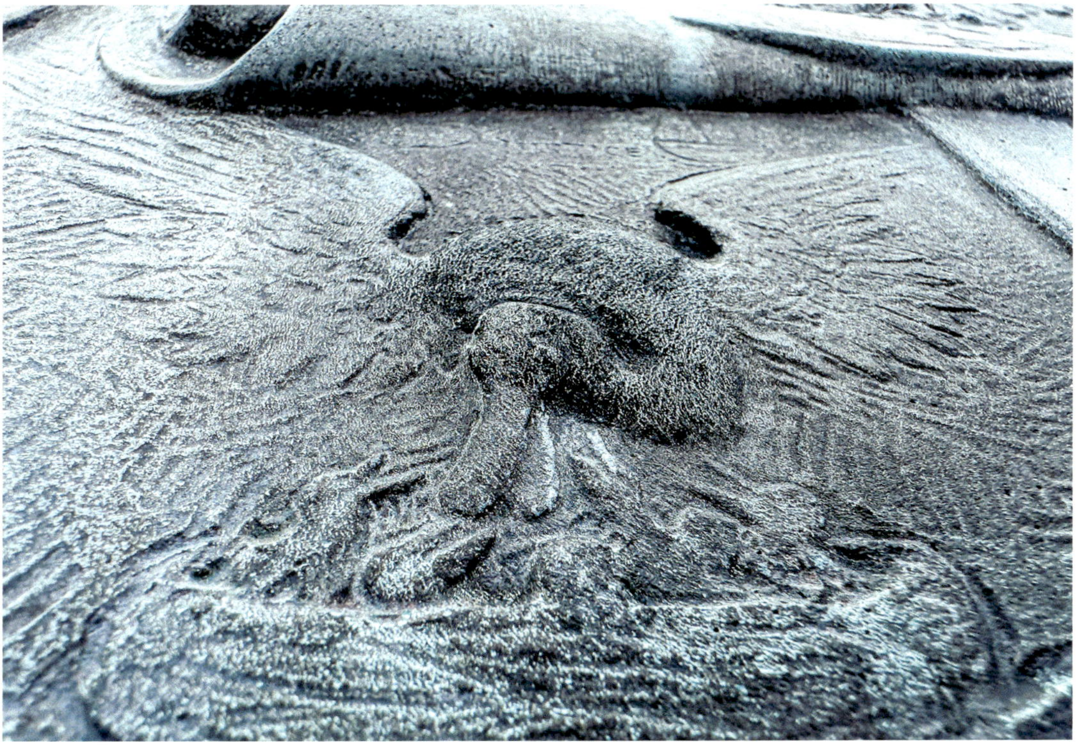

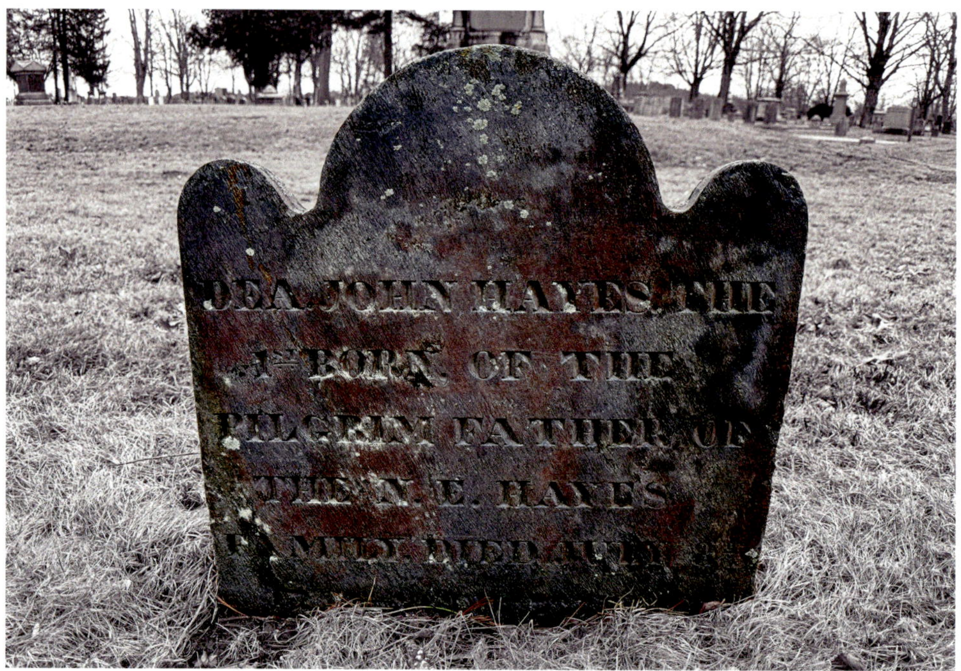

First born of the Pilgrim Father of the N.E. Hayes Family.

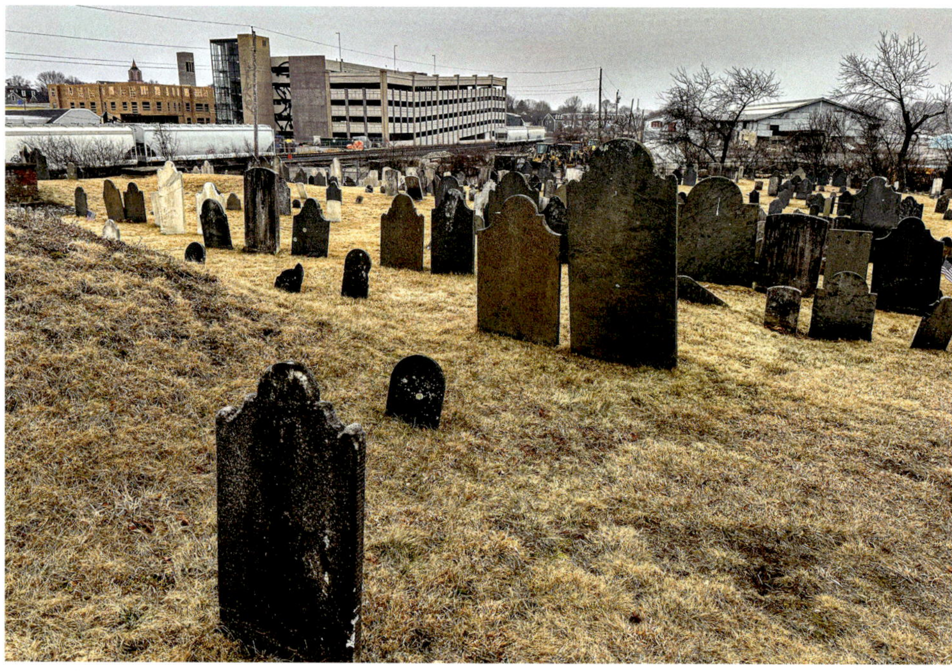

North Cemetery is the second oldest burial ground in the city. While the cemetery sprang up in the 1750s, the parking garage behind it is a much more modern addition to the landscape.

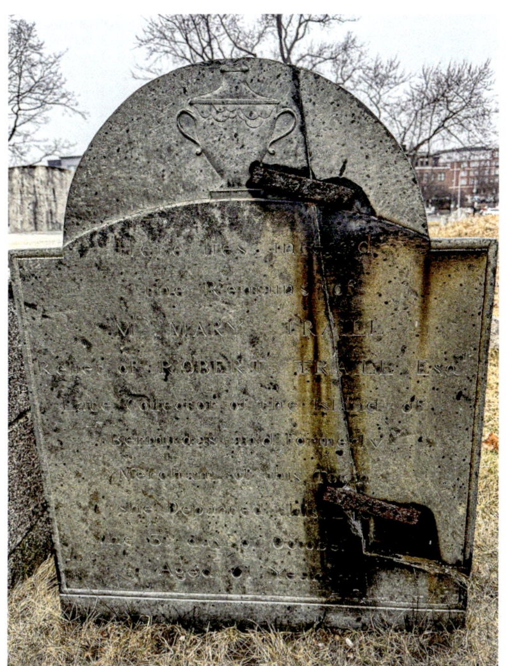

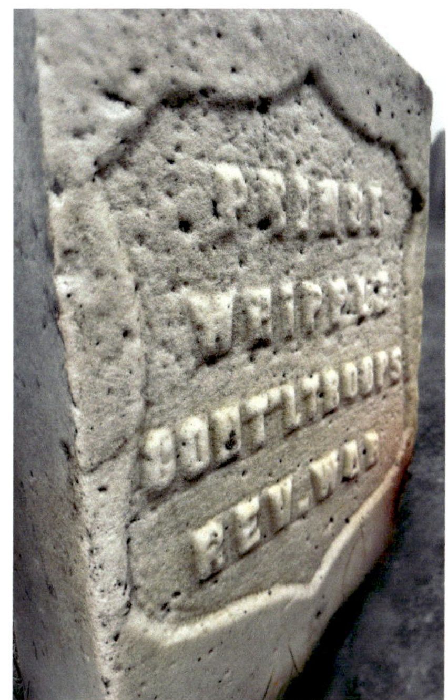

Above left: Maintenance of stones that have stood for centuries is a difficult task.

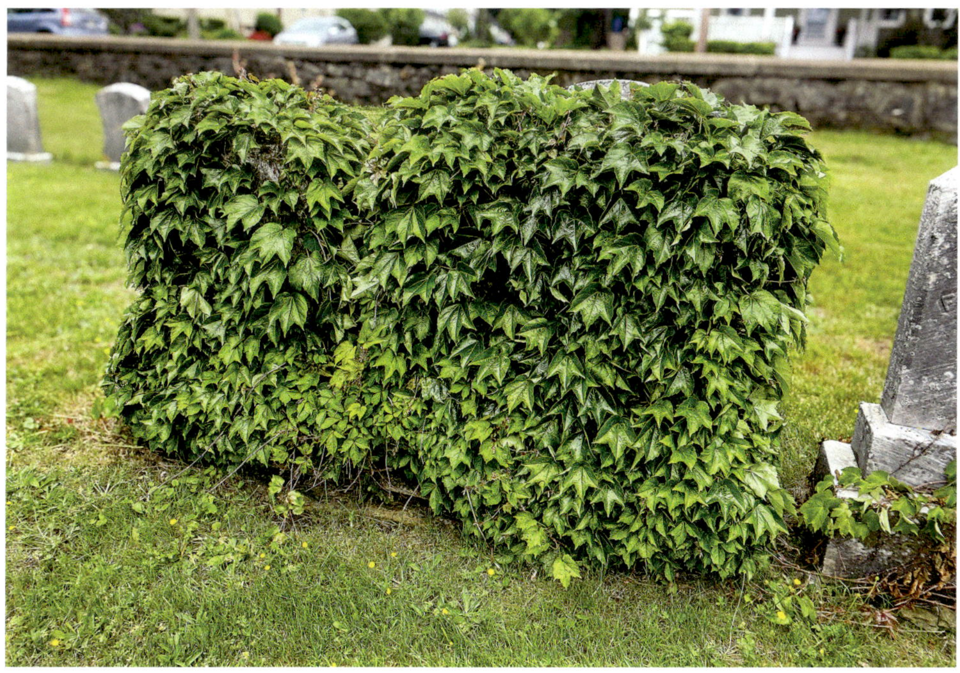

Never underestimate ivy.

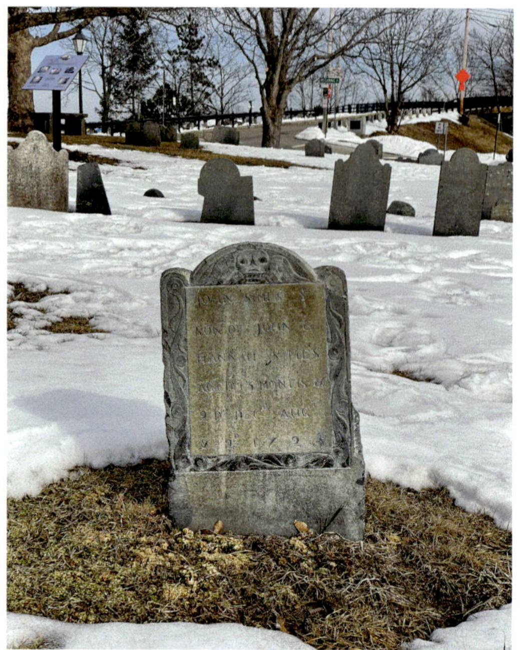

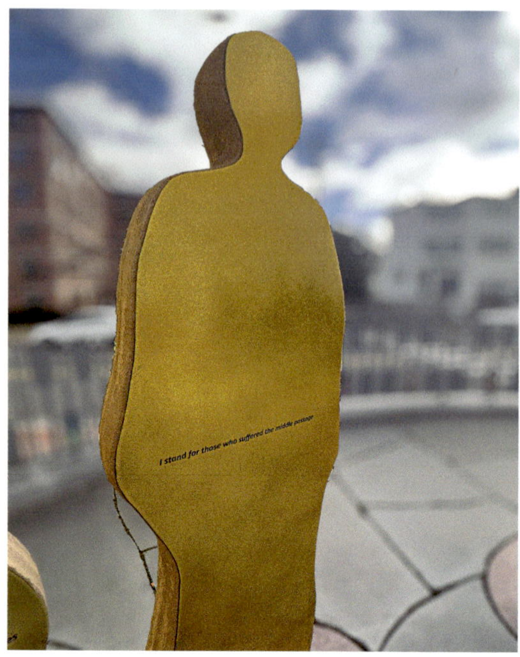

Above left: The 1700s and the modern world intersect alongside the Point of Graves in Portsmouth, New Hampshire. Ancient stones looking up on traffic and parked cars.

Above right: This stunning memorial sits above what was once the burying ground for people of color in Portsmouth, NH. The original burial ground held several hundred freed and enslaved peoples.

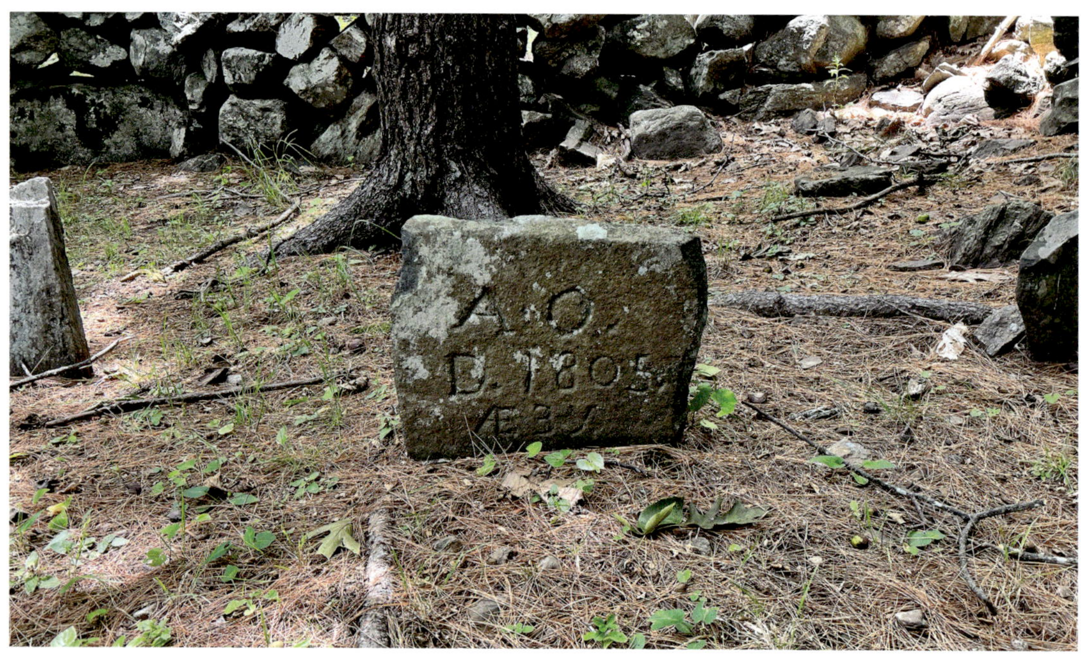

4
Rhode Island

Aquidneck Island, Roodt Eylandt, Aquethneck, Isle of Rodes, The Ocean State

The smallest state in the United States has proven resilient and unique across its time—from the native populations and their relationship with the land and waters that make up this area, which was and is made up of areas of islands from colonial usage and modern times. Rhode Island was once home to the Pequot, Nipmucs, Niantics, Narragansetts, and Wampanoag indigenous groups. Through bloodshed, slavery, and other inhumane practices, the colonization and expansion of what would become Rhode Island left the indigenous peoples to see, over the centuries, their land virtually nonexistent today. The first major change toward colonization began in Massachusetts, where a young man, unhappy with the status quo, set out on foot to the "undiscovered" areas to the south. Mr. Roger Williams had been run out of Massachusetts over religious persecution. His new home, he planned, would offer refuge from such situations, and would offer more religious liberty. Upon arriving in the areas that would one day make up central Rhode Island, Roger Williams took control in a way that was different from all the other colonies; he worked with the native peoples to negotiate for the land. Of course, this historic retelling is told through the prism of those who would inherit that land and who would aid that reduction of native peoples from it. Whatever the truth may have been, this story has been retold, celebrating Williams, and spreading the state motto of "hope."

When exploring the burial grounds of Rhode Island, you are treated to a cornucopia of history, folklore, exceptionalism, and darkness. In addition, you will frequently find epitaphs indicating that those buried beneath them were members of the Mass Bay Colony or the Commonwealth of Massachusetts. Rhode Island, with its small size, massive waterfront lands, and farmable lands saw a number of boundary changes across time. The Ocean State, a phrase that would become synonymous with the formal name, also offers some unique burials and memorials. It is a state with many on-farm family plots, public and private plots, and burying grounds dating back to the 1600s with still legible markers. Roger Williams himself, who set out on a journey to explore and colonize this area, did not stop with his death at seventy-nine in 1683. Being laid to rest on his property would be just one step in what is, hopefully, his last journey. The next interruption of his rest would occur around the year 1740 when his grave was opened, reportedly unintentionally. In the late nineteenth century, Williams' "remains" would travel from his home to a family crypt in the North Burial Ground, also within the city of Providence. His next move, in theory his last move, was made in 1939, more than 250 years after his death, when what remained of Williams, mostly dirt from his first burial site, was placed beneath a statue of him on a hill where the founder is able to peer out over his state.

The history that is told by those dead and buried residents was for some time lost and difficult to track. Thankfully that unfortunate neglect of the burial grounds in the state has been largely rectified in recent times. The Rhode Island Historical Cemetery Commission has set upon identifying and preserving the lost or nearly lost Rhode Islanders. This project has seen them catalog and maintain large common burial spaces, family plots, and even known single burial spots. While these burial spaces include fair-sized dedicated public spaces, they also include many spaces that are far smaller, or spaces that have been lost to nature. Driving the just-over 12,200 square miles across Rhode Island, it is not uncommon to see a historic marker and gravesites in yards, business plazas, alongside roads, and anywhere in between. Sitting high above a mall in North Smithfield, a long set of stairs leads to one of the many small family graveyards. In Newport, just outside the active downtown area sits the graves of both free and enslaved people of color. Moving back to the north of the state, inside a picturesque cemetery in Burrillville, the grave of a woman, a wife and mother, sits with the base only. Bathsheba Thayer Sherman, retroactively known as the "witch" of *The Conjuring*, had her grave marker removed from the cemetery due to vandalism. Today, the base is the only relic to reflect that there was a real Bathsheba, beyond the hocus pocus of the Warrens and Hollywood. The lore around Mrs. Sherman includes an alleged relation to a Salem Witch Trial victim, her presence for children who died unexpectedly, and unfortunate ends for herself and her son. The results of twenty-first-century interest in these tales of Bathsheba have been mixed at best, intentionally misrepresented at worst.

In Rhode Island, the history of the state told through its buried dead is as expansive and varied as the growth of the one-time chartered colony. The modern state is overpopulated and overbuilt. As a hamlet of Boston, it now draws in residents who have been priced out of the city area. Grave marker artwork, tombstones, and burial practice that have evolved over the centuries mirror the state's growth from unspoiled native lands, to farmlands, and now its designation as a Tech Hub. The burial ground's variety and preservation of tombstones reflect the prevailing attitudes of the nearly thirty-nine decades that have passed from the 1636 settlement of Roger Williams and our modern day.

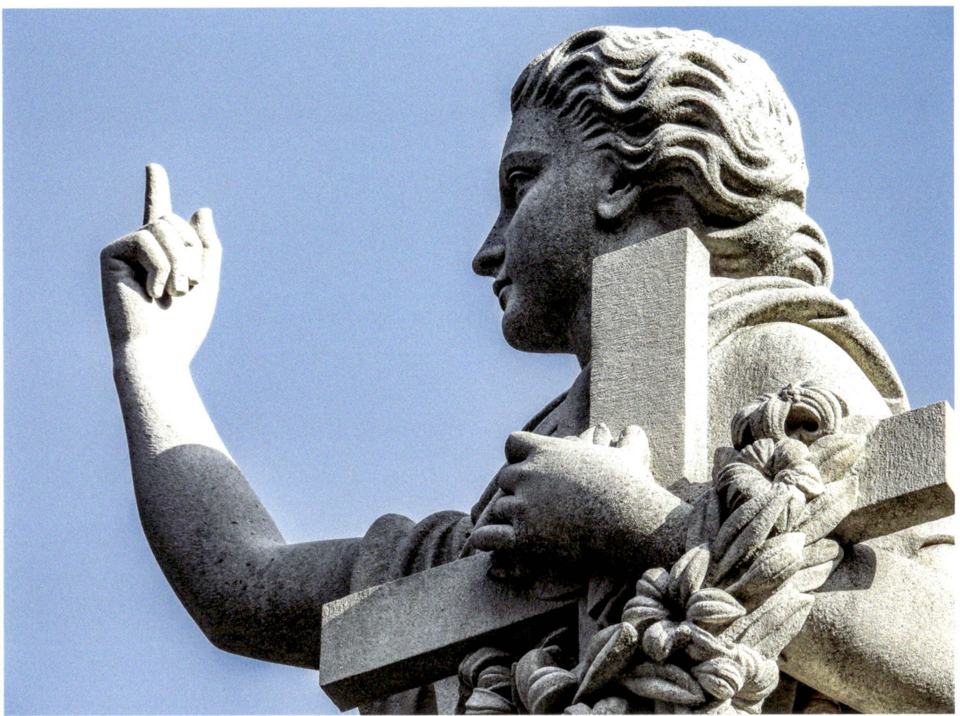

Swan Point Cemetery in Providence, Rhode Island, sits on a 200-acre site. Inside the cemetery is home to stunning pieces of art.

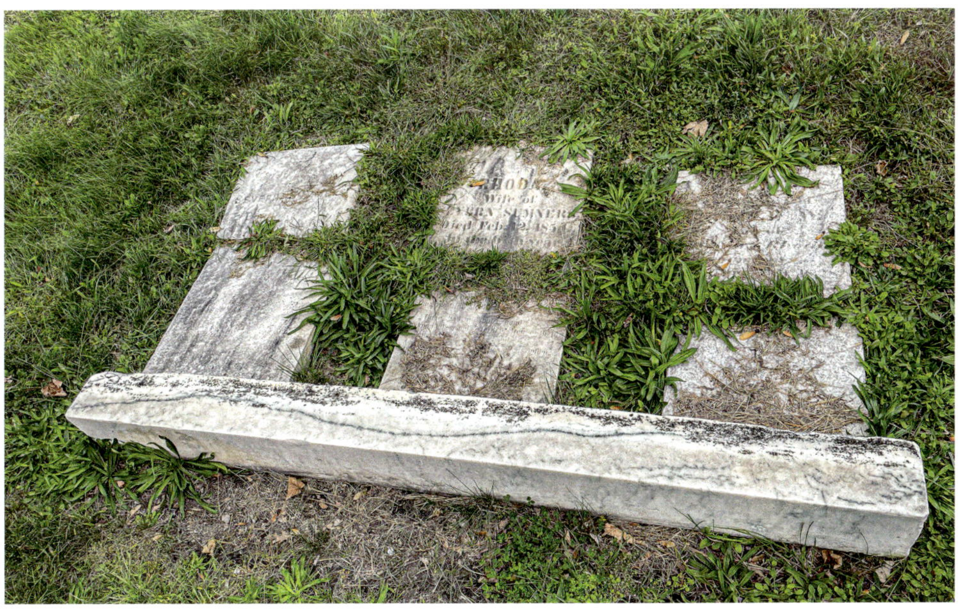

North Burial Ground's extensive history, in the city of Providence, has resulted in this city owned and operated burying ground featuring many monument styles across the centuries.

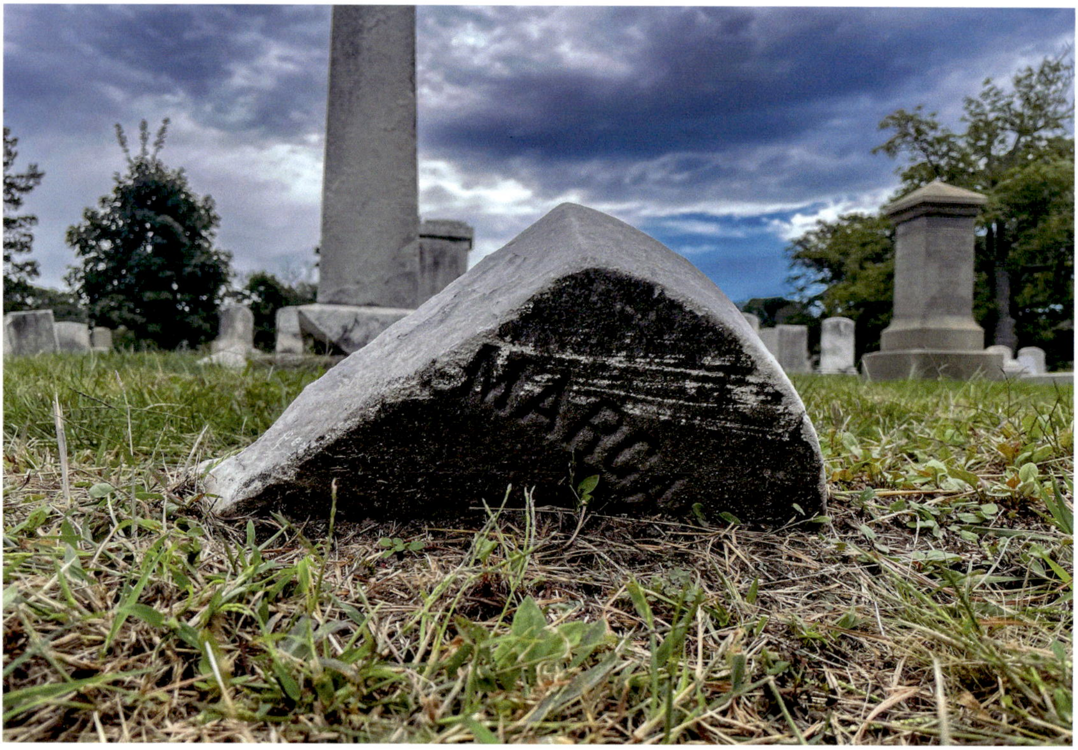

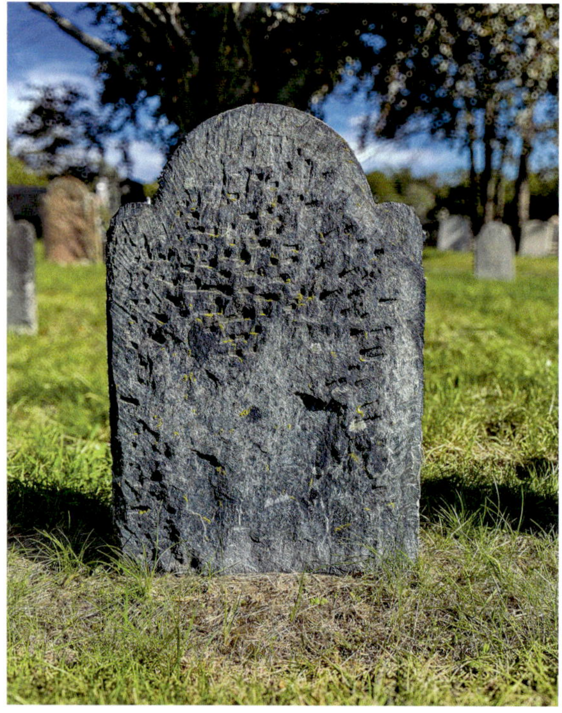

Above: Family lots, like this one, are ubiquitous through the landscapes of New England.

Left: This stone tells a drastically different tale today than the one intended when it was first placed. Inside the Crandall Family Lot in Westerly, Rhode Island, many gravestones have become lichen havens. Lichen is unusual in a number of ways, including its ability to grow on or in areas that could not support root-based growth.

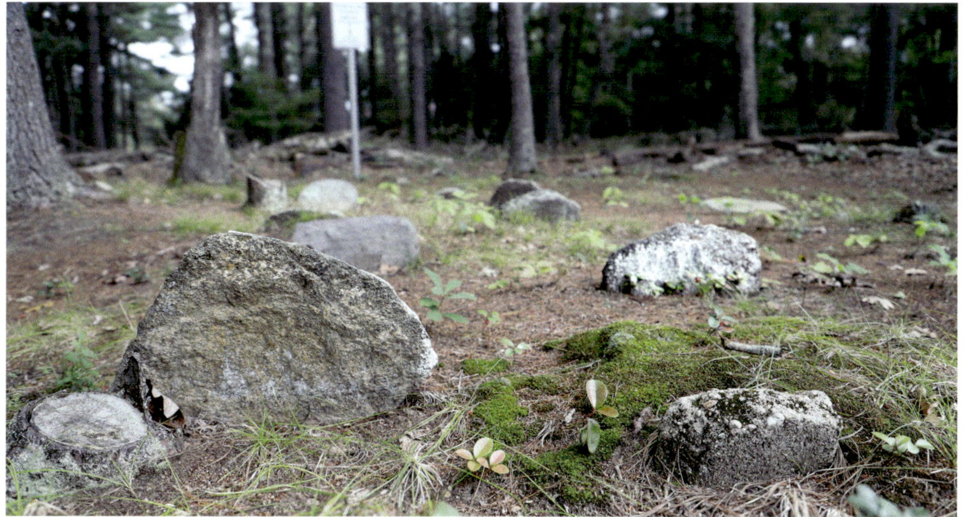

Alongside a busy Woonsocket street down the berm and into a surprisingly natural area, inside a busy city, sits this burial ground. The Friends Church and Burial Grounds sit beneath a significant tree cover and provides a picturesque garden for those dead Friends. Only a small number of the Friends' participants chose to have grave markers accompany their burial, with the rest choosing to be buried without a marker, allowing them to dissolve back into nature with minimal disturbance. The approach used for the burying grounds has left it difficult to accurately distinguish rocks from grave markers.

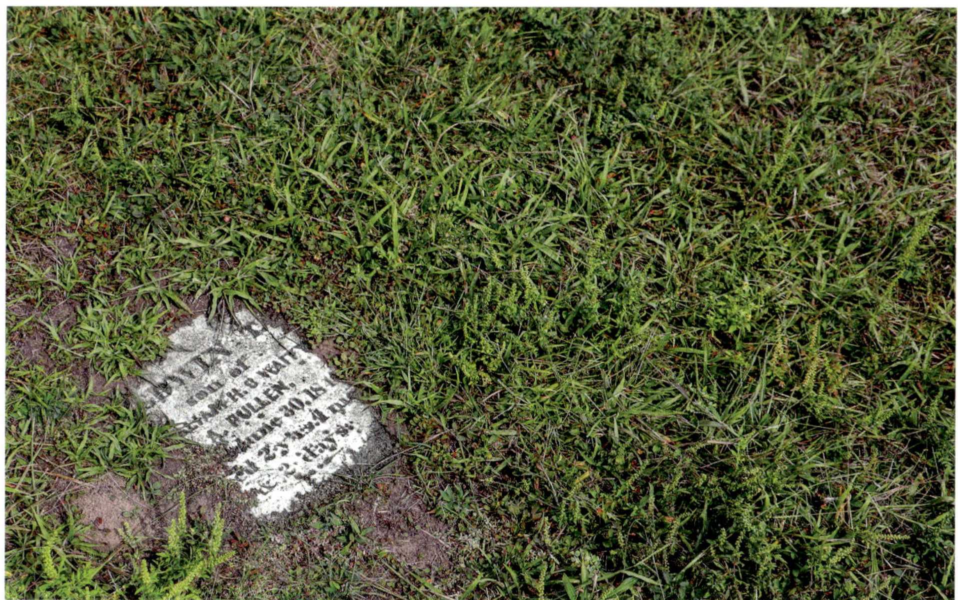

With hot and humid summers, wet and cold springs, warm days and cool nights during the autumn, and freezing temperatures and heavy wet snow in the winter, it is easy to see how tombstones are destroyed.

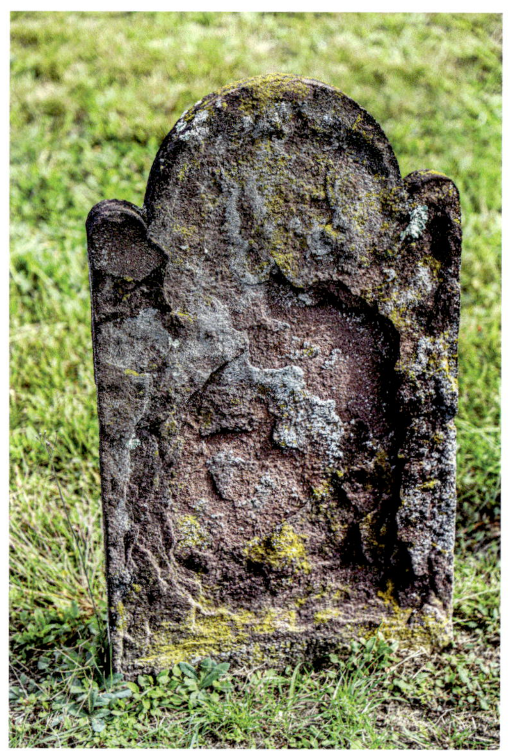

Left: With more than 40,000 grave markers spread out over 110 acres inside Providence's North Burial Ground, markers like this have been feasted on by time and weather.

Below: There are many notable Rhode Islanders buried inside the more than 3,000 cemeteries. Among the gravestones spread across all those cemeteries a plethora of unique stories have been etched into the graves for the future to observe. Captain Fry notably died travelling from Batavia (known today as Jakarta), capital city of Indonesia.

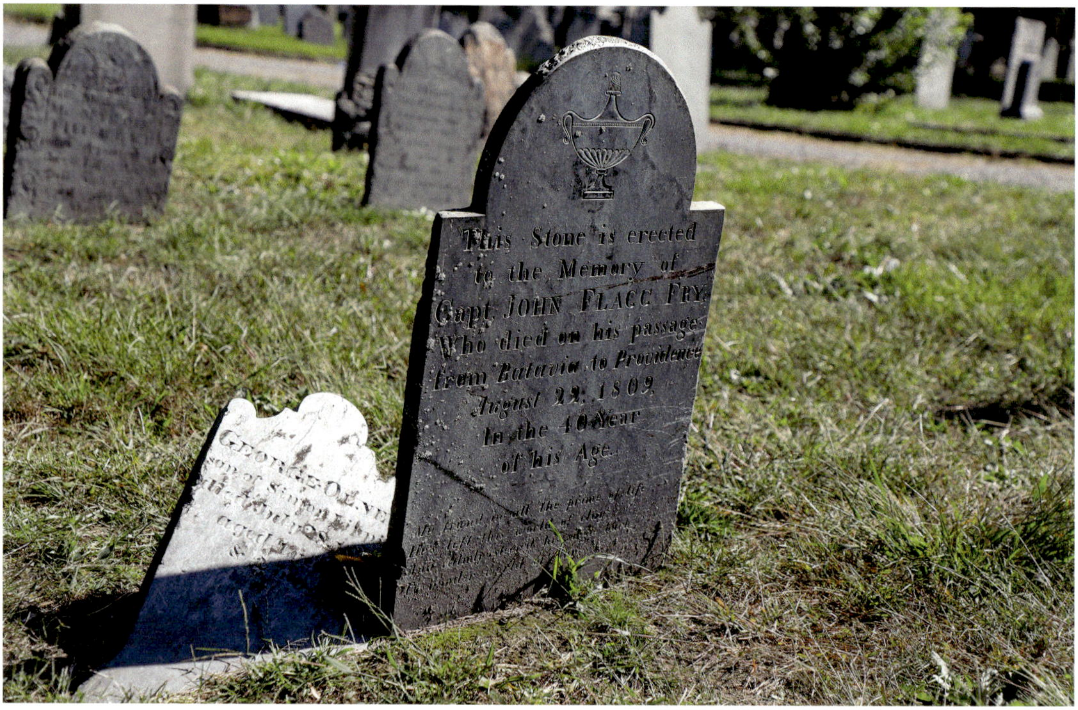

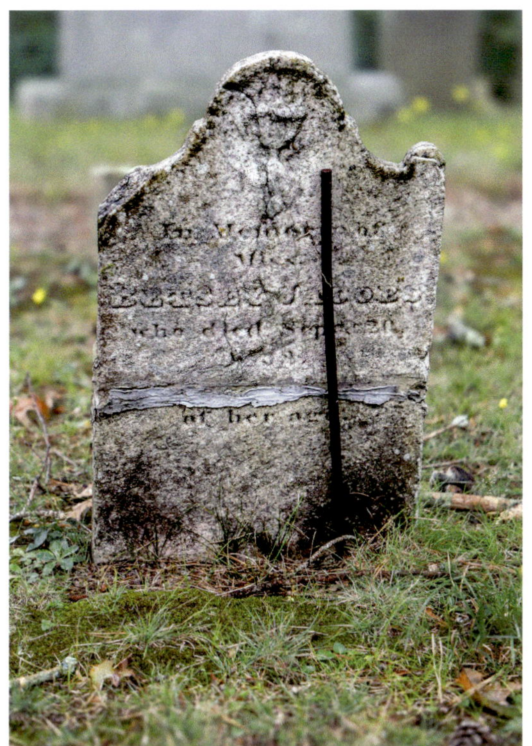

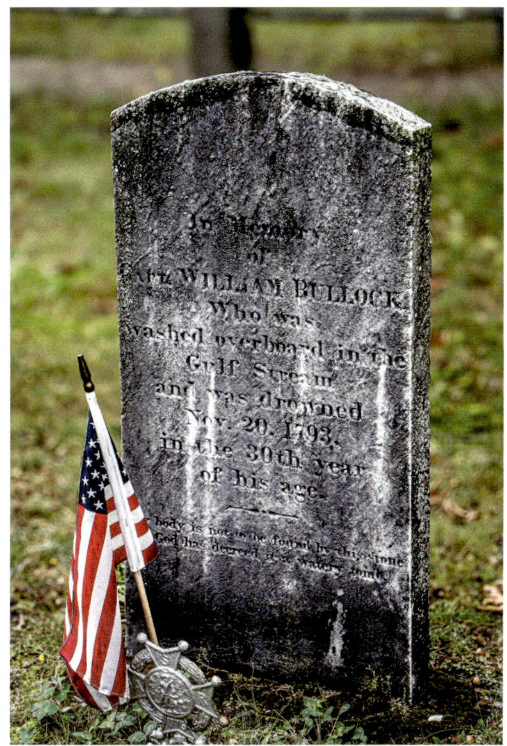

Above left: Ancient Little Neck cemetery in East Providence, Rhode Island, has operated for 370 years, so far. Many of the citizens of colonial Massachusetts and eventually Rhode Island have laid on these grounds beneath their markers. As time marches on, it has become common to see headstones throughout the region held together in a multitude of creative ways. Betsey's marker is held together with a bonding agent and a rebar stake; while unusual, it has been effective in delaying the destruction of this well-worn stone.

Above right: Captain Bullock, lost to the sea. The captain, having drowned after being washed overboard, is noted to now rest in a watery tomb.

Right: The concept of the race against time is frequently referenced with regard to one's lifetime. As this marker attests to, so too does the lifetime of a tombstone.

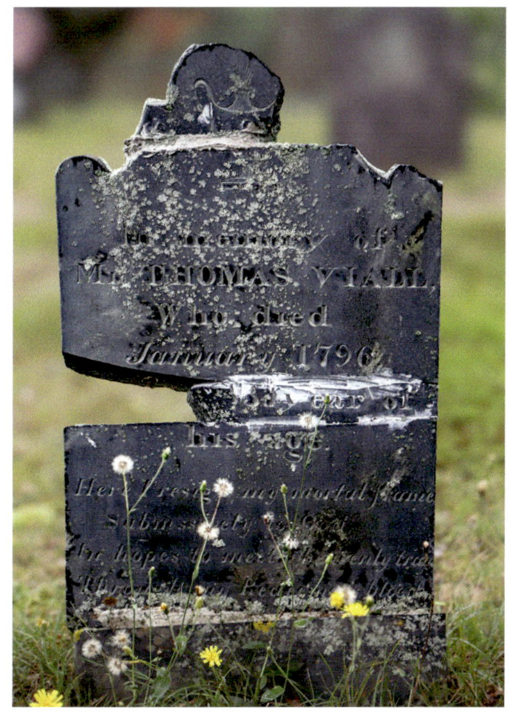

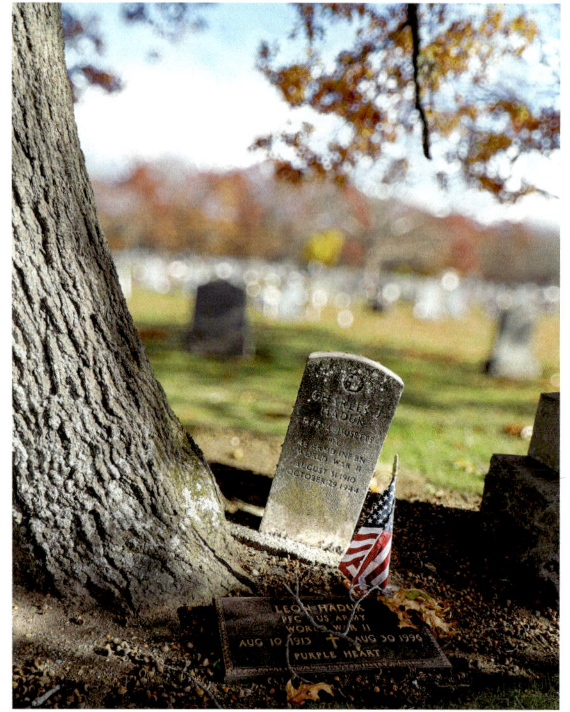

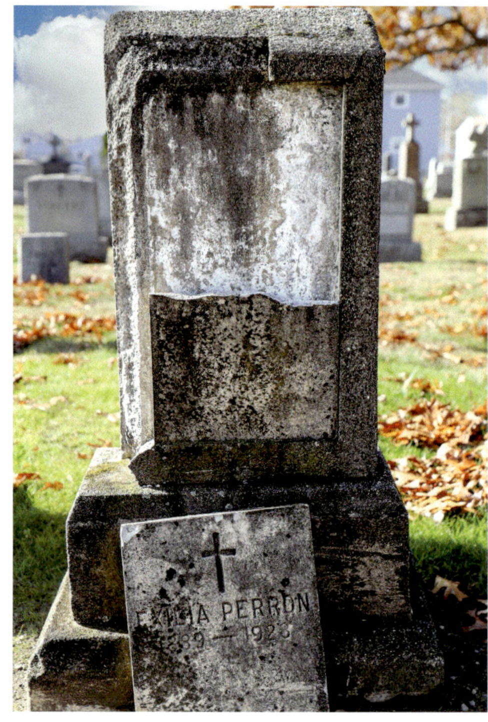

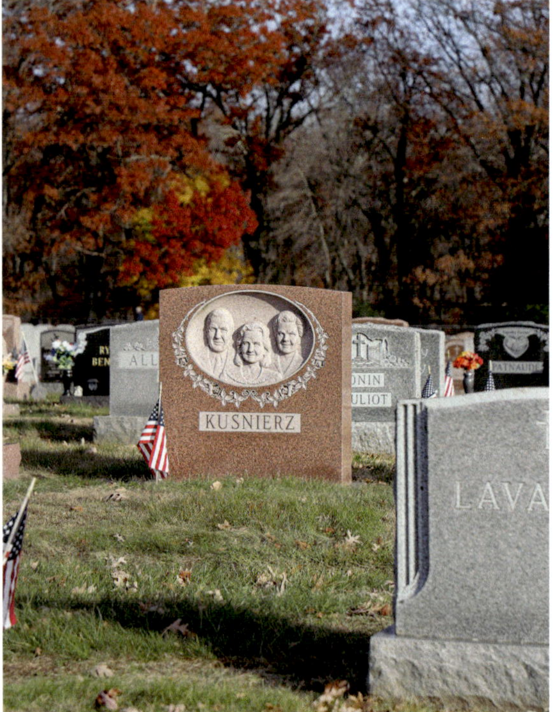

Above left: Charles and Leon Haduk both fought in World War II, and today their graves are fighting against time and a large tree.

Above right: Face has not been saved.

Left: Gravestones for many are a final way to remember a lost loved one. Other times they are a testament to achievements. Some are simple with only a first name or dates alone. On the grounds of the Gate of Heaven Cemetery in Rhode Island, this family chose an incredibly unique approach to memorializing their lost family members.

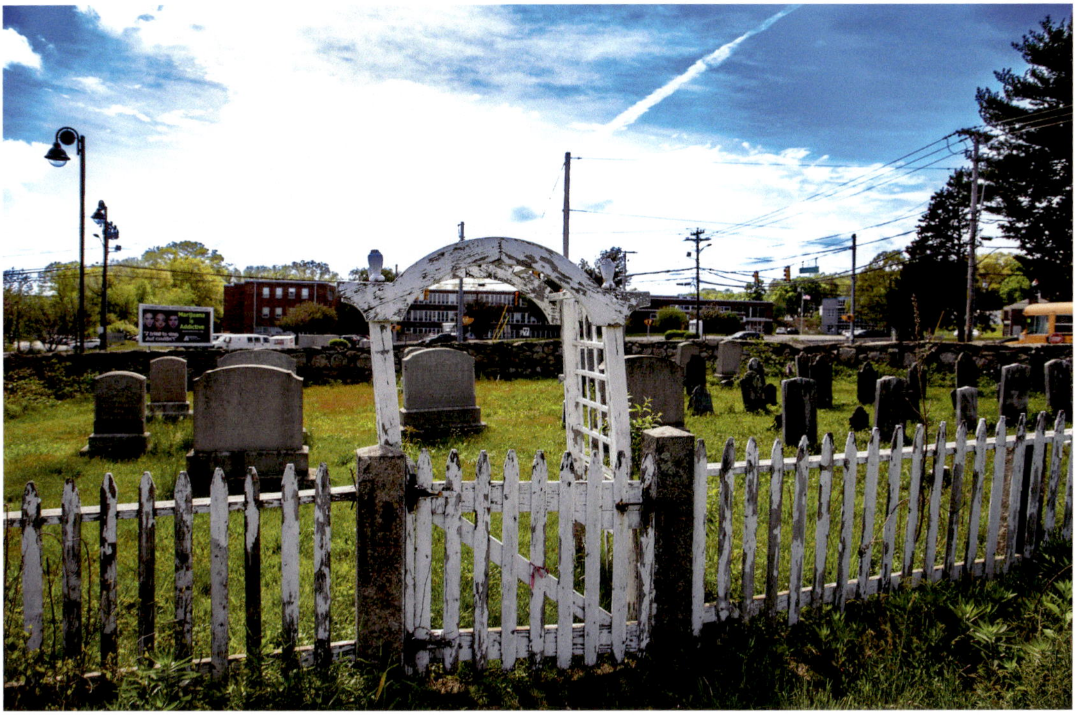

Above: This family cemetery once sat on the property of those buried within. Standing at the burial spot today, looking at the Johnston Middle School, across from the High School, and inside a small mall with a pharmacy and coffee shop to its side.

Right: The grave of Mercy Brown, arguably the best documented "vampire" in America.

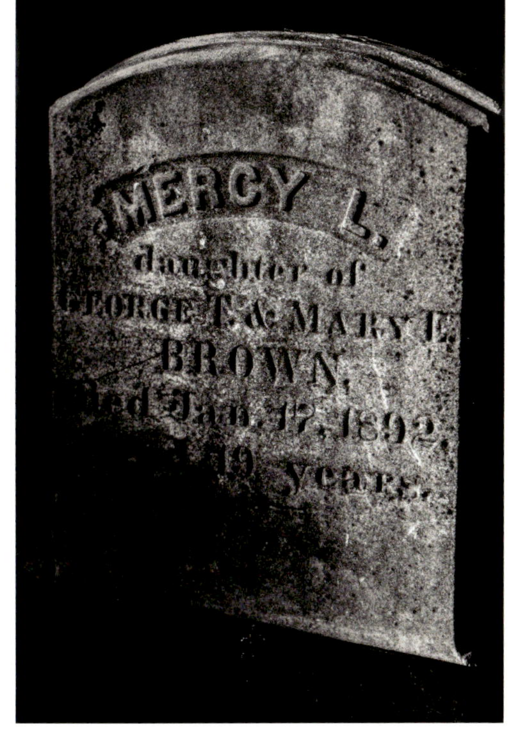

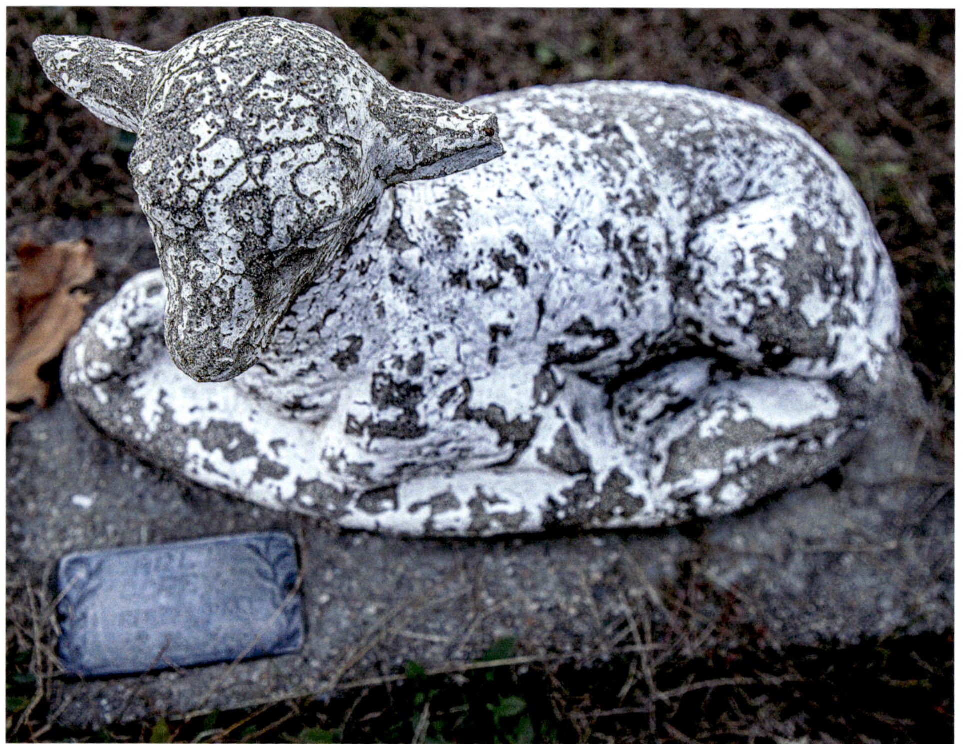

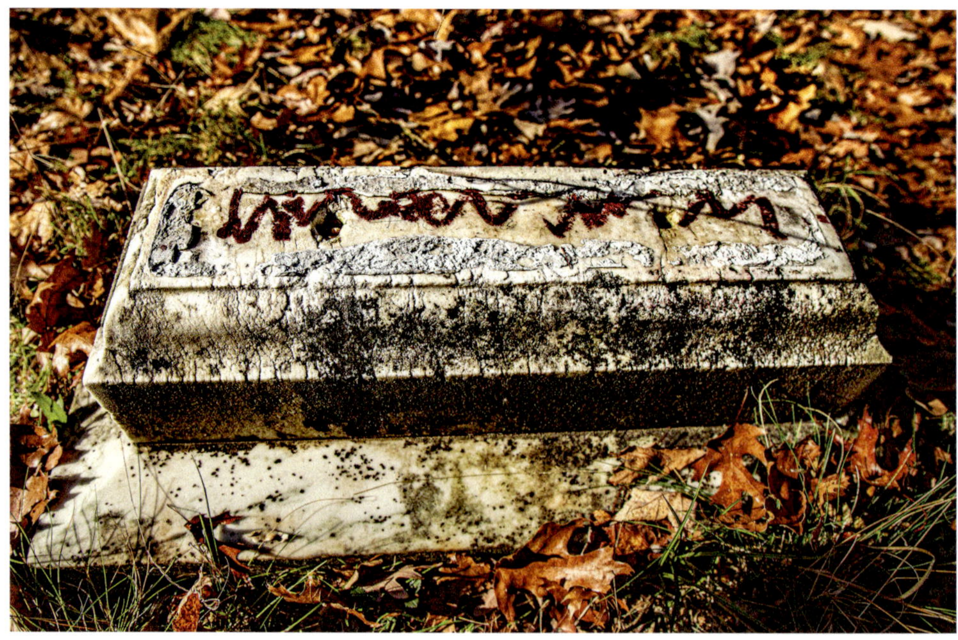

Bathsheba Sherman died in 1885. Centuries later, her tombstone would become a target of those wanting to tangle with the "witch" of *The Conjuring* films.

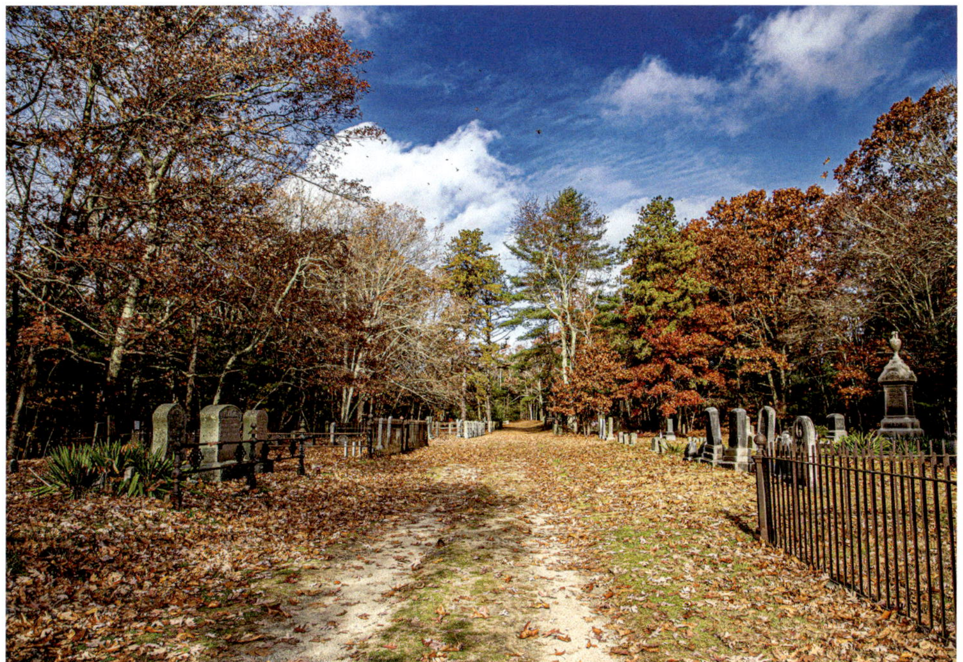

The Riverside Cemetery on Halloween 2022. Thanks in part to the film series *The Conjuring*, this site has become a Halloween must.

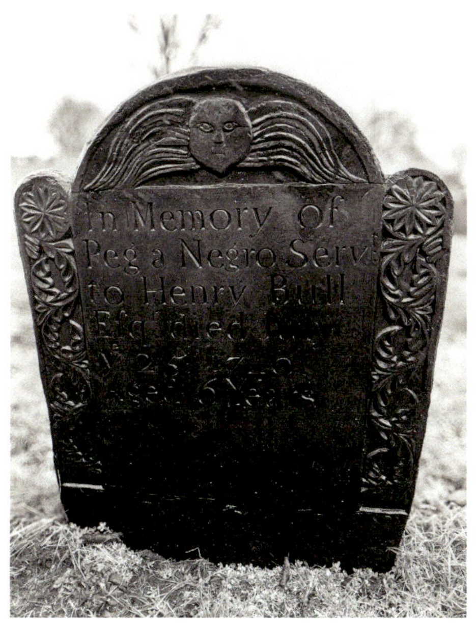

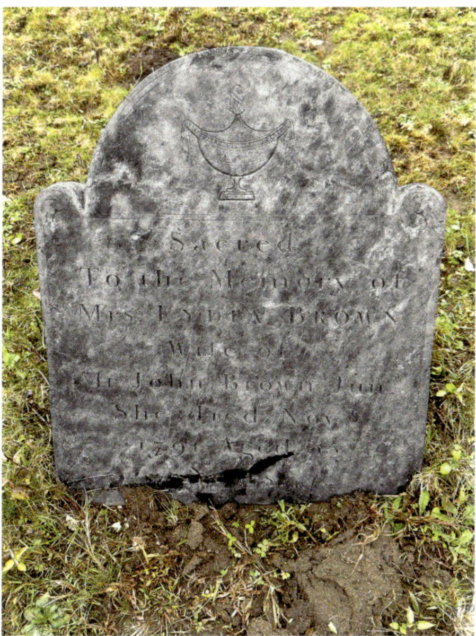

Above left: Peg, a six-year-old enslaved person.

Above right: The Brown family lot sits, currently, inside a farm animal sanctuary, West Place.

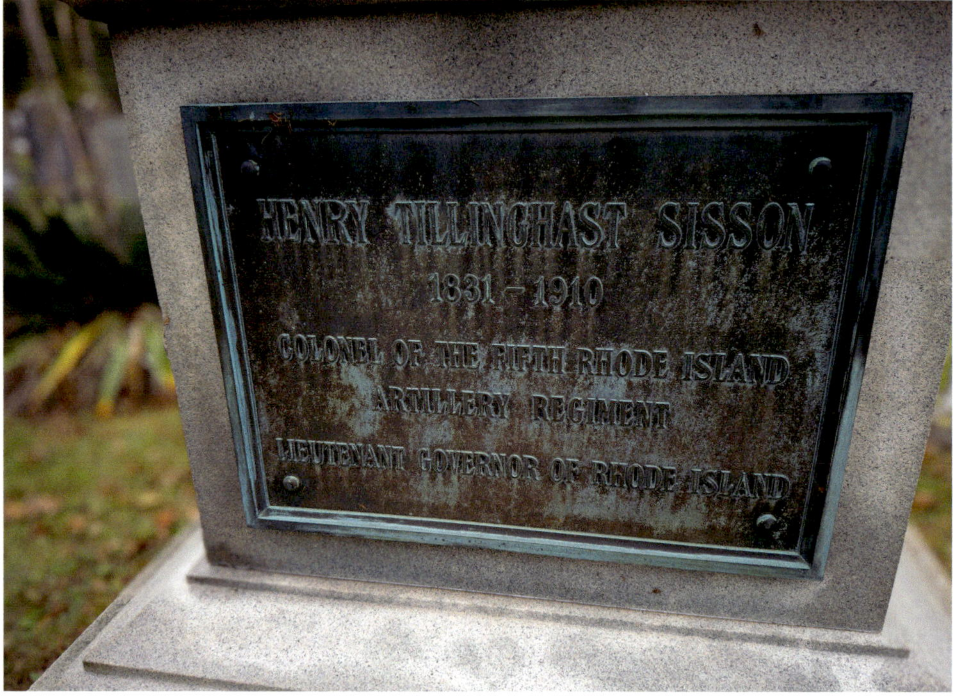

The lieutenant governor of Rhode Island, Sisson, was a resident of Little Compton, Rhode Island—a small oceanside town in the southeast of the state.

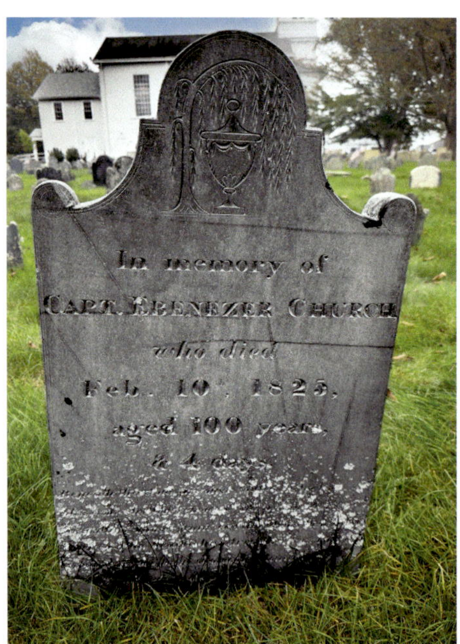

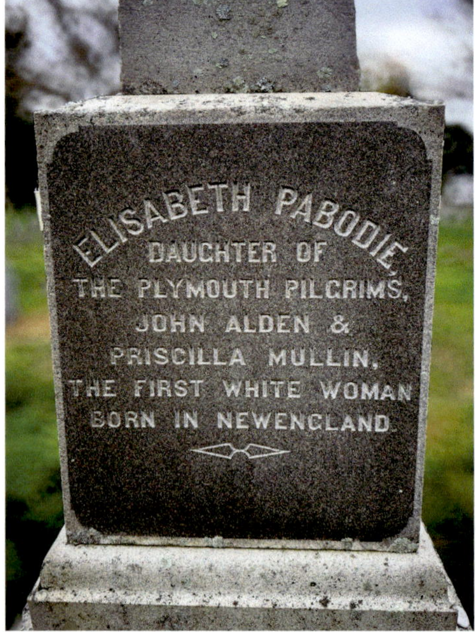

Above left: 100-year-old Captain Ebenezer Church.

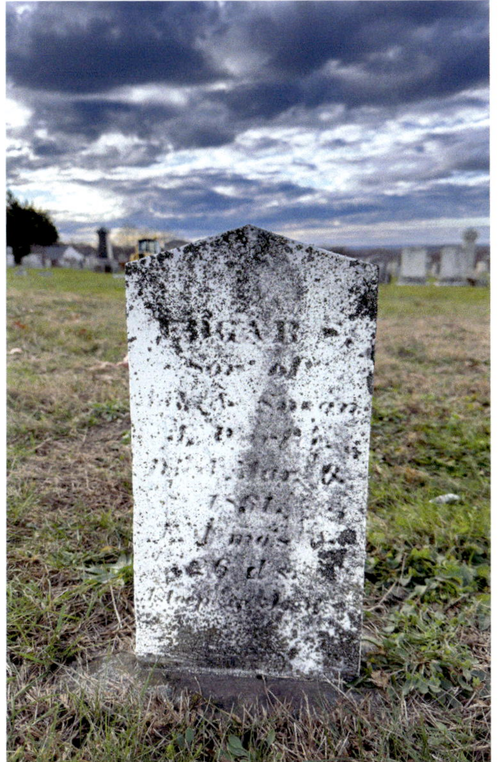

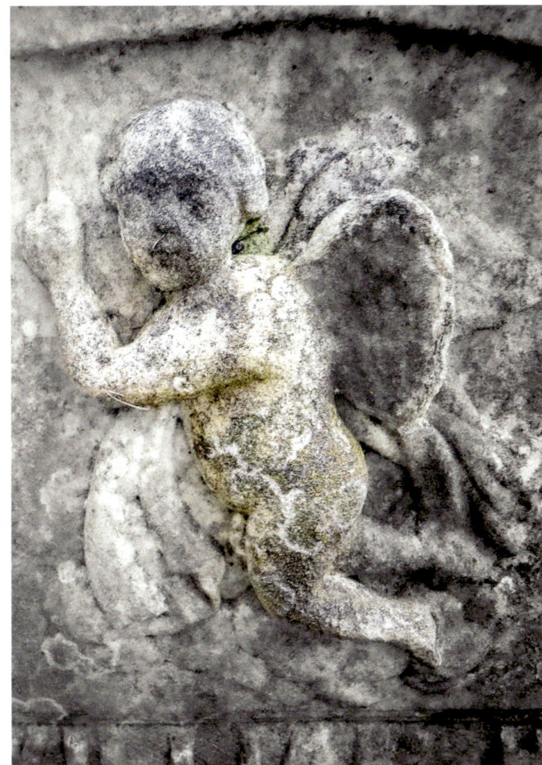

Right: Inside the locked burial ground of the upscale town of Bristol, Rhode Island, a surprising amount of destruction has happened to the markers of the dead.

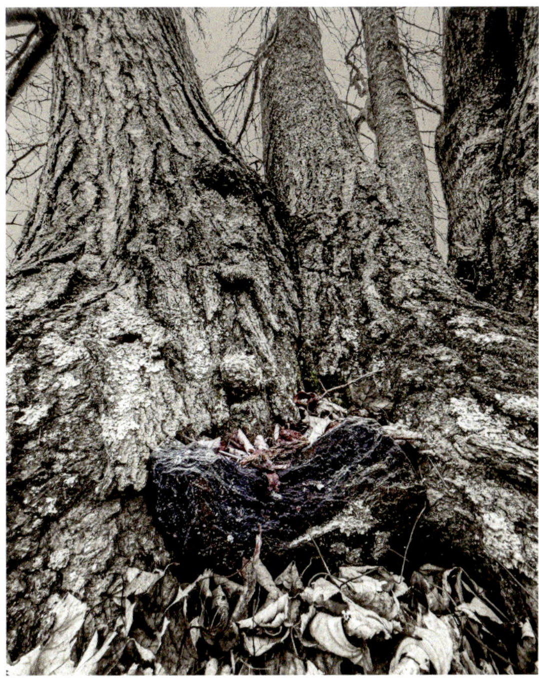

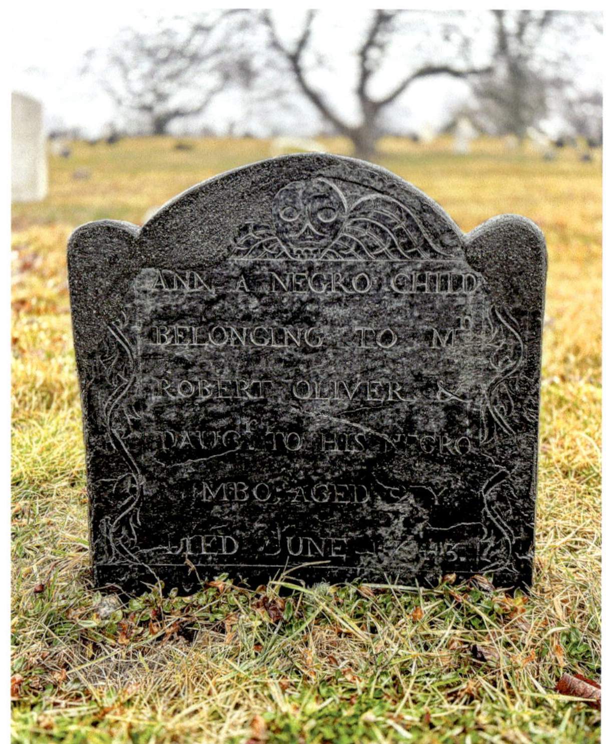

Left: Ann was born to her mother, Mimbo, and under the "ownership" of Robert Oliver. This marker in Newport, Rhode Island, is also standing in Dorchester, Massachusetts. The story between the duplication from 1743 has yet to be answered satisfactorily.

Below: Emily McLean, 1888–1942. A temporary marker not meant to last nearly 100 years holds on by duct tape and creativity

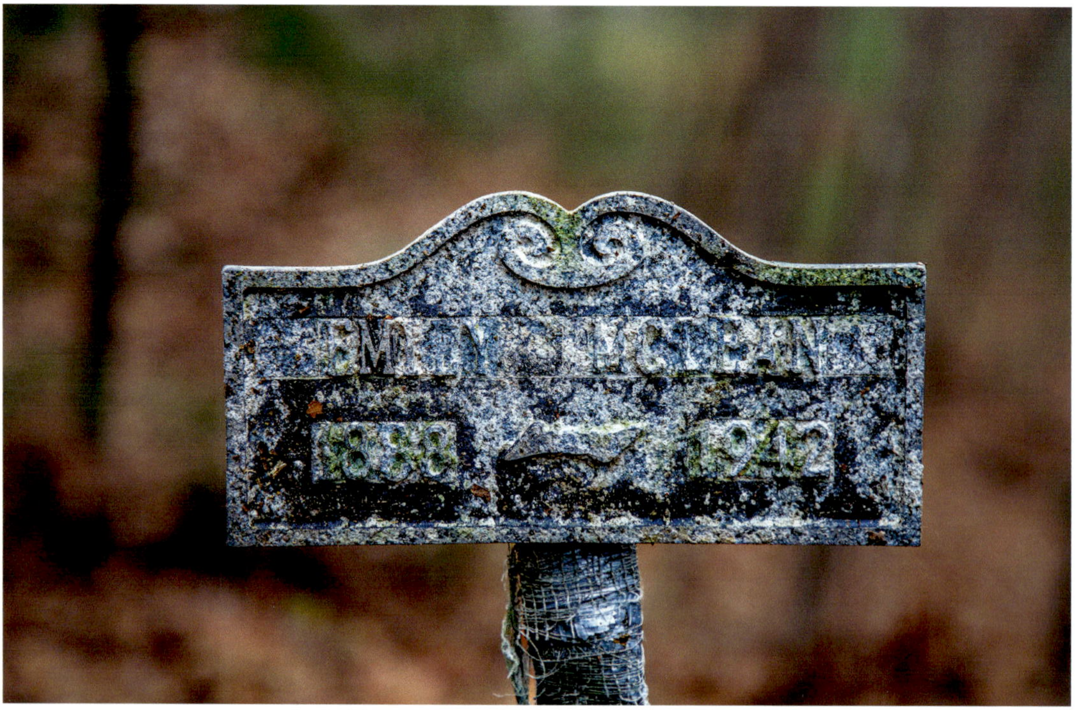

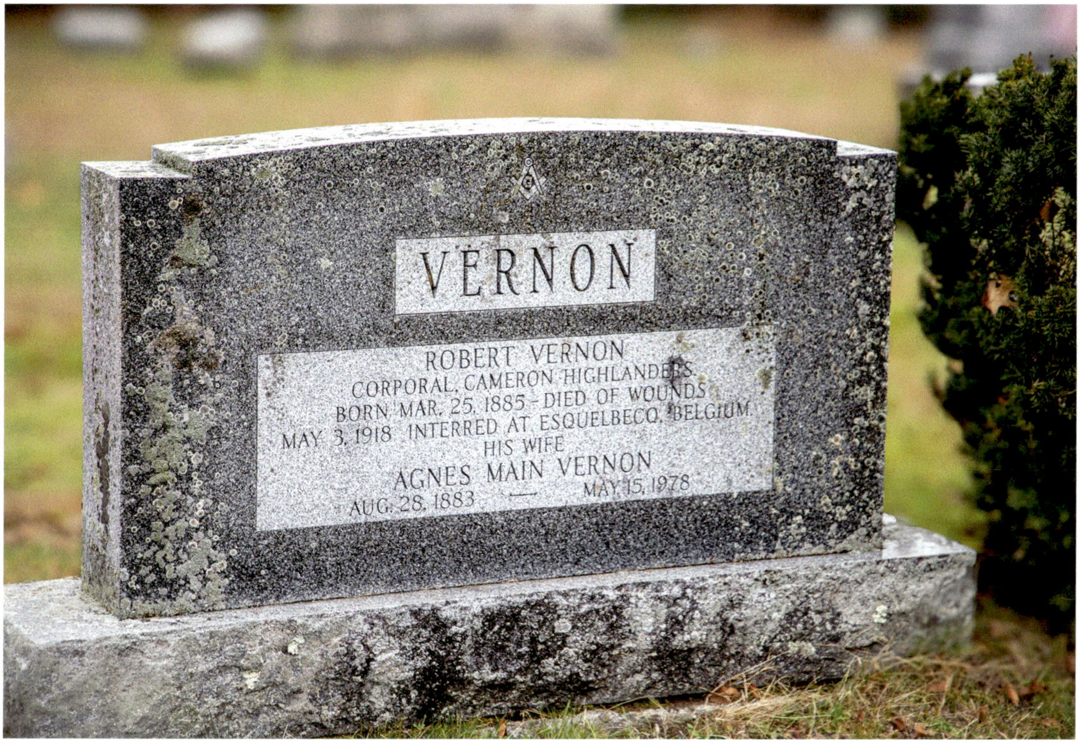

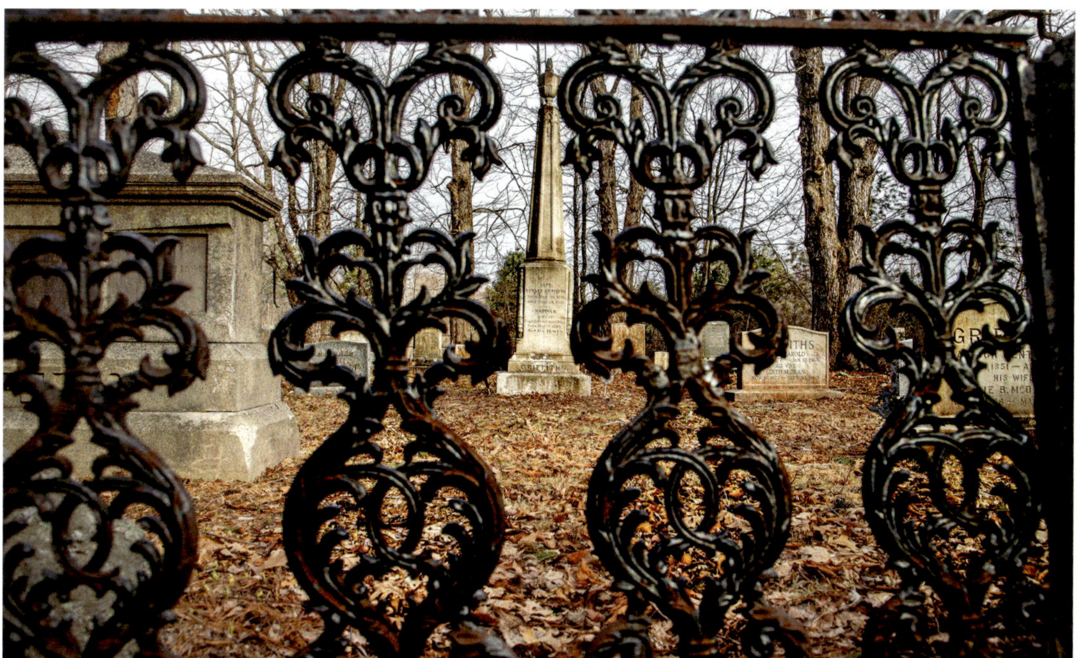

The Griffiths family cemetery as seen through their gate.

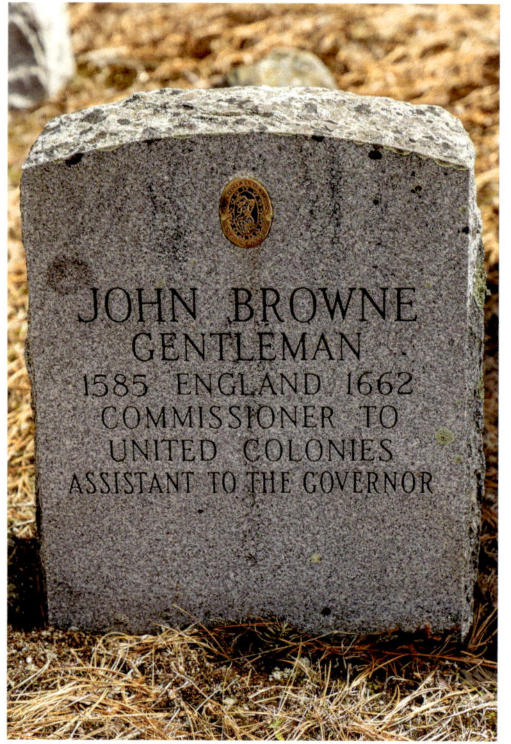

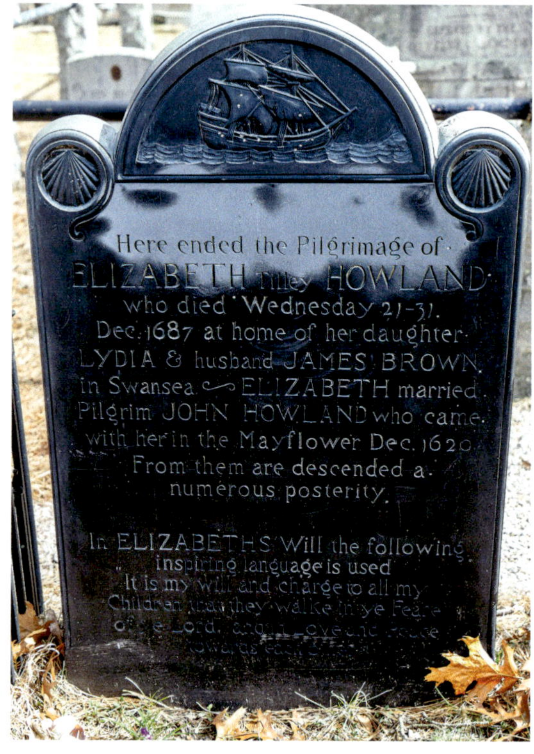

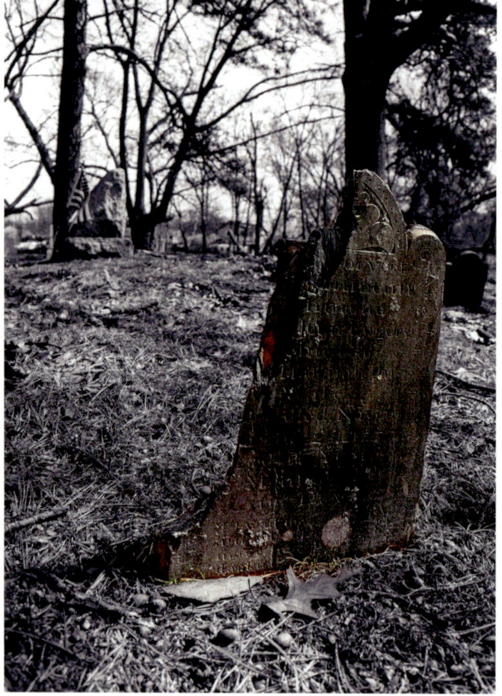

Above left: Wealthy in life, simple in death.

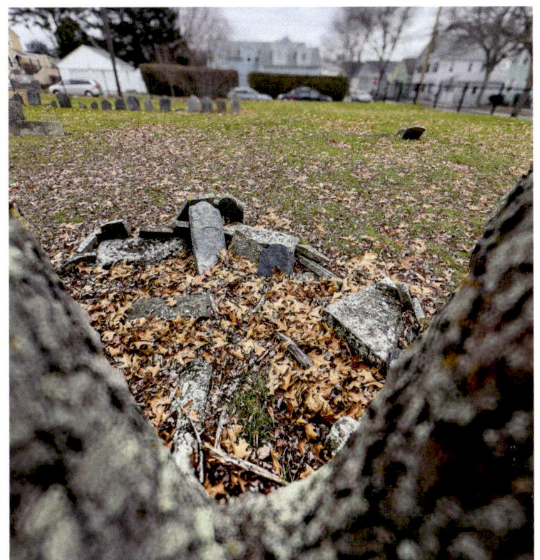

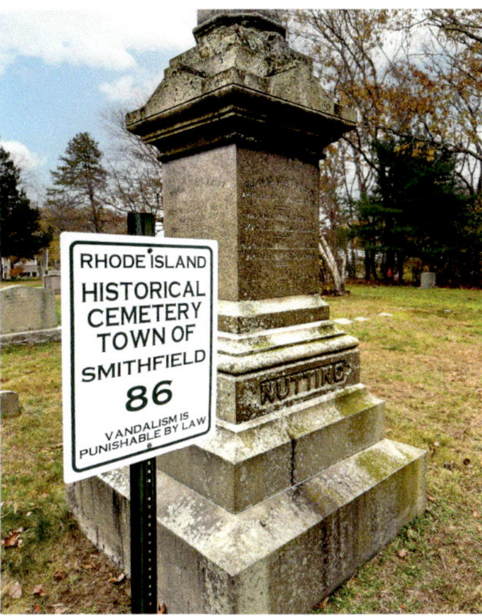

Above left: Even in affluent areas like Bristol, Rhode Island, it is not uncommon to find piles of graves stacked together, further deteriorating.

Above right: Since establishing a program to track and care for cemeteries in Rhode Island, it has become common to see a lot such as this. Dr. Thomas Nutting Lot has also been assigned an updated name as this one has; Rhode Island Historical Cemetery Town of Smithfield 86.

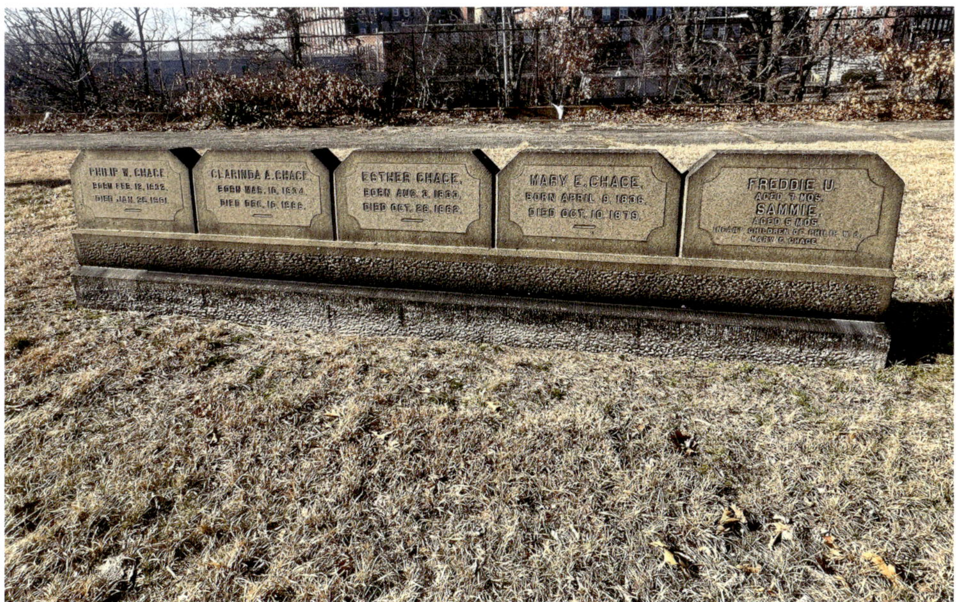

Many families travelled from Canada through New England following millwork. Many factory buildings still stand today, some empty, some rehabilitated into new use, and some crumbling to their death in plain view.

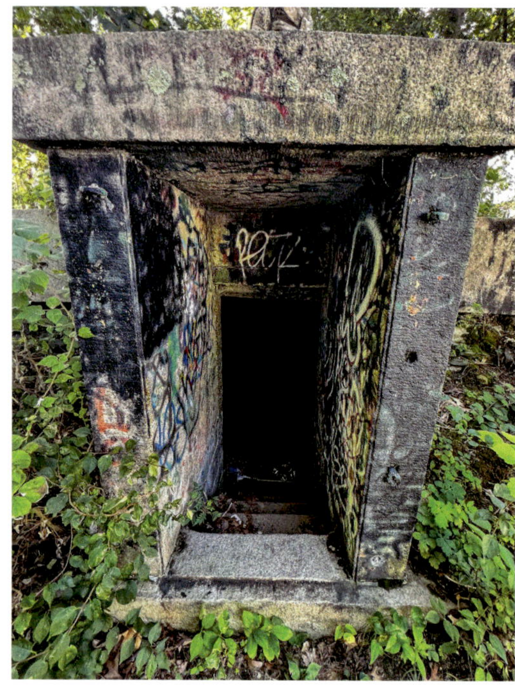

What was once a crypt inside this small family cemetery is now used to practice graffiti art, hide underage drinking, and generally be a creepy remnant.

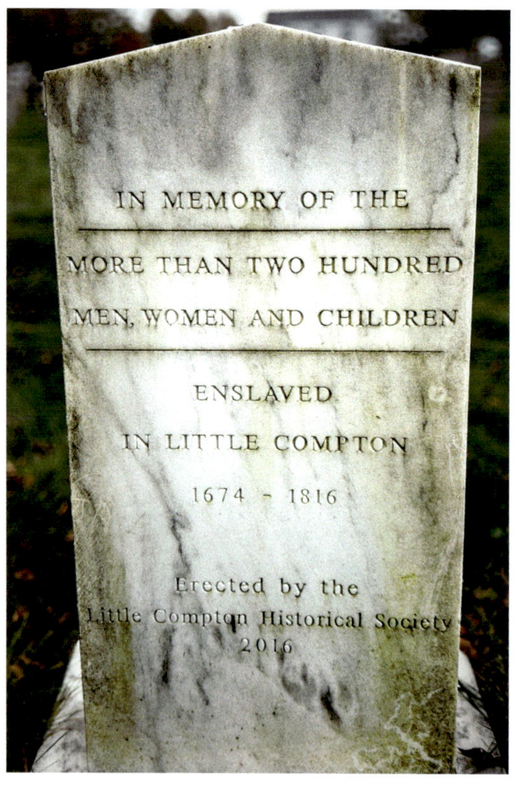

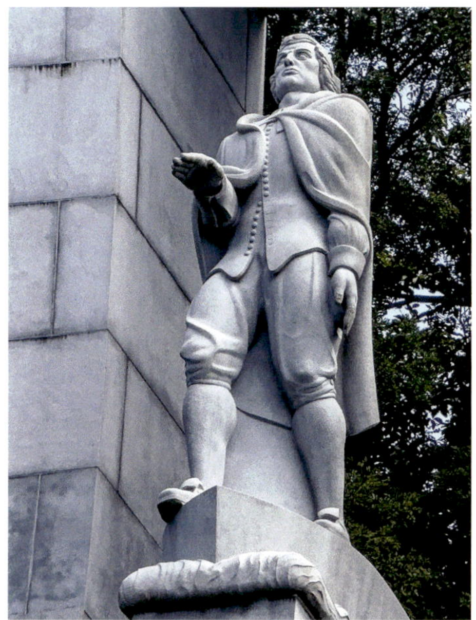

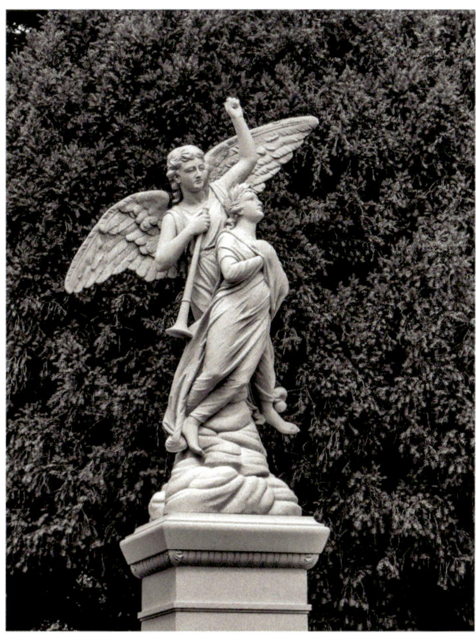

Above left: The remains of Roger Williams, the colonial founder of the state of Rhode Island, can be found below this 14-foot statue.

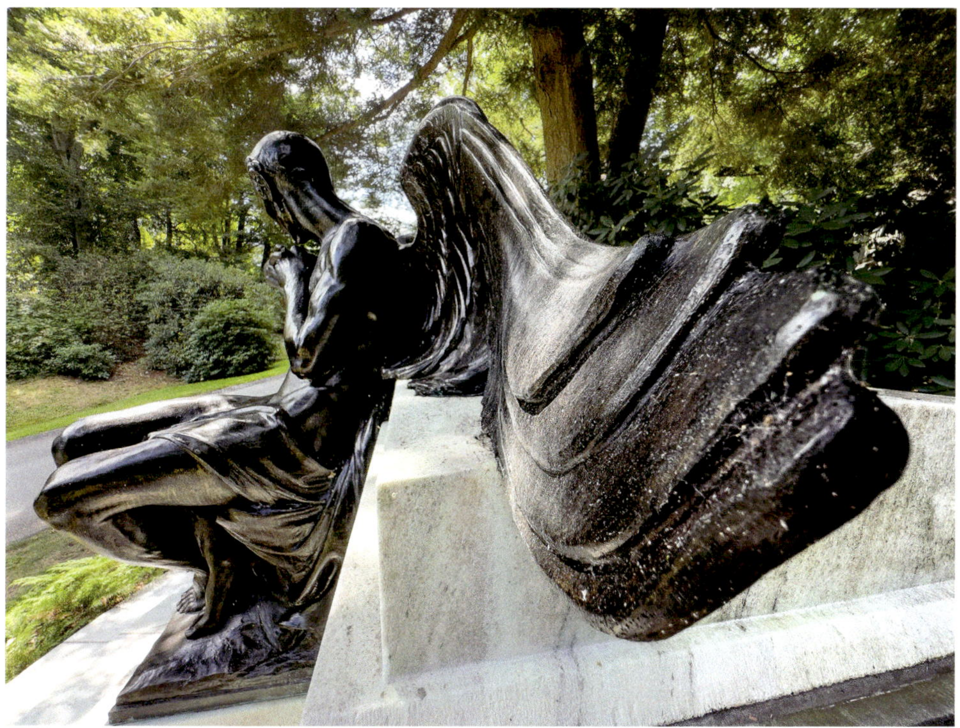

The wings of an angel outstretched.

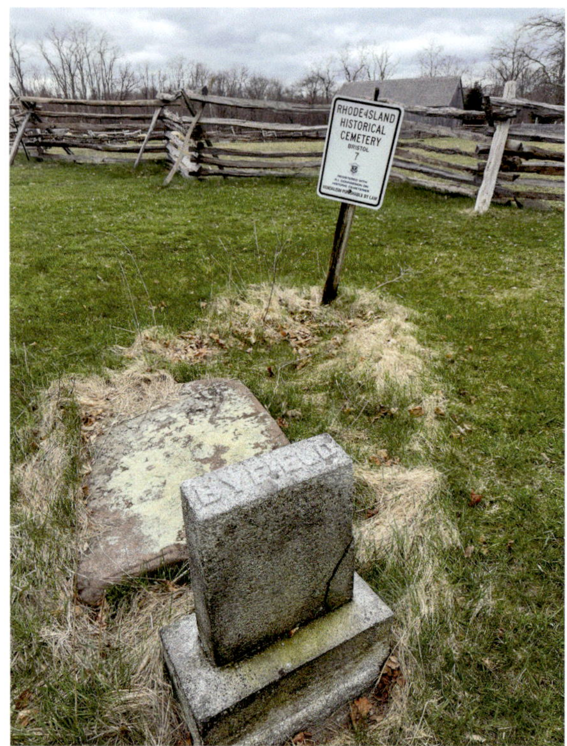

Left: Byfield. The lone grave making up historic cemetery Bristol 7. Horse, person, prank—we may never know.

Below: Dorcas.

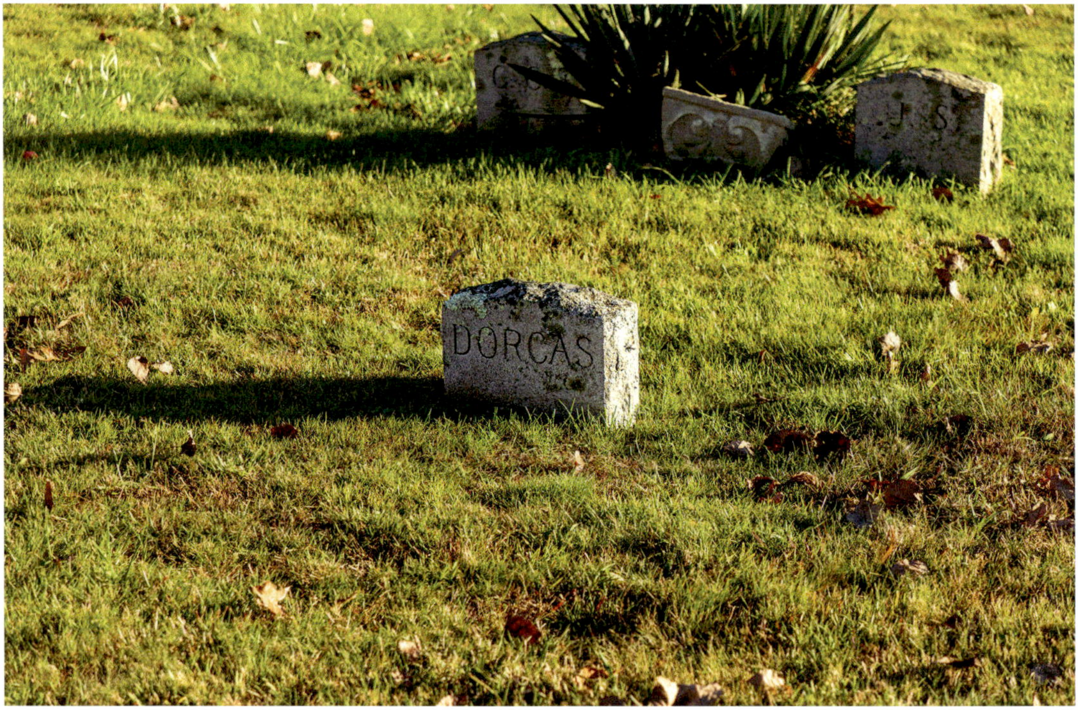

5
VERMONT

Republic of the Green Mountains, New Hampshire Grants, Green Mountain State

While exploring Vermont, most visitors are struck by the amazing views of mountains, waterfalls, and trees. Vermont, a very popular location for leaf "peepers," has seen its forests decrease statistically from nearly 80 percent of the entire state a century ago to 4,500,000 acres today. The weather of the Green Mountain State is one of wide differences. With cold snowy winters, wet springs and autumns, and warm, humid summers, survival in the state, like those of its sister states, has been a challenge to contend with across its history. The drastic changes in weather conditions and temperature, proving enough to challenge even the most adventurous person, is only the outer layer of what Vermont weather can bring. Seasonal heavy rains can cause flooding as well as the snow-covered peaks of the state which, when defrosting, push water down from the mountains to the valleys. Another of the many challenges for the people, dead and alive, is the turn from mud to frozen solid ground. The oldest known grave in the state dates to 1762. Compared to its New England neighbors, Vermont's oldest documented grave is nearly youthful. The markers and stones that have been erected in the approximated 2,000 cemeteries and graveyards across Vermont are easy targets for modernization, weather-related issues, and general apathy. As expansion runs wild and the wooded areas of Vermont are threatened, it seems inevitable that the many burying grounds of the state will continue to be encroached upon.

Visiting the state and its burial grounds, you will find many notable people, unique markers, mountain-side burials, and modern graves. Included is the 30th president of the United States, Calvin Coolidge, buried alongside his family in Plymouth Notch. While the 21st president, Chester A. Arthur, was born in Vermont, he was laid to rest in the Albany Rural Cemetery in New York. A long drive up a mountain side ends at a sprawling multi-level lodge, known as the Trapp Family Lodge. Here you can find villas, suites, and the Trapp Family Cemetery where members of the famous singing family who fled the Nazis are buried. The resting places across Vermont are a final home to many poets, victims of war, entertainers, endless people of significance for the state, country, and world, and of course a Flavor Graveyard in Waterbury dedicated to Ben & Jerry's ice cream flavors that are no longer with us. Ben & Jerry's Flavor Graveyard filled with graves of flavors and epitaphs and dates of their run, proving succinctly how intertwined cemeteries are with modern life. Vermont, a state with a less than 25 percent representation of rental homes available across the year, is a state that means to be a home to those who come to stay and end up being longtime residents. Thankfully, given the relatively small urban sprawl as compared to many of the other New England states, Vermont's burial spaces are likely to continue in their intended use without being negatively affected by modernization. This leaves one major opposing force at work against the graves of modern Vermont: the weather.

Vermont, not unlike its neighbors, has a complicated history. Before the colonization of this area by Europeans, native settlements stretched over thousands of years prior. From there, both French and English settlers began occupying the densely wooded area that would become Vermont. Farmland would become a major use of the lands of the state. From its beginning as an aboriginally settled area, to its colonization, and on to its participation in the Revolutionary and Civil Wars, and then on to the modernization of the twenty-first century, Vermont has been and likely will remain an area of transformation and importance. The Vermont of today brings visitors from all over both the United States and to its north, Canada. Those who explore today's Vermont find a vibrant art community, breweries and cideries, and unlike its neighboring New England state, the vast expanses of wooded mountains and beautiful lakes still stand. Traveling from Brattleboro to Burlington, it is no surprise this area was once disputed by New Hampshire and New York.

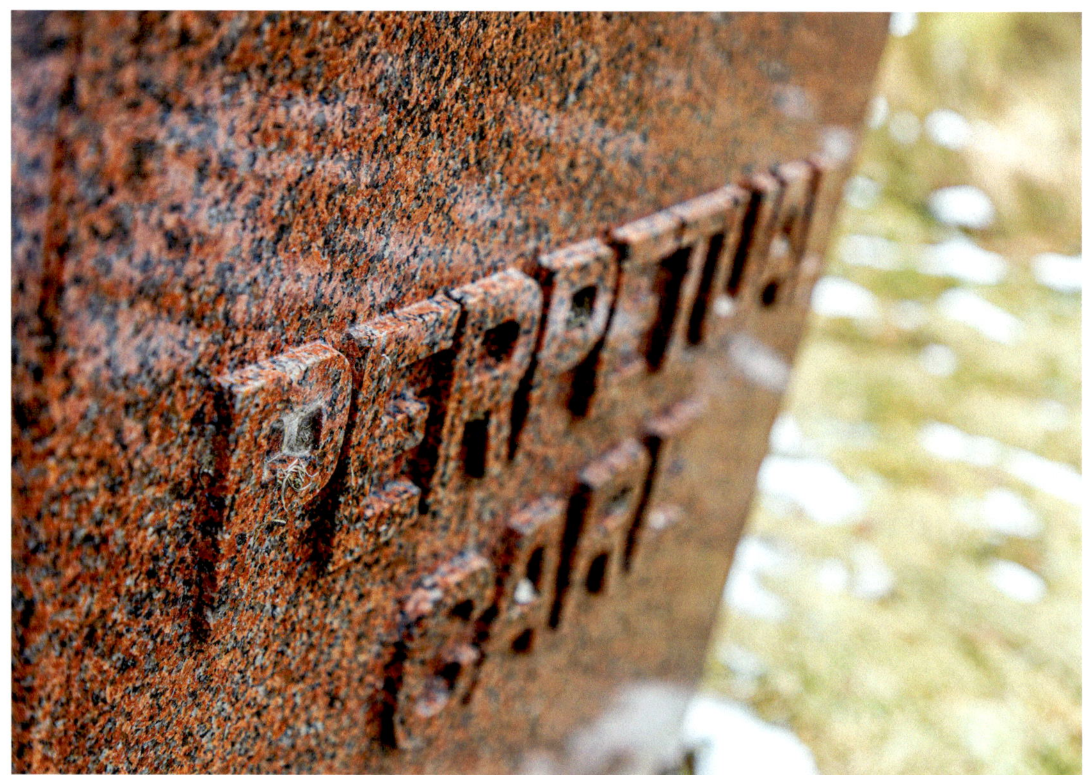

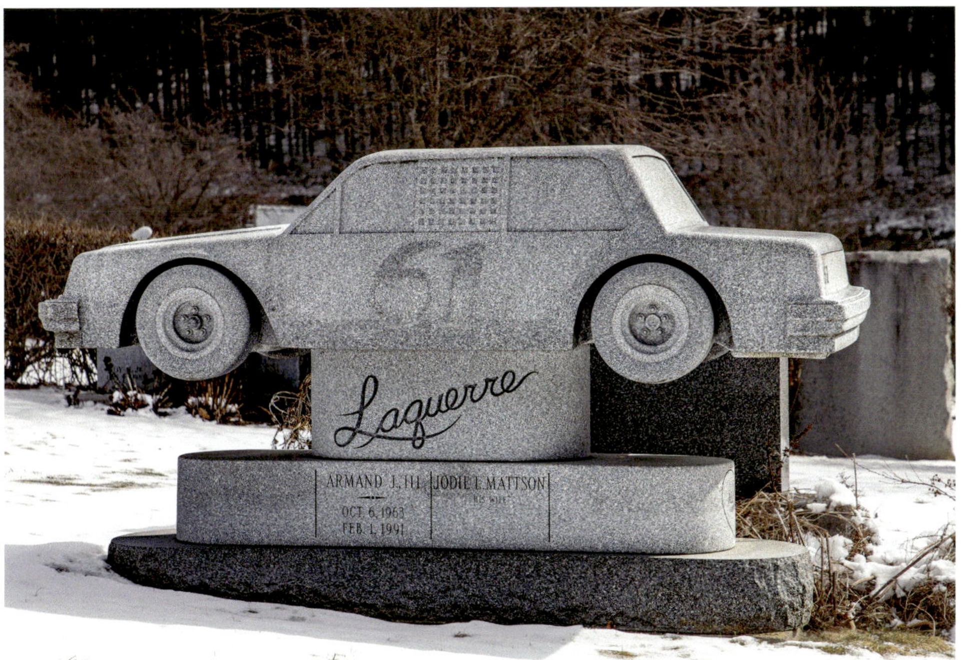

Hope Cemetery in Barre, Vermont, offers grave markers that are larger than life, to put it mildly.

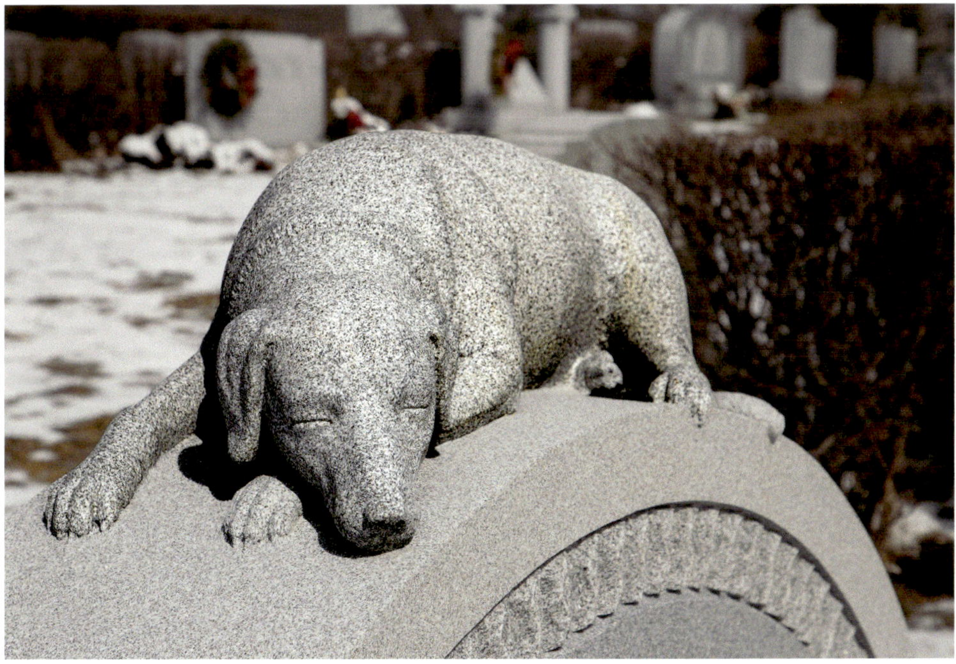

One could not hope for a better overseer of their final resting place than a dutiful dog.

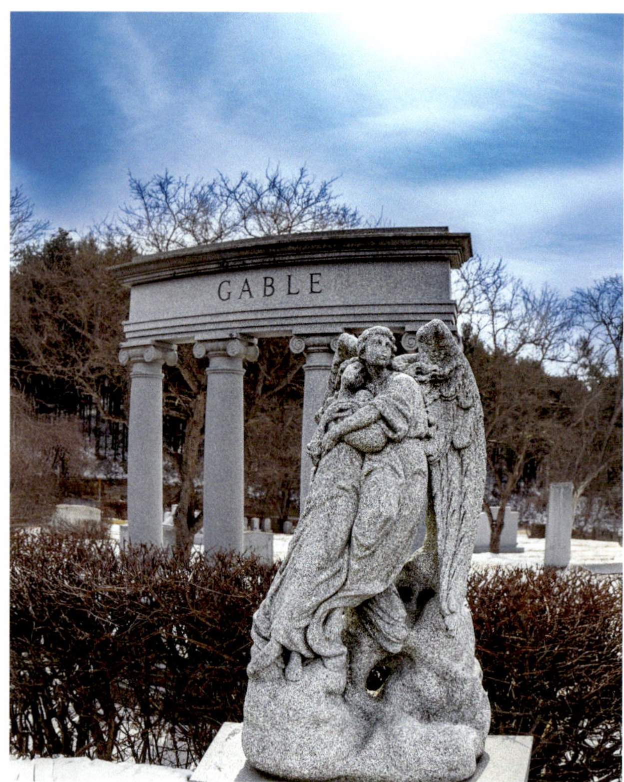

Below: The Thomas children, according to their gravestone, drowned in a flood in 1927. Buried beneath the stone includes eleven-year-old Ralph, nine-year-old Clyde, seven-year-old Dean. Carroll, five years old, is detailed on the grave as having never been found.

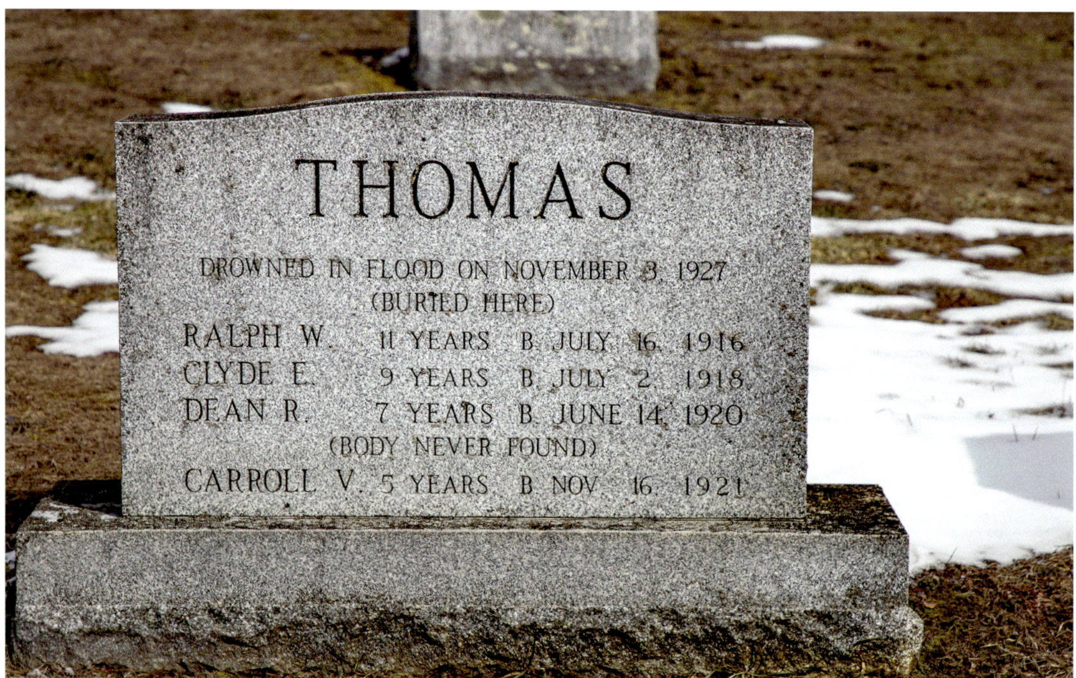

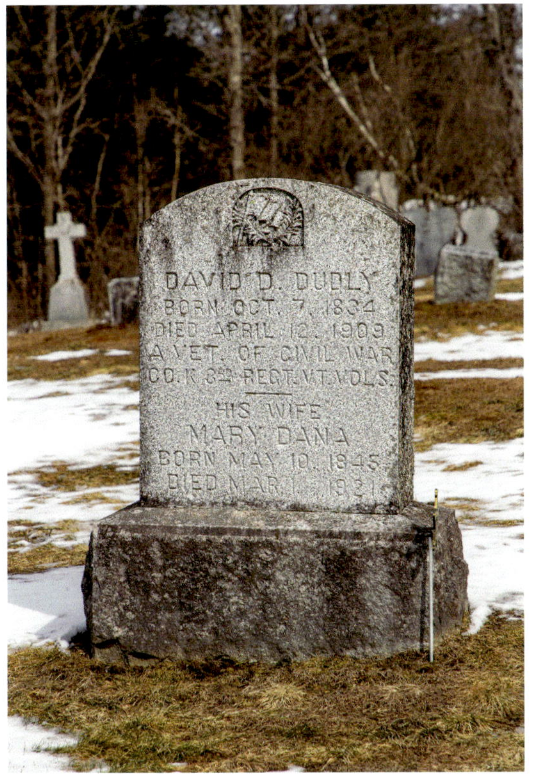

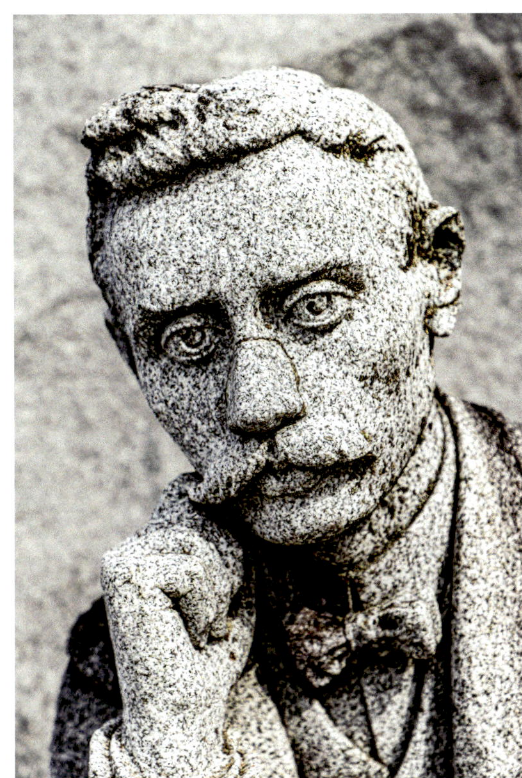

Above right: Even among the amazing artworks that top the graves inside Hope Cemetery in Barre, Vermont, imperfections brought by time are still visible.

Right: Born in Barre, Vermont, died in Germany, buried in Holland, and finally rested in Barre, Vermont.

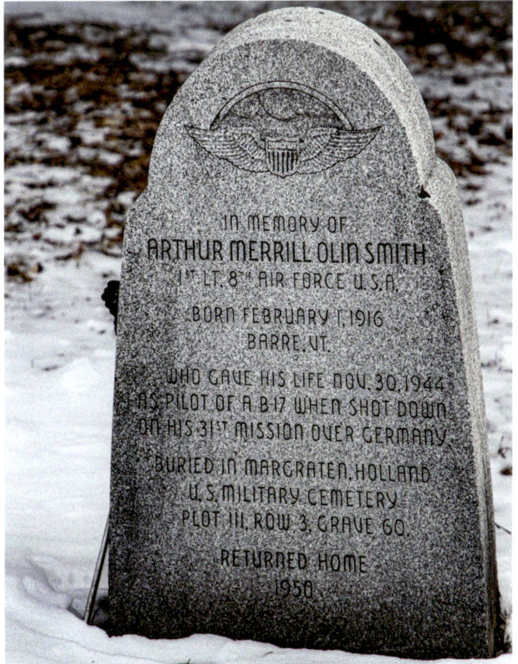

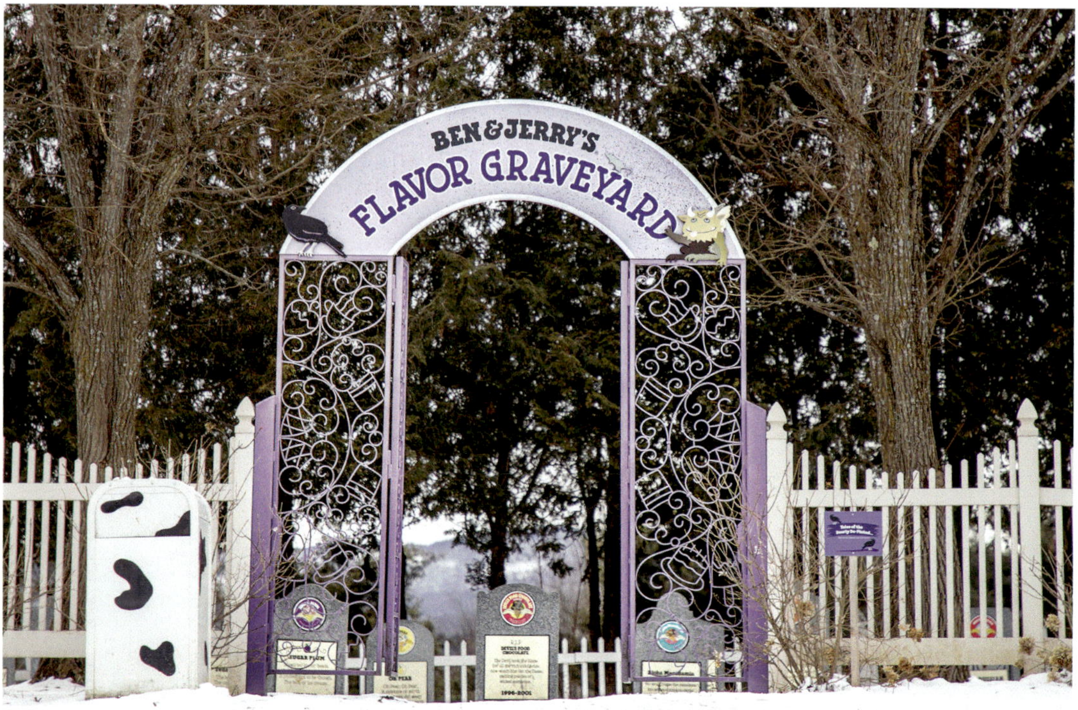

Above: In New England, home to many notable graveyards and cemeteries, even the ice cream industry has bought into the burial concept. Visitors to the famous ice cream company can walk the flavor graveyard on top of a hill and view the many flavors lost to time.

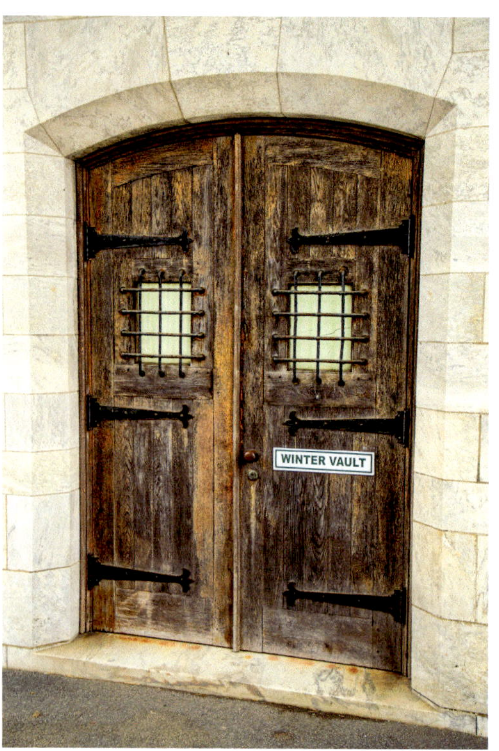

Left: The winter vault of this cemetery sits behind at the entrance of Green Mount Cemetery. Considering the often-frigid winters of New England spaces like these have been, historically, important in preserving the local dead until the ground thaws and can be cut into.

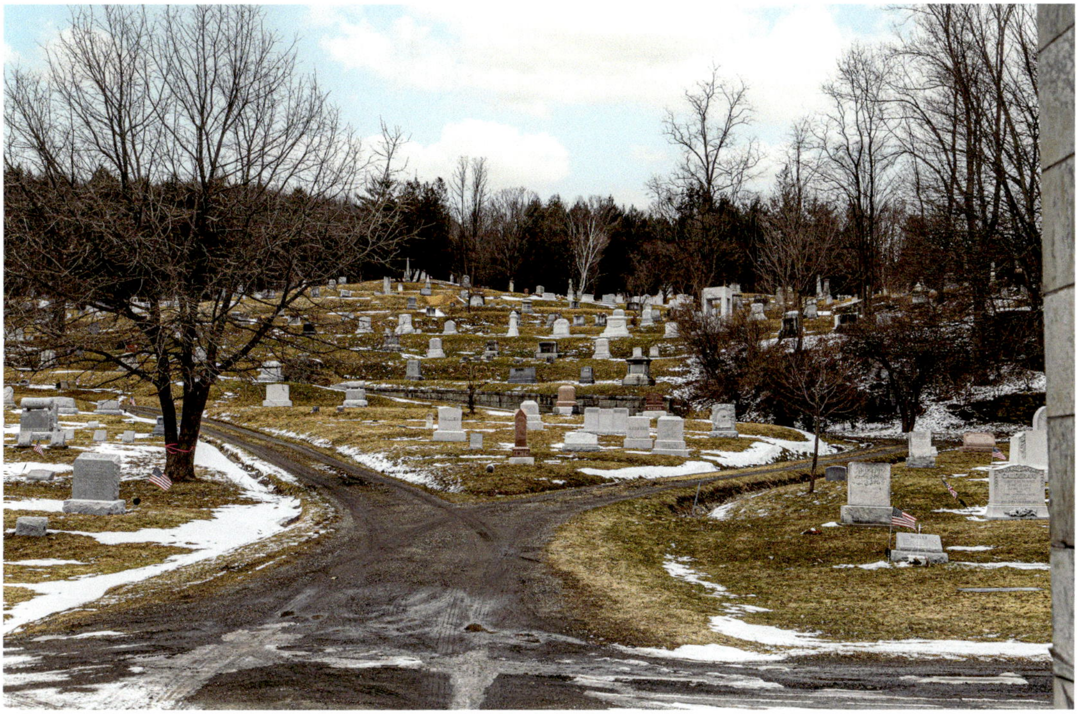

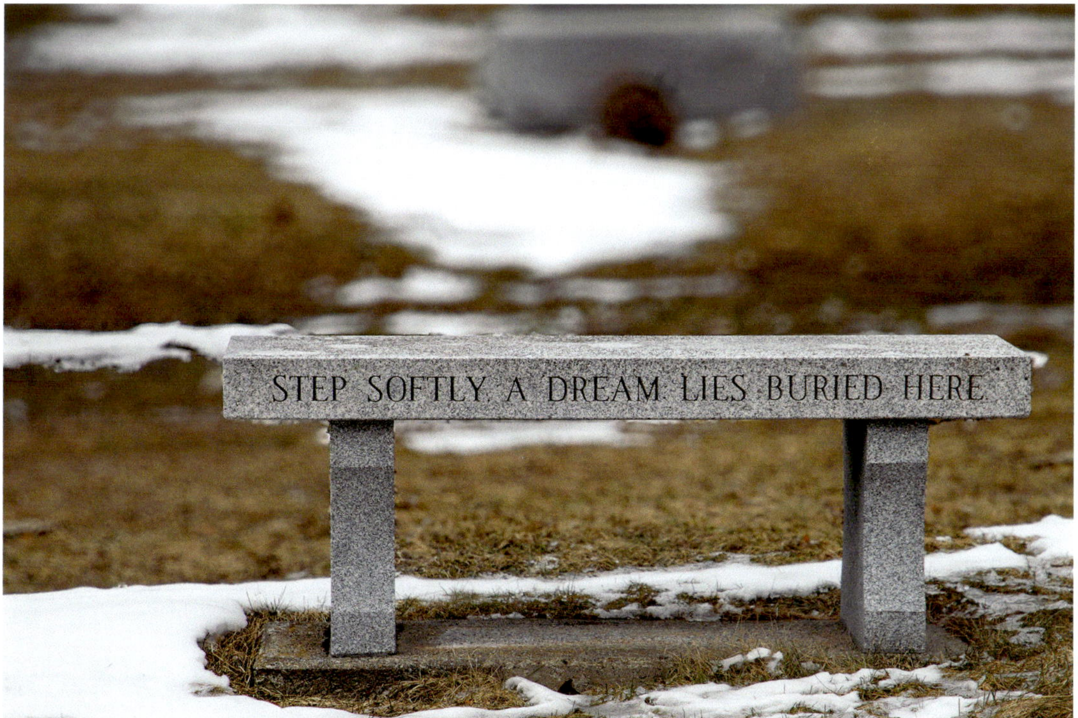
STEP SOFTLY A DREAM LIES BURIED HERE

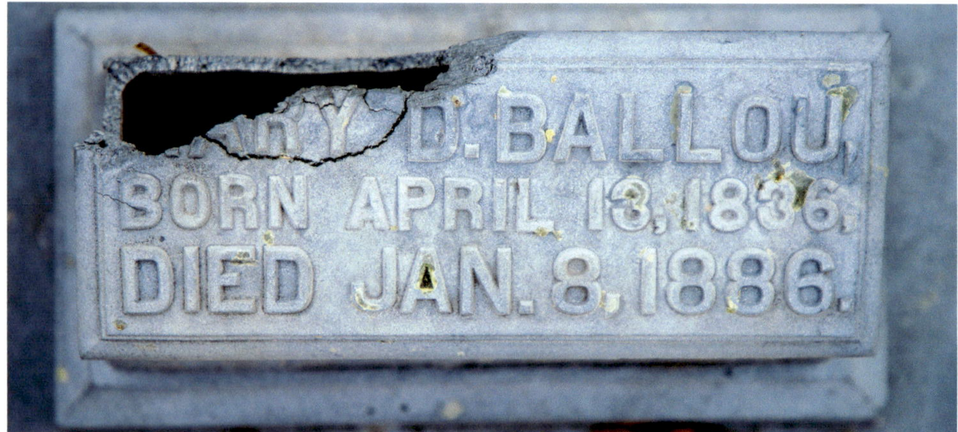

Above: Anyone exploring the buried dead of New England is likely to find unique headstones such as this one. White bronze grave markers, which are made from zinc, were a popular option for a period at the end of the nineteenth century. These so-called stones are a stunning color of muted blue, the inscriptions, typically, are as legible as the day they were erected. Especially unusual and cost saving, they are hollow.

Below left: Little Margaret, something of a local legend in death. An only child, her parents chose to honor the seven-year-old with a custom gravestone that would be as close to a photo of her as it could possibly be. The detail is stunning, showing the strands of her hair, the bridge between her nose and upper lip, her pearls, and the lace of her dress.

Below right: Black Agnes, one of the most notable residents of Green Mount, has a number of stories behind him. Agnes or Thanatos or Black Aggie are some of the names assigned or associated with this unbelievably ornate grave. The man buried beneath this supposedly haunted statue was generally despised by his community after making moves that redirected an estate that was meant to be gifted to Montpelier to himself.

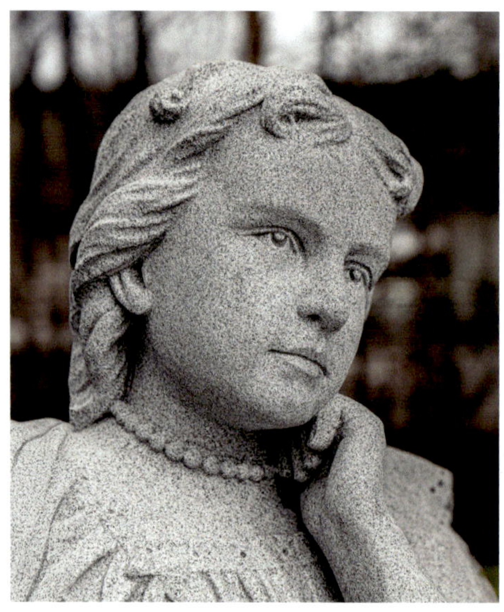

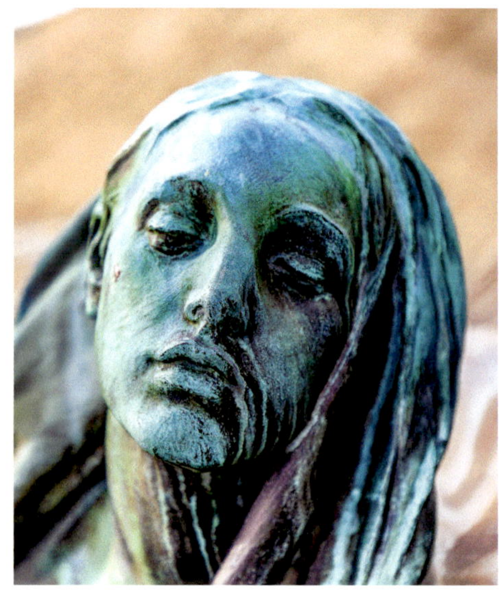

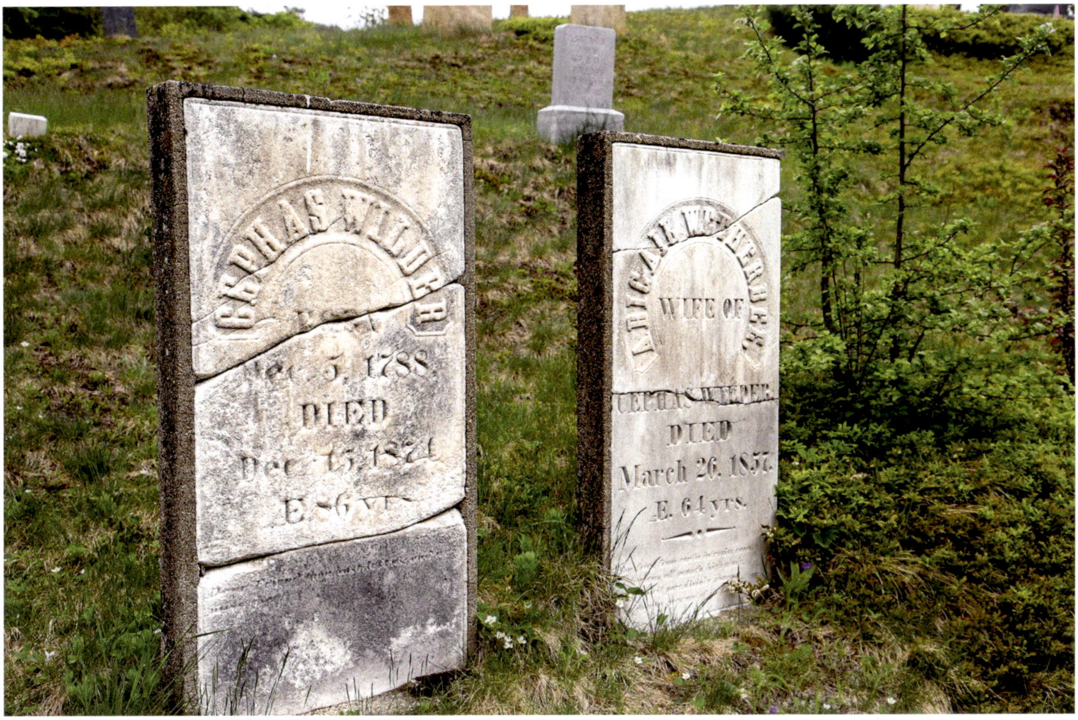

Right: The 30th president of the United States, Calvin Coolidge.

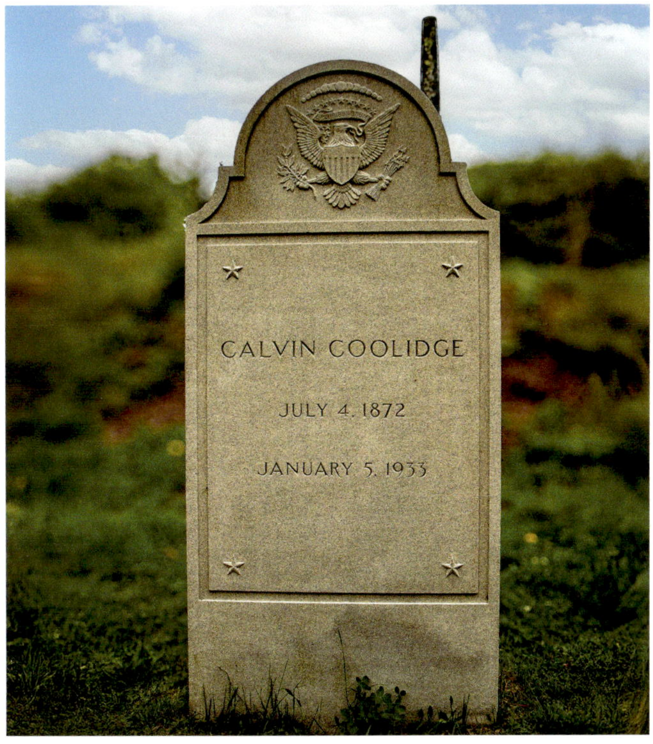

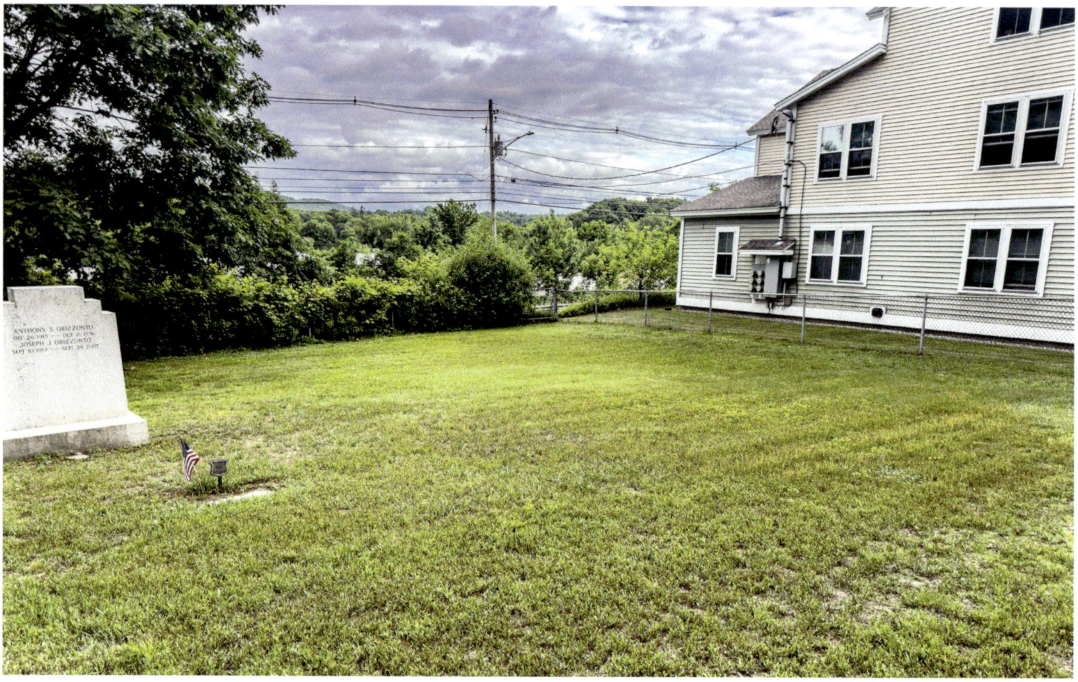

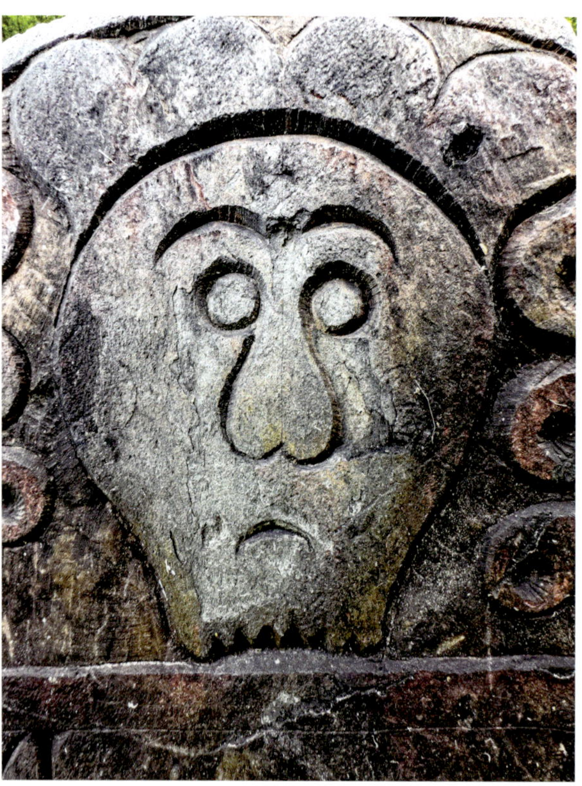

Above: Local legend claims that this section of the small hillside graveyard is a burial mound of native people. As such, they say, no burials have been placed here as to not disrupt the burial mound.

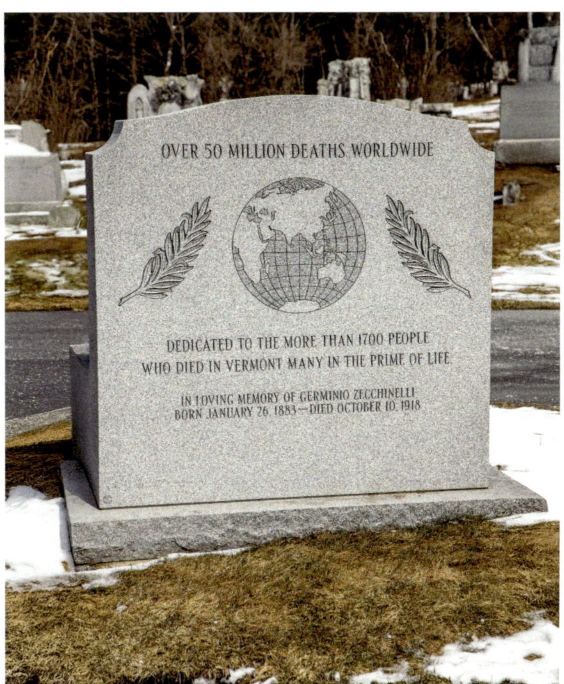

Below : "Strew gladness on the paths of men. While we have time, let us do good."

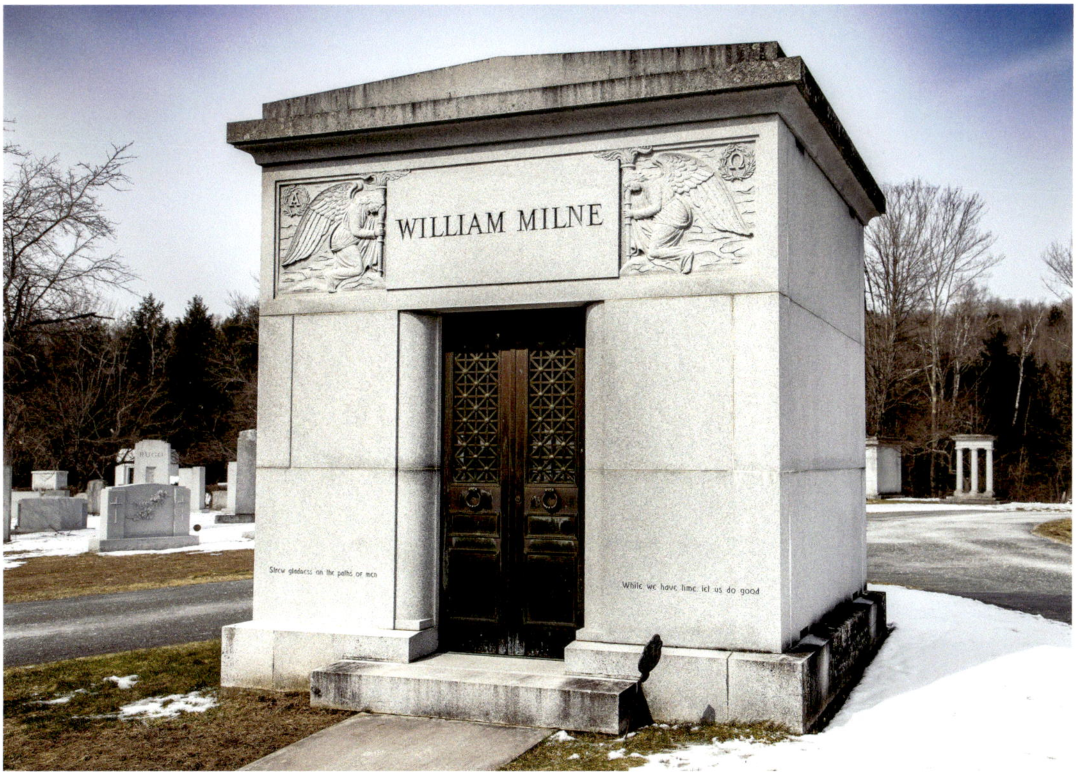

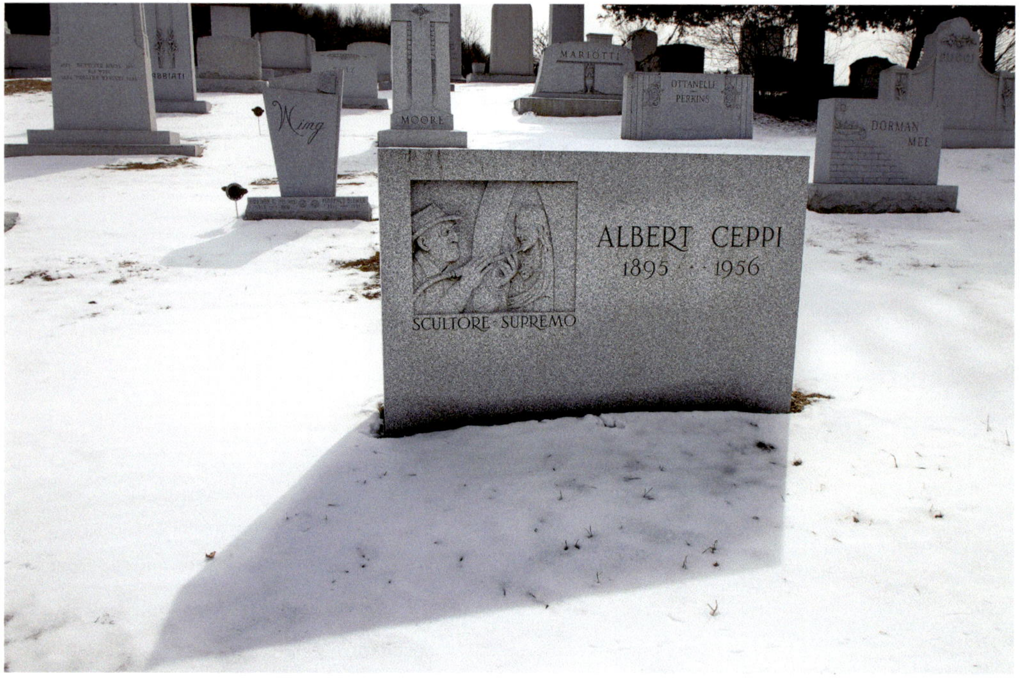

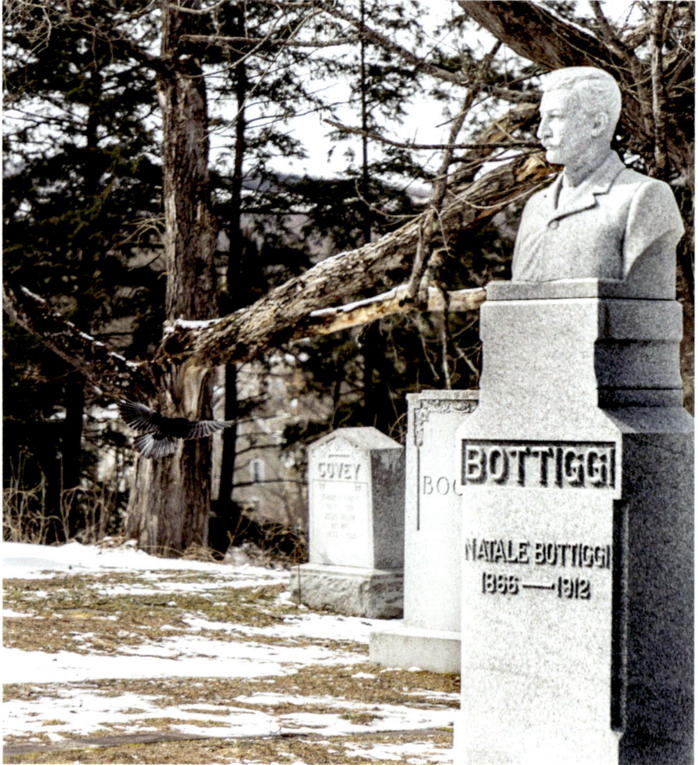

Above: A carving on a granite marker of a carver of granite markers.

Left: Birds, frequently found in graveyards because of the quiet open spaces, are also said to have a connection from the dead to their next life.

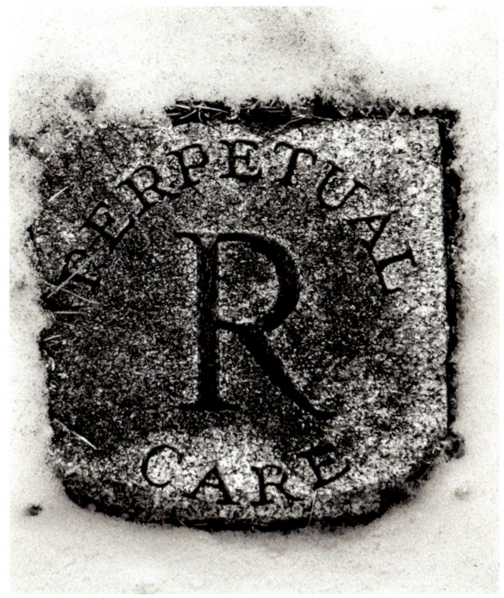

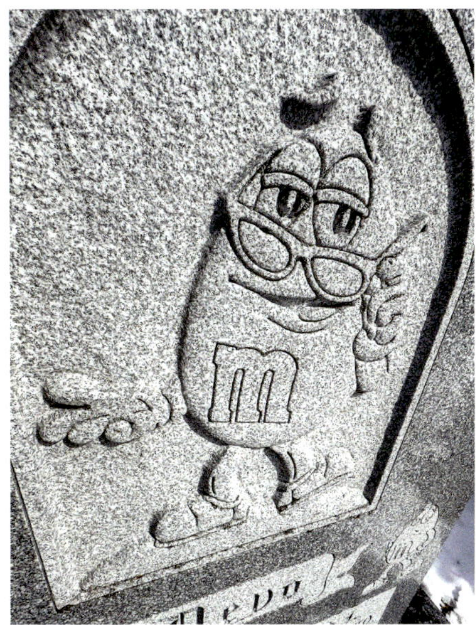

Above right: As society changes over the centuries, the unique carvings of death markers change with them.

Below: Wife and husband, together forever.

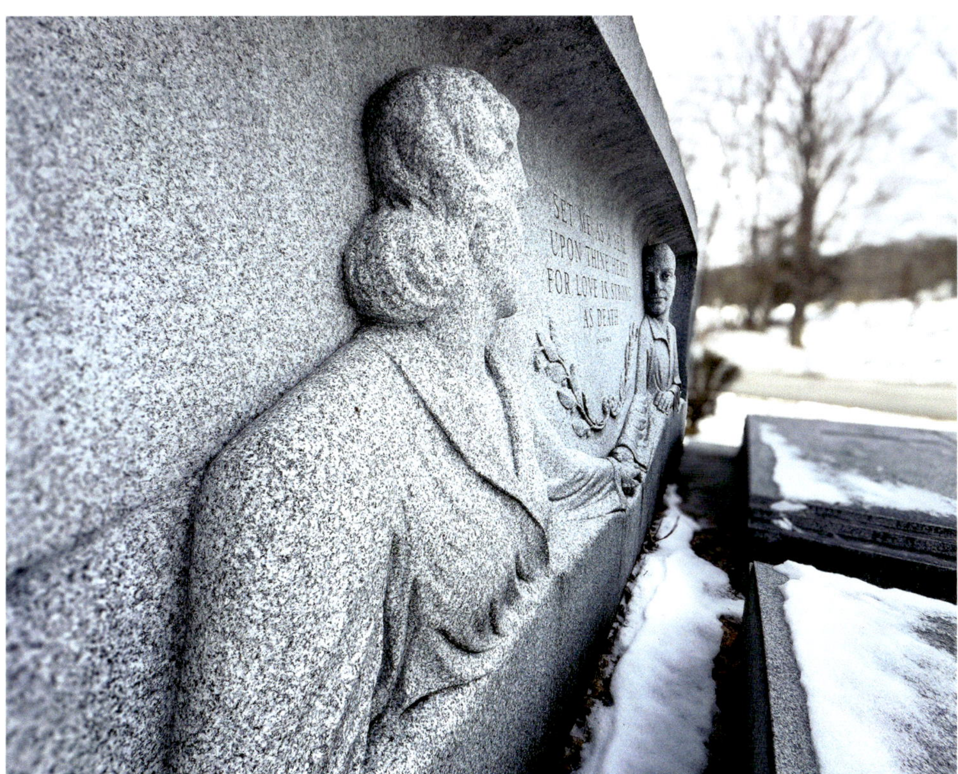

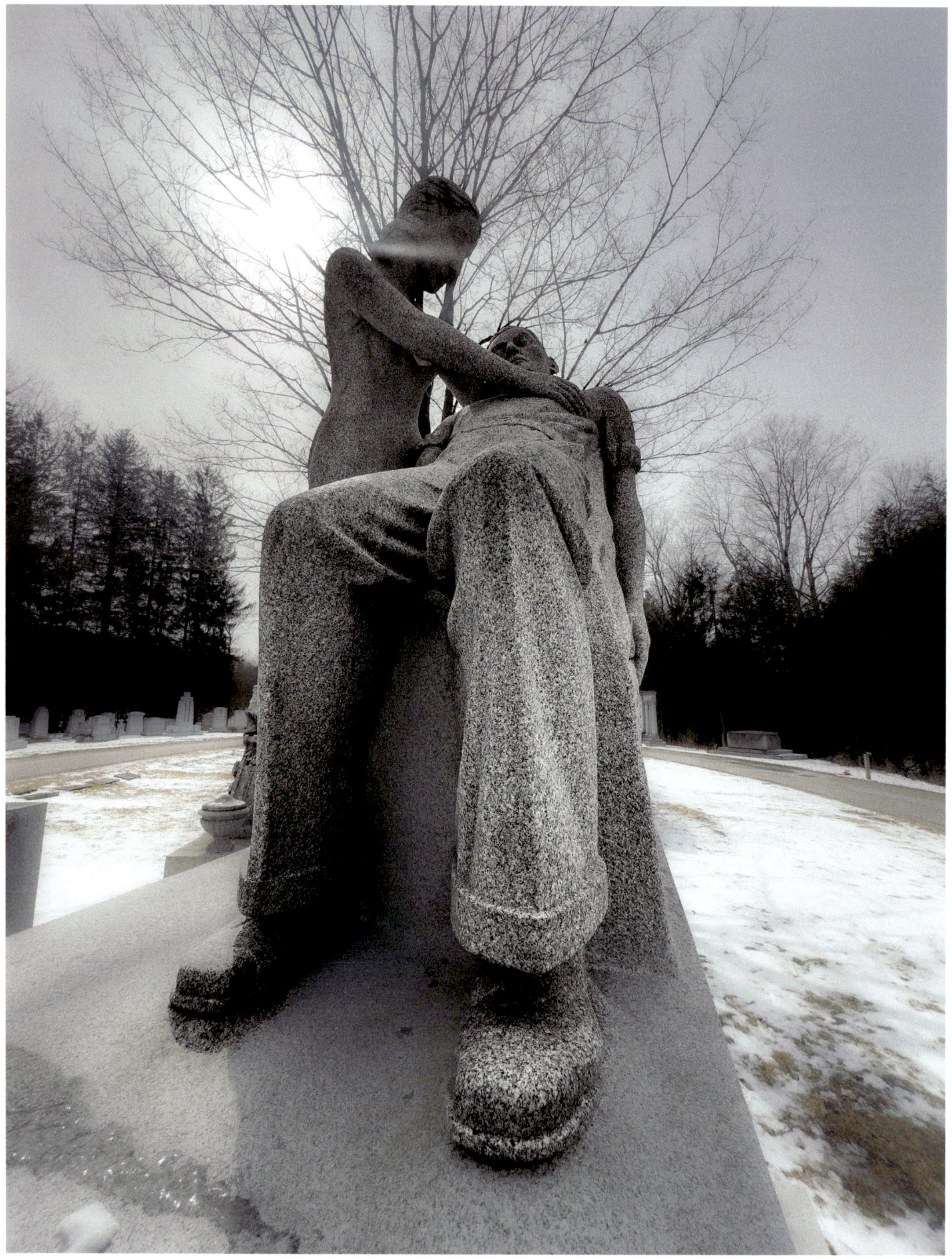

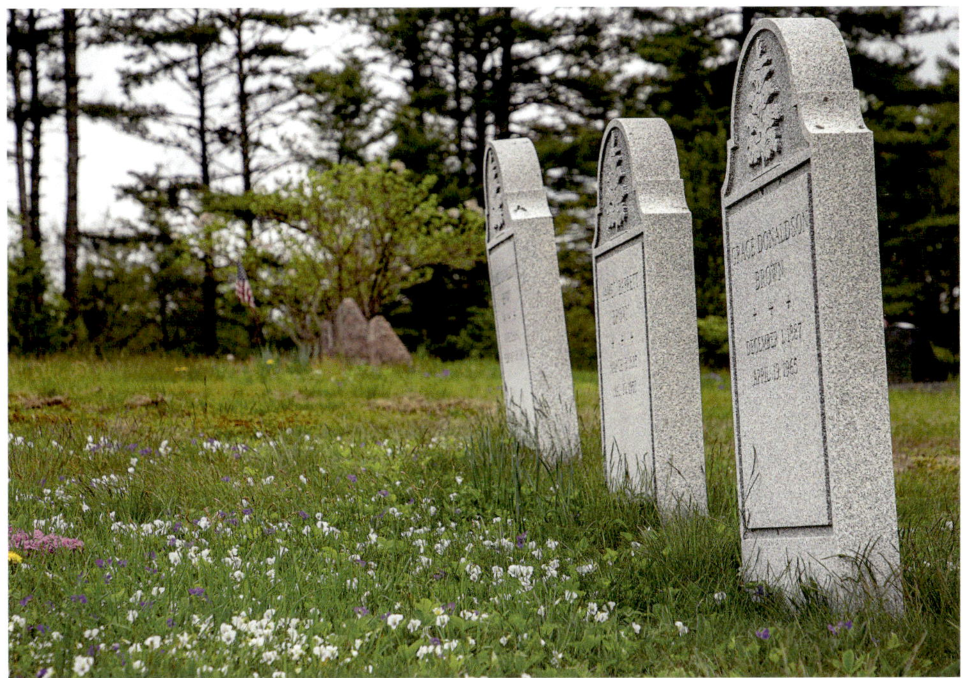

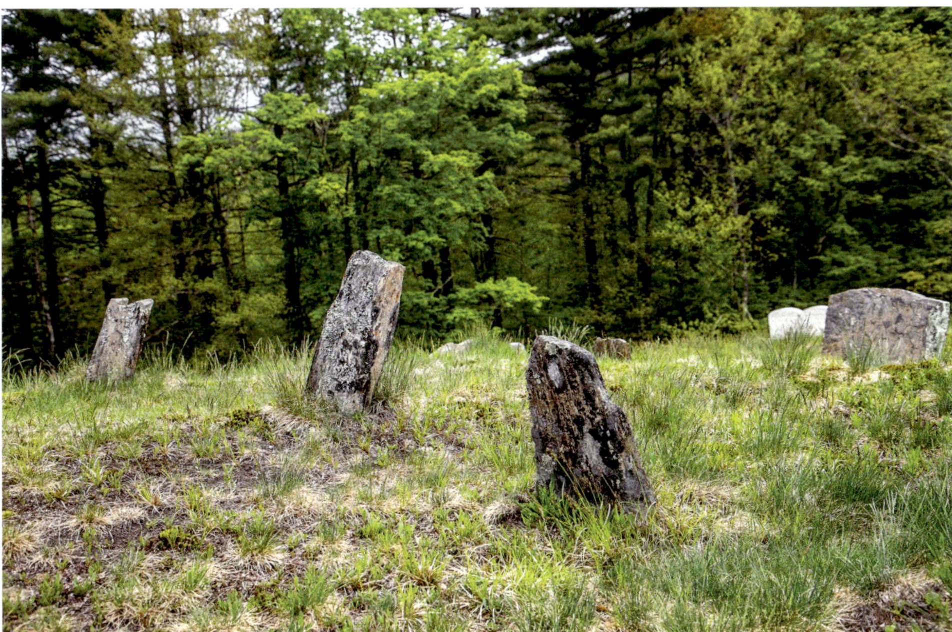

In a cemetery with more than 1,000 people buried over a couple of centuries, the battle between memorial and time rages on. While some residents, like the 30th president of the United States, bring attention to the small-town burying grounds of New England, even that attention cannot undo time.

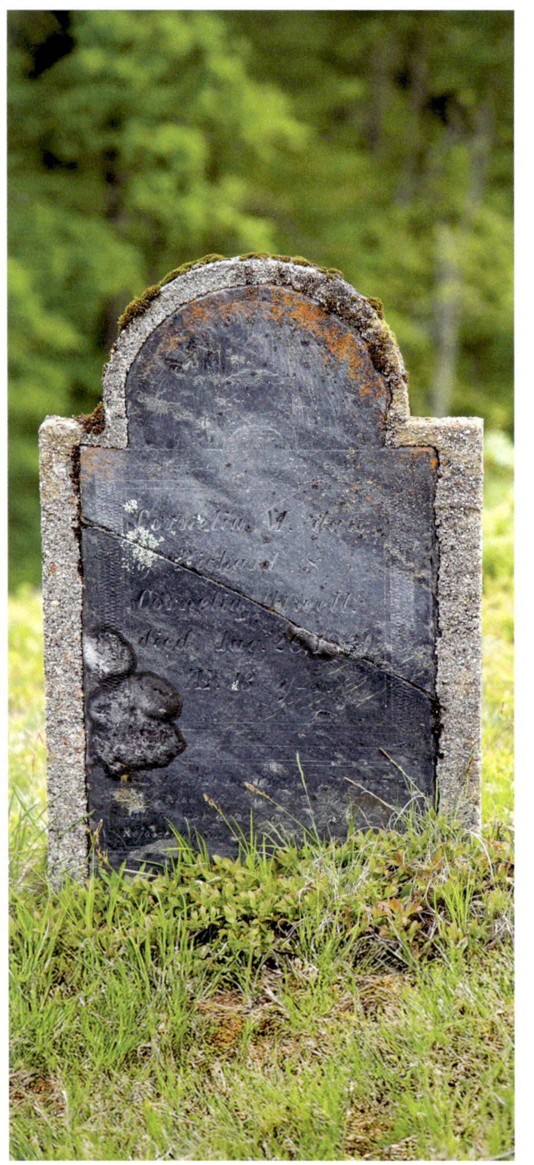

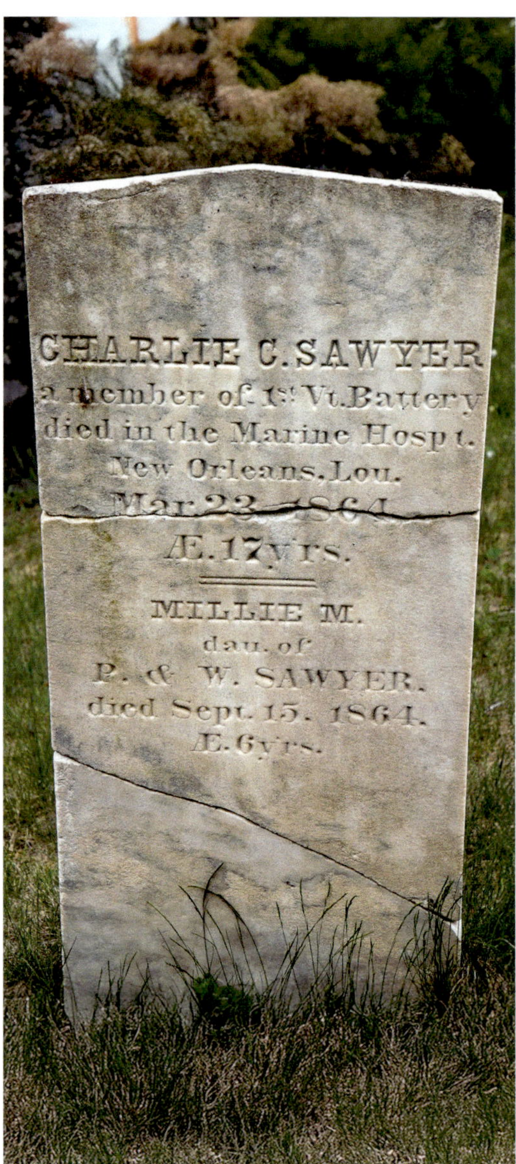

Above right: Lucky are those who evade the cold bitter tap of death on their loved ones.

6
Maine

Maynland, Province of Maine, Province or Countie of Maine, The Pine Tree State

Maine, once abundant with nature that provided life to the native inhabitants and wildlife, has, like its neighbors, seen many changes. From its original state of lush forests, waterfalls, lakes, rivers, and mountains to the transition to farming, Maine and its landscape continue to evolve based on the needs of those men and women who call the state home. As the nation changed, so did Maine, slowly but surely. As farms began to sprawl out across the state, tucked into the great wilderness, burials too changed. The burial methods of the earliest known inhabitants of the region, believed to be Ice Age hunters, took place in the caves. Others used riverbeds, burial mounds, and countless other rituals to lay their lost ones to rest. With farming came new practices, farmers with their expansive acres of land to maintain now set upon utilizing what they and the government of the day deemed to be their land. As these farm-centered families came to the richness of the state, so too did the need to commit the dead to final rest. Family farm burial lots preserved generations of those who had lived off the land they were now buried in. The evolution of the outside world saw change continue in Maine. As time passed, family farms saw their lands reduced, sold in part or in whole, lost to the banks and lenders that had financed them, and of course lost to modernization. Traveling U.S. Route 95, which spans from Florida all the way up the East Coast and ending in Maine, you will find burial lots not only on the small back roads but even along the major highway route. Traveling just south of the Kennebunk rest stop on Interstate 95, a family plot straddles the highway, divided by a fence and a barrier. For those who stood there so many years ago mourning their lost ones, it would be entirely inconceivable to entertain these changes. This adds another layer to the uncertainty that surrounds death; what will the future look like and how will it impact those buried, will they be robbed of the promise, gone, and never forgotten?

Inside the more formal burial grounds across the nearly 500 municipalities that help make up the state, the memorials range from the inventive to the ostentatious. Hand-carved gravestones sit in the shade of elaborate statues, with their arms reaching high to the sky. In the long, cold New England winters, those buried under flat stones are absent for several months a year. Those with the ability, drive, want, and determination to erect grave markers that climb up toward the heavens stand memorialized all year round. During the warmer months, Maine still has the upper hand on death—as grasses, weeds, and shrubs all grow and overtake even some of the upright markers. The gravestones of children, parents, families, and individuals, with enough time, are only allowed to be remembered at the mercy of the elements yet again. In a way, burials, cremations, funerals, and other rites of passing are meant, culturally, not to grieve the loss but instead to celebrate the life, the essence, and for many, the final journey of their life.

One thing has remained consistent across New England's history—time stops, largely, for two things: birth and death. Most people never have the chance or the reason to see their grave marker or location while they are alive. Some do, insisting on planning and controlling their future; arguably due to a worry about what will happen if they do not manage those plans or because they want to control this final aspect of their life. Across Maine, people of nearly all backgrounds have been committed back to the earth at the end of their life. Some of those who return to the ground, where all things grow from, imagine that specific moment as a stop on their way to some version of an afterlife. Others go into death and burial with a certainty that their existence has ceased and will never exist again, on this plane or any other. People of great historical significance are rested alongside those who had a great impact on their family, community, or their own life. Death, as it is said, does not discriminate. Enslaved people, minorities, natives, immigrants, teachers, leaders, lobstermen, and more, who are indeed remembered by a tombstone are differentiated by the living. Mass graves, unmarked graves, family plots, communal cemeteries, and other burying grounds show how centuries-old markers have stood the test of time in their battles against the weather, nature, and time. These same areas also provide a unique glimpse into each area, the cultures that thrive or thrived there, how the communities changed over time, and, perhaps most importantly, how humans treated humans. If a culture is to be judged, it seems worthy to judge how the living members of that culture treated, judged, accepted, celebrated, or villainized their dead.

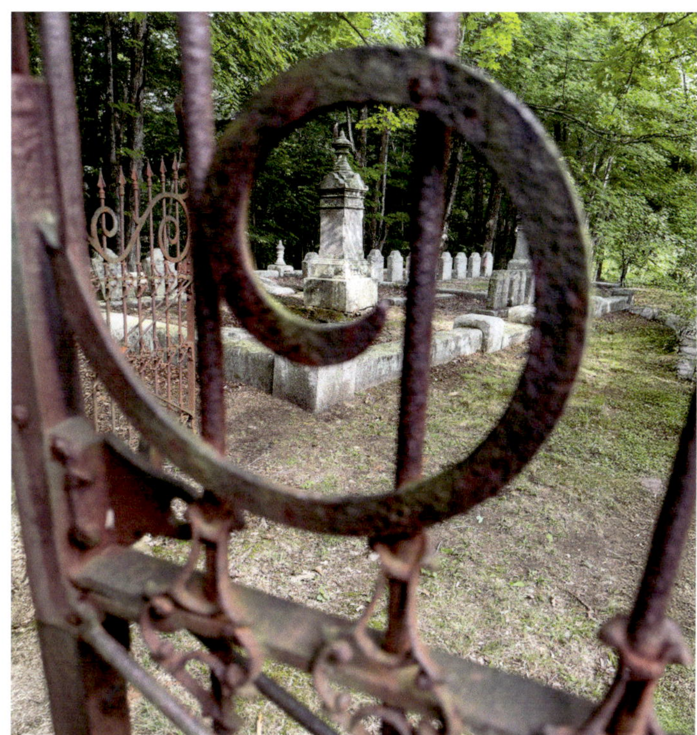

Below: This memorial stone was erected to remember the victims of the Candlemas Day Massacre. During a raid carried out by the native people of the area on the colonial residents of York.

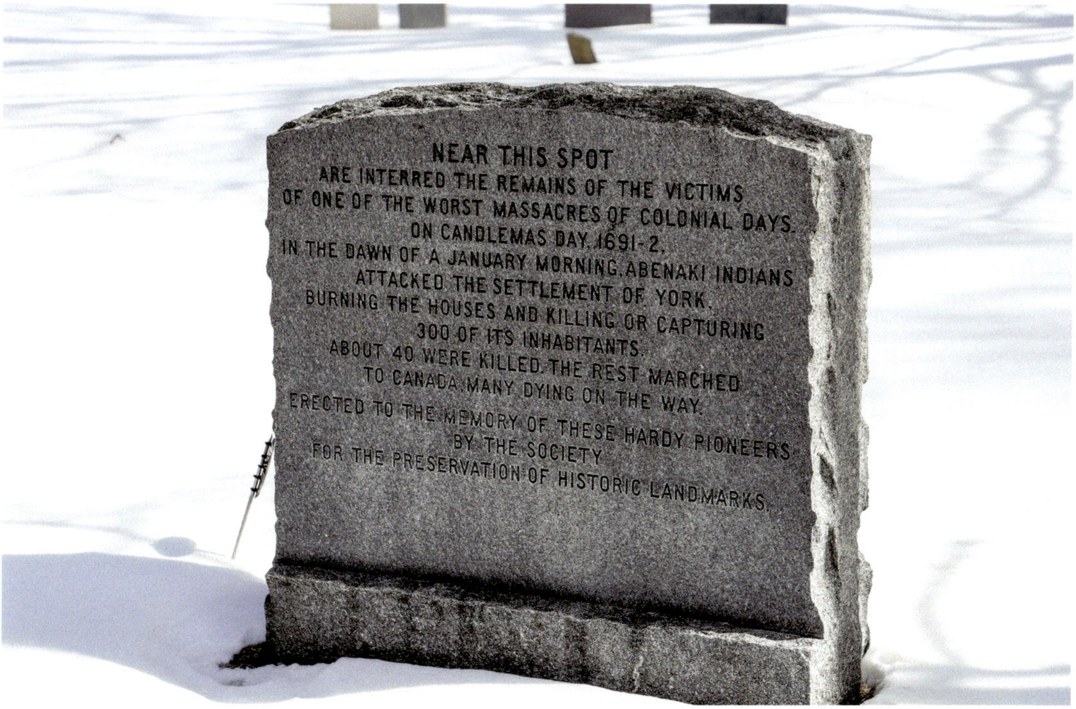

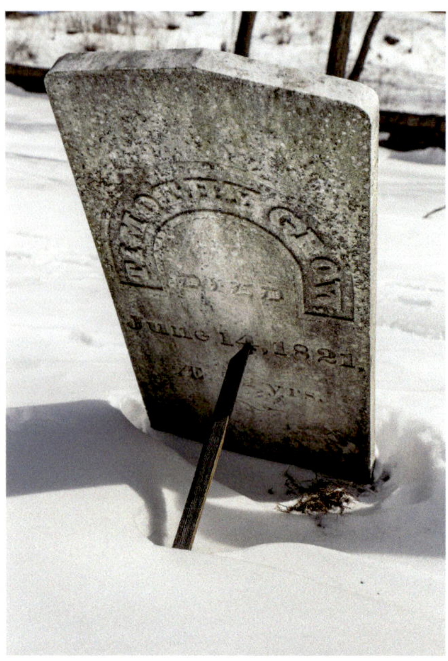

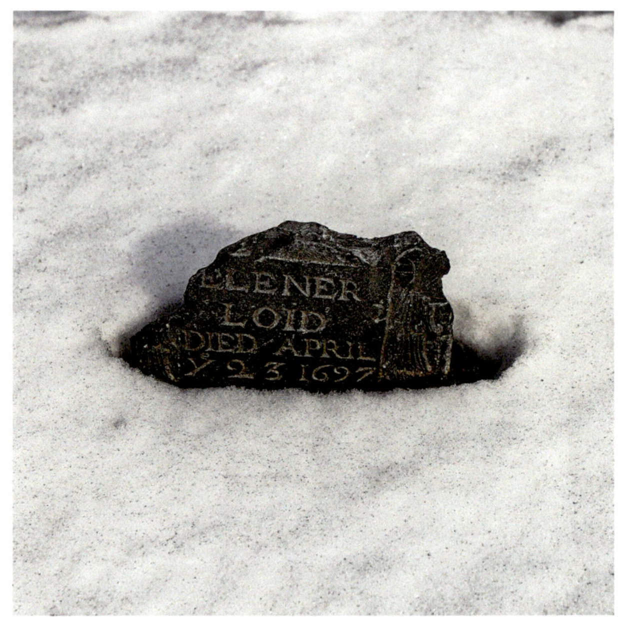

Above left: Mr. Grow's headstone has been resisting its extinction in a manner not commonly found; a simple wooden stake has taken on the responsibility of attempting to prevent the headstone from what might be its last tumble.

Above right: April 23, 1697.

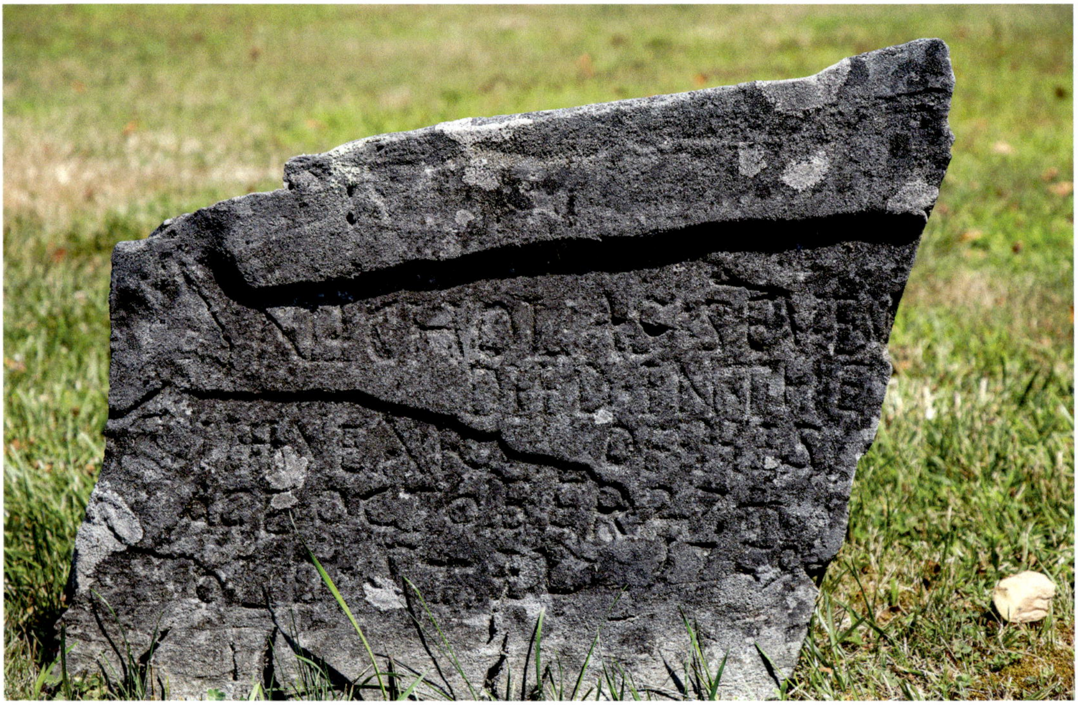

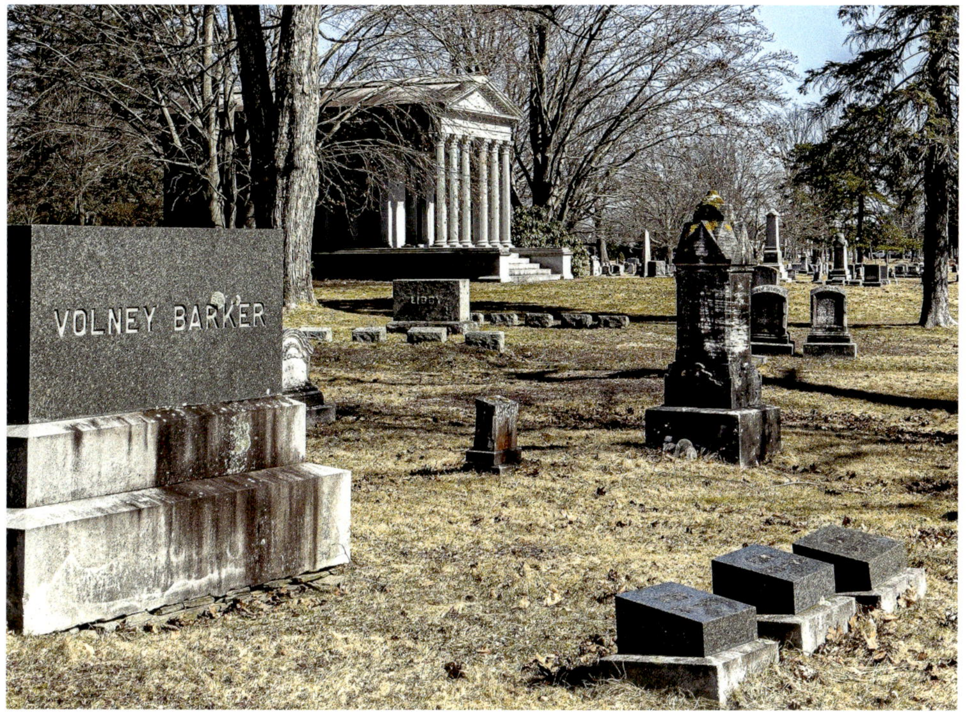

Above: Evergreen Cemetery in Portland, Maine.

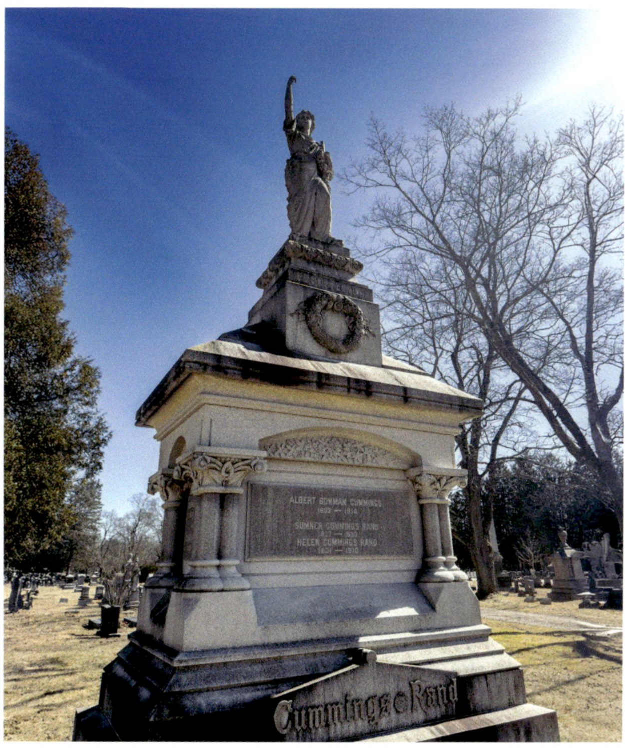

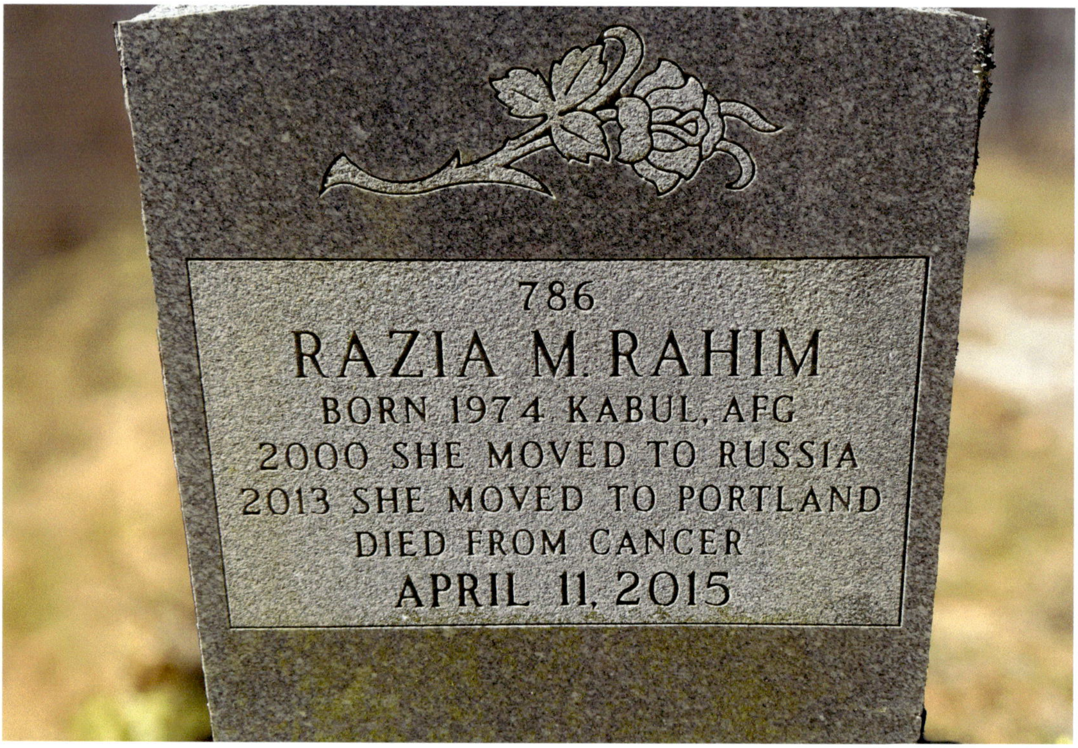

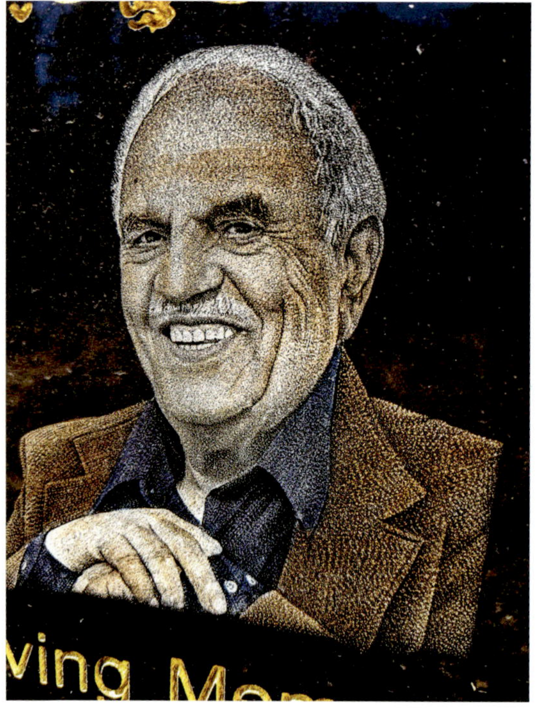

Above: Born in Kabul, moved to Russia, moved to Portland, Maine.

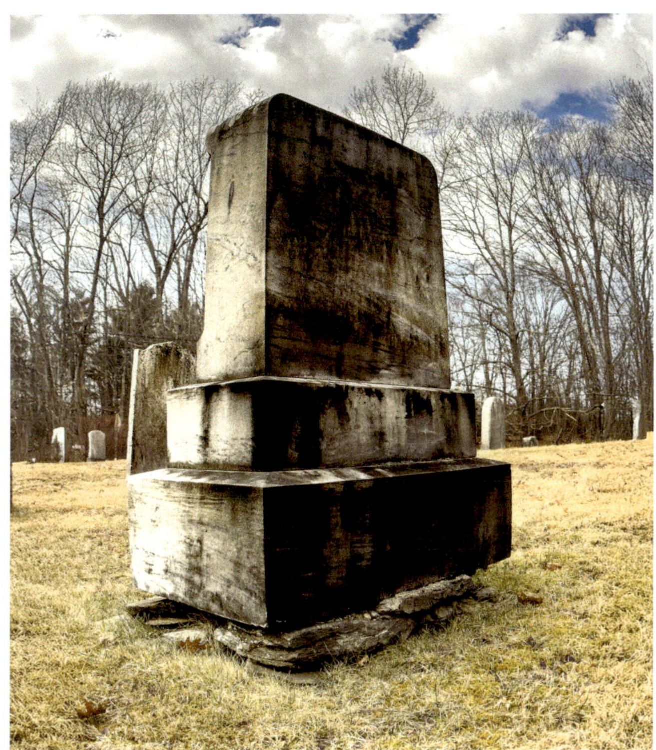

Right: Held up by stone.

Below: Families buried within feet of the street.

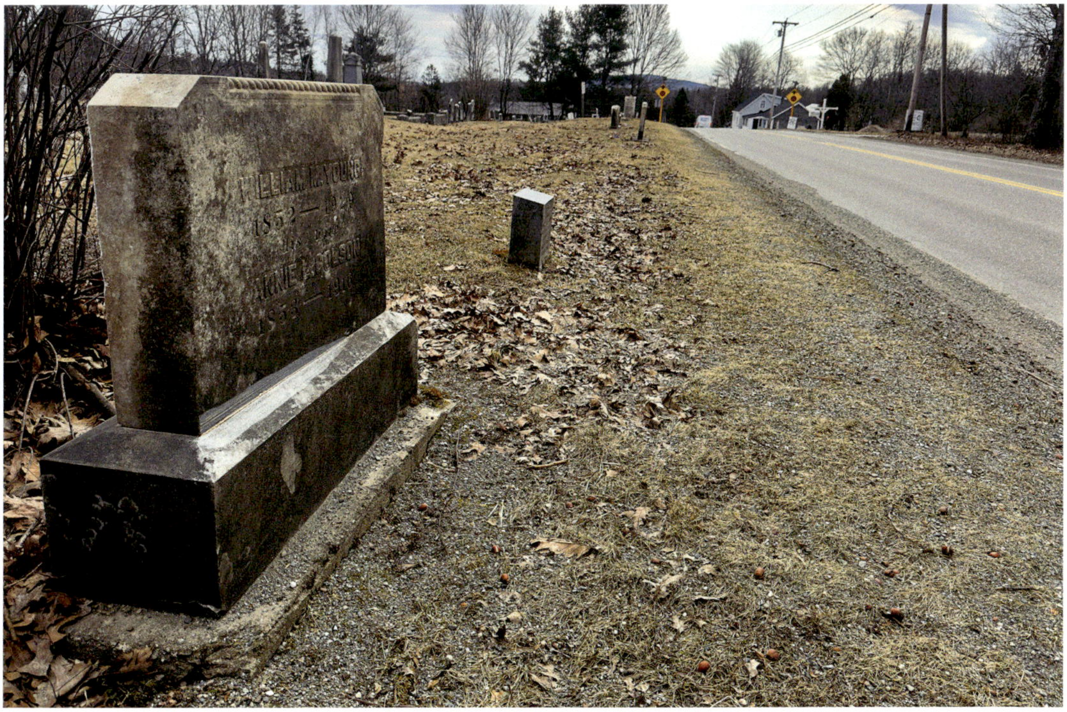

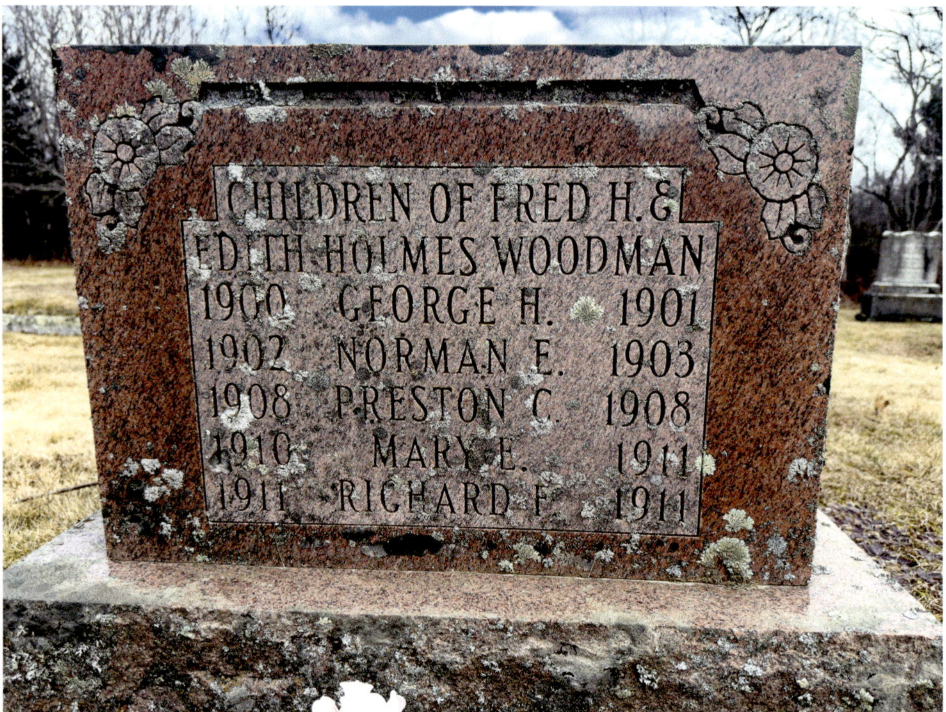

Inconceivable loss in eleven years.

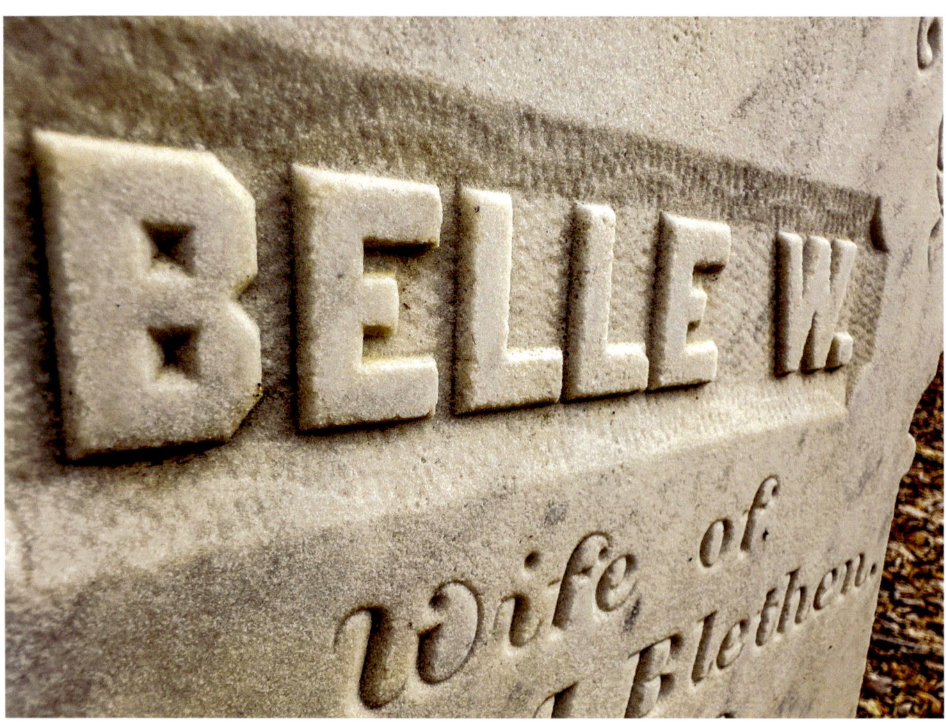

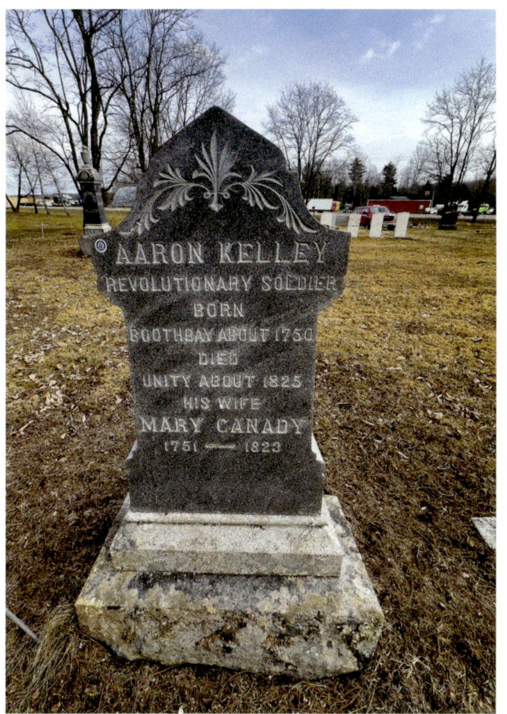

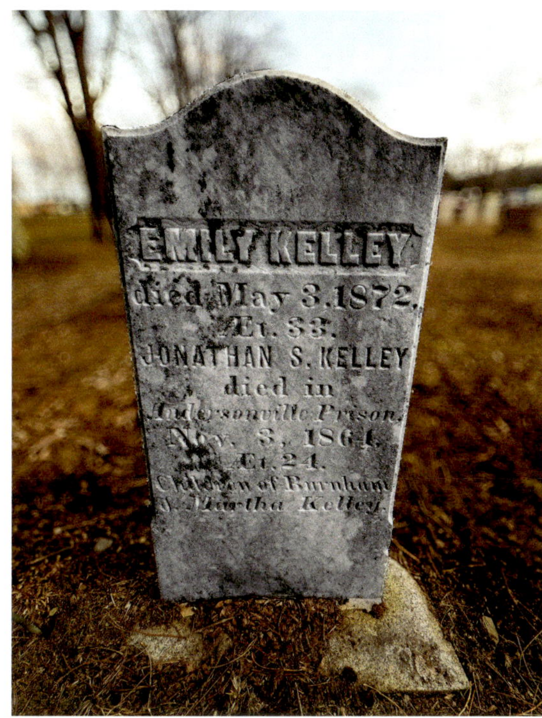

Above left: Inside the Fowler Cemetery in Unity, Maine, there are an unusual number of war veterans buried, especially when considering the small population the town has maintained for centuries.

Above right: Emily and Jonathan Kelley, siblings. Jonathan died, as the marker states, in Andersonville Prison.

Right: The Buck family, having founded the town of Bucksport along the coast of Maine, were notable. Arguably the most notable being Colonel Jonathon, the patriarch. Across many years, a stain that rests under the Buck name on the colonel's gravestone appears, as per the legend, as a foot or leg or shoe. The legend accuses Buck of having burned a woman accused of being a witch, and it is said that her leg rolled out of the fire.

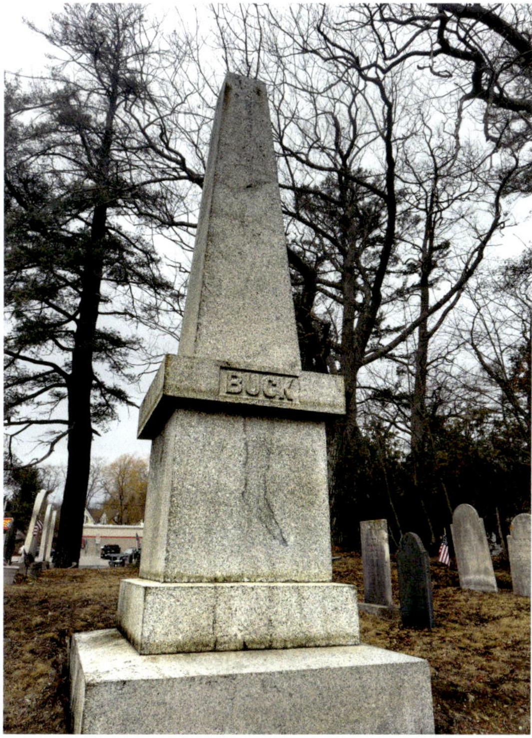

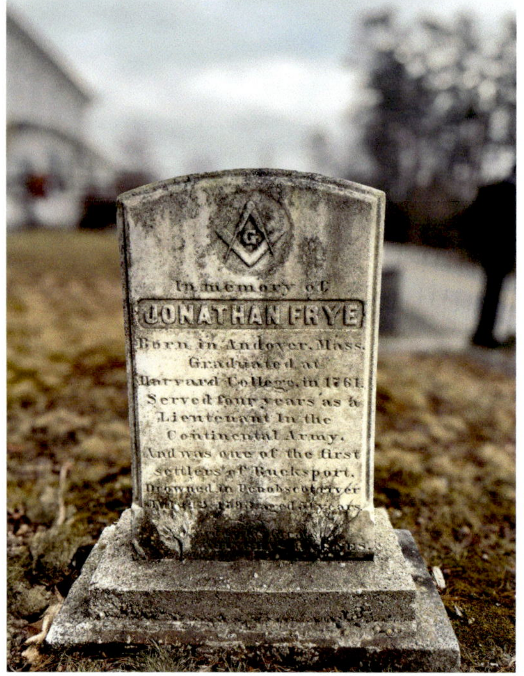

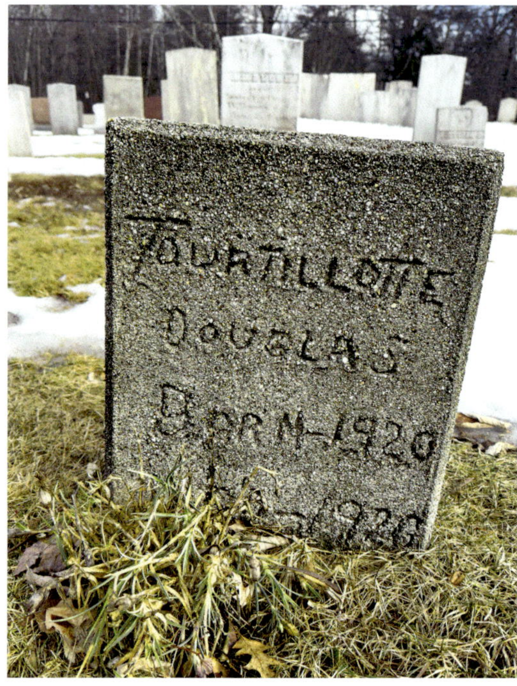

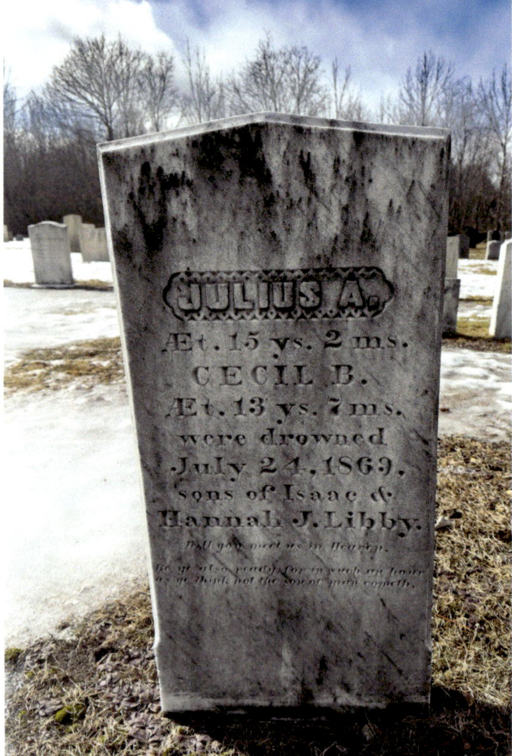

Above left: Mr. Frye, a veteran of the American Civil War and an original settler of the town of Bucksport, met his death, drowning in the Penobscot River.

Left: Hannan and Issac's sons drowned on July 24, 1869.

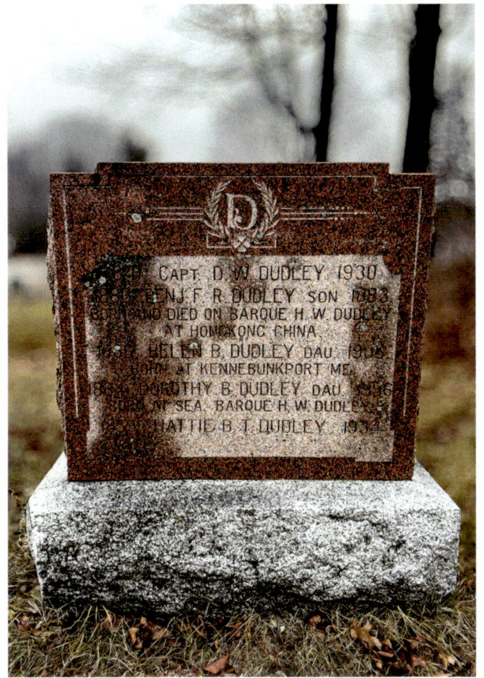

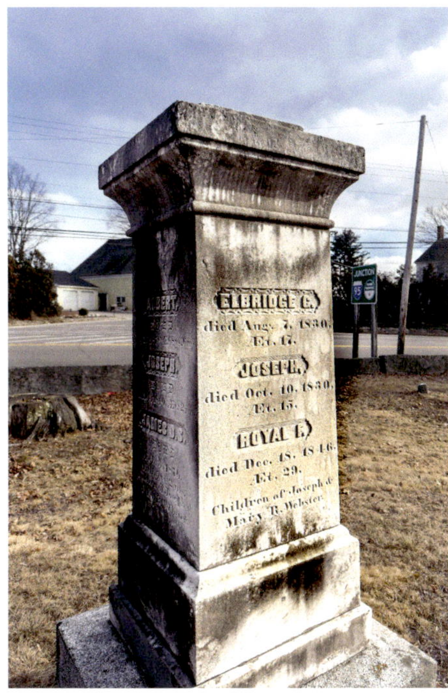

Above right: An onramp to U.S. Interstate 95 is not something one considers running adjacent to their loved one's burial spots.

Below: Laura and her husbands, Arthur and Walter.

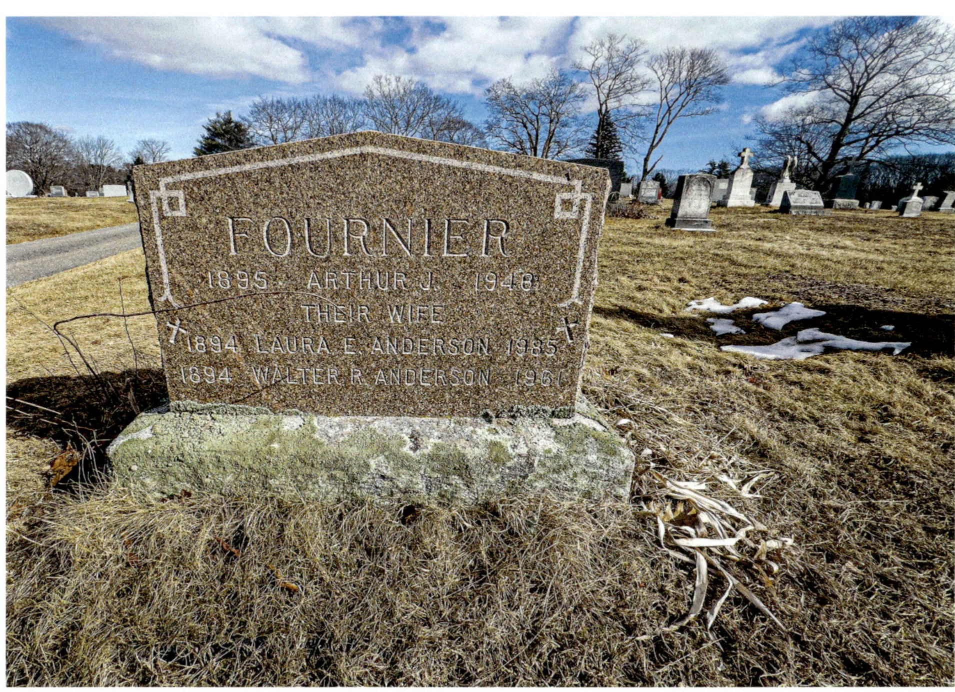

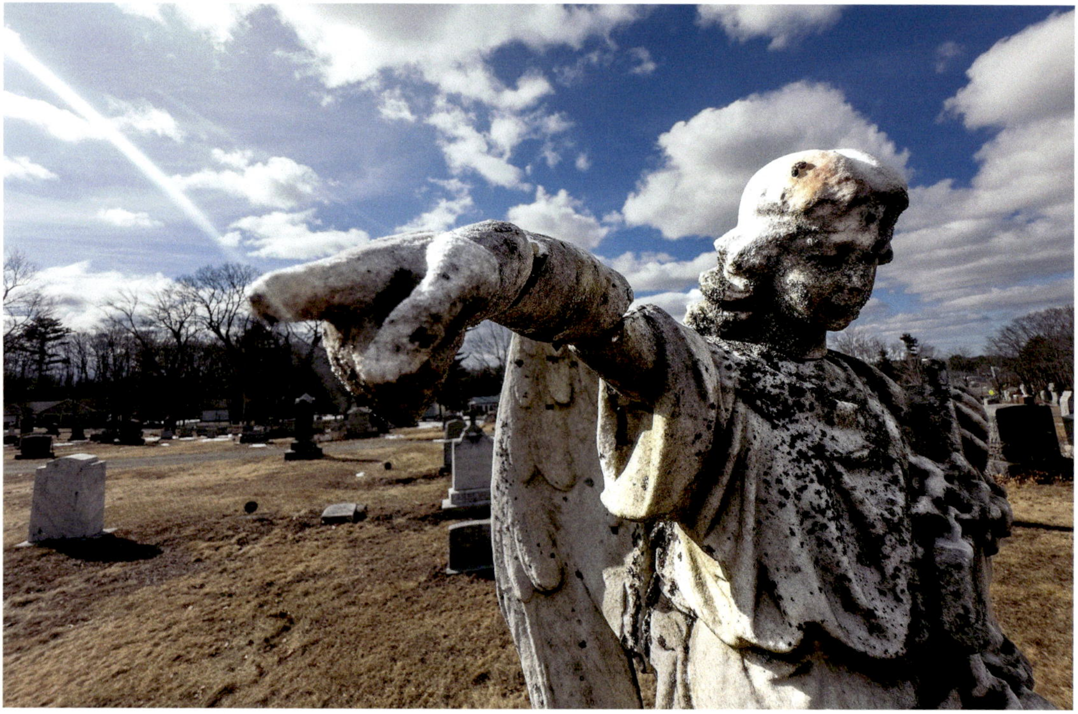

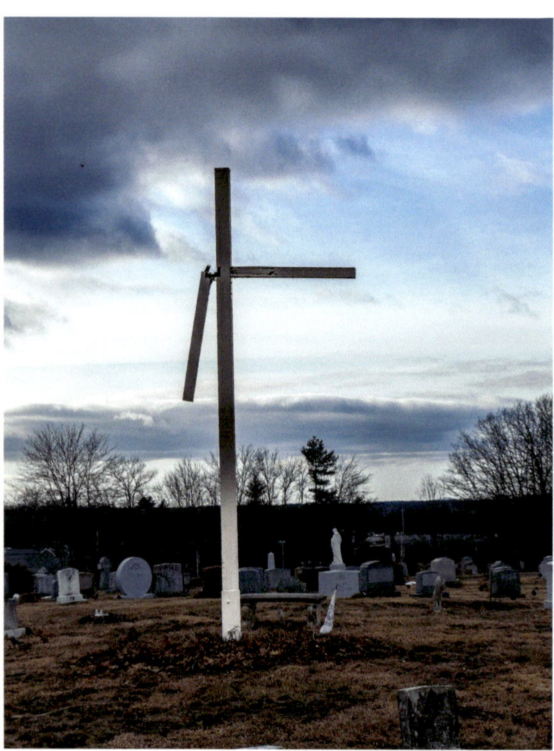

Left: A wooden cross stands above an area of the cemetery dedicated to children. As happens in New England, the weather's impact is unpredictable.

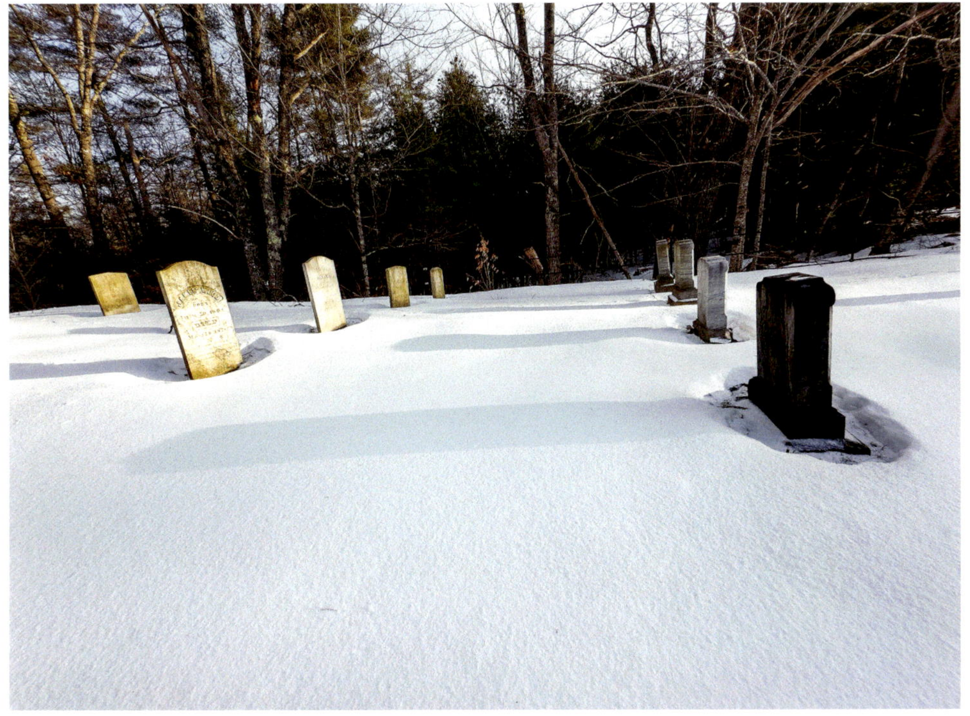

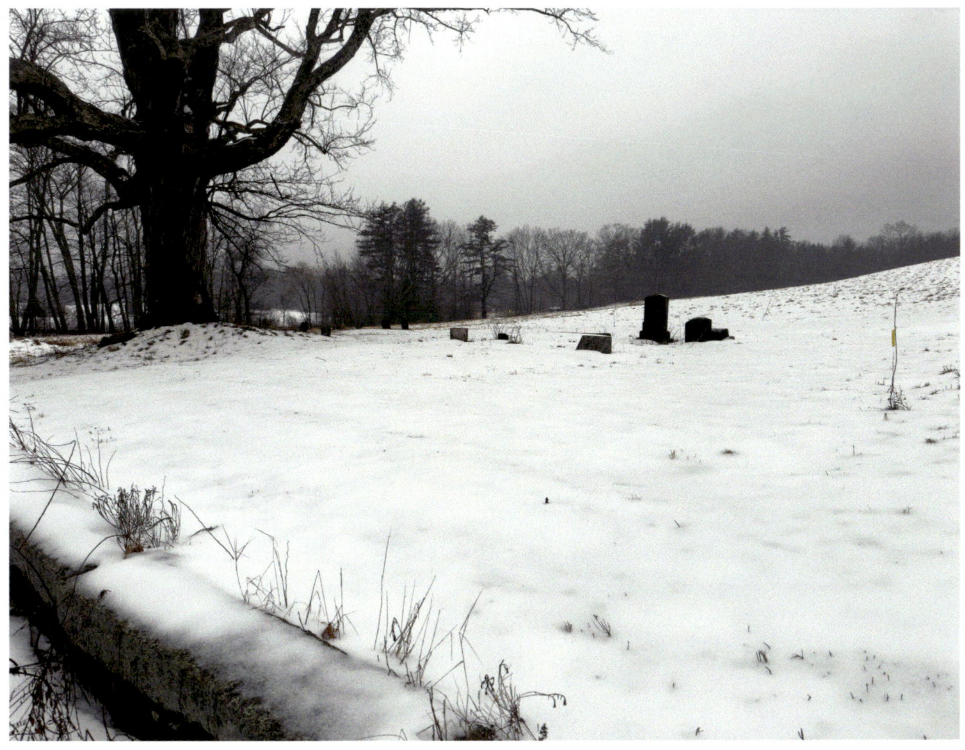

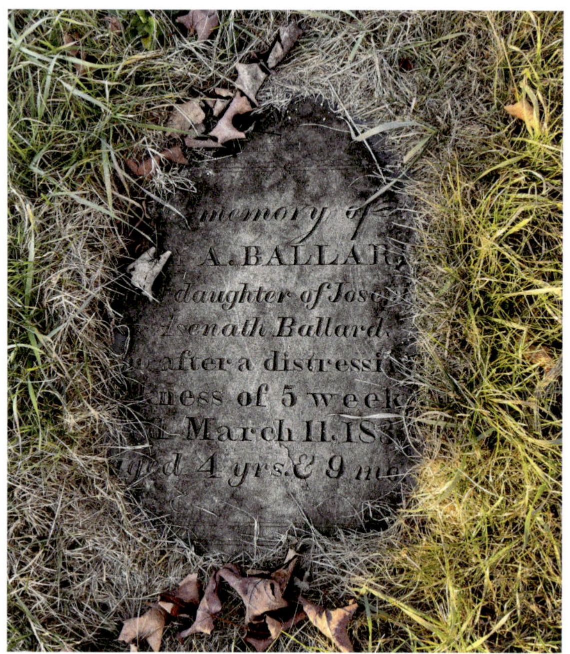
memory of
A.BALLAR
daughter of Jose
senath Ballard
after a distressi
ness of 5 week
March 11. 18
yrs.& 9 m

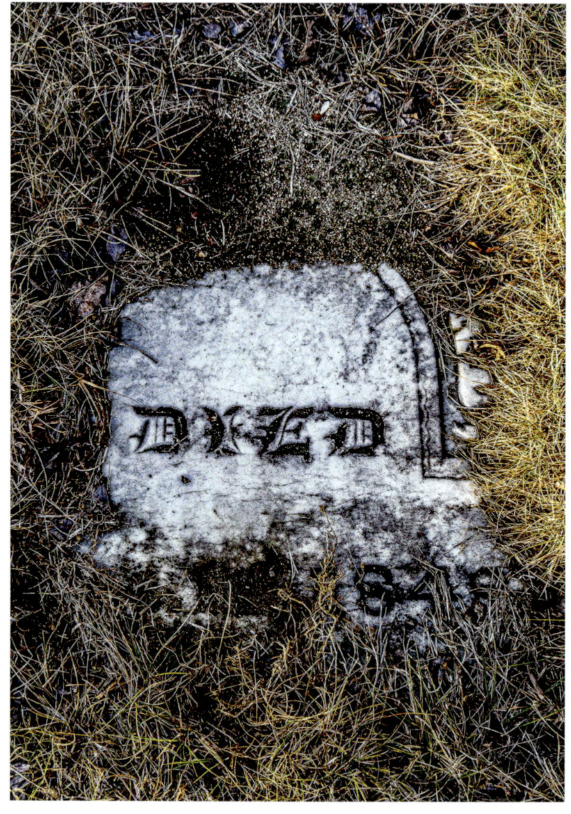
DIED

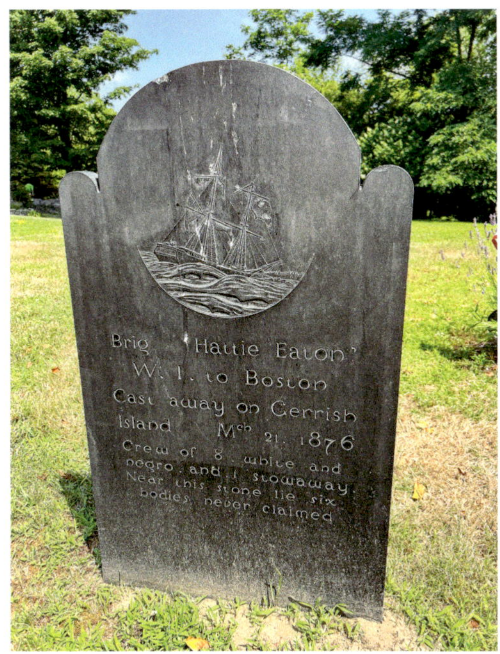
Brig 'Hattie Eaton'
W. I. to Boston
Cast away on Gerrish
Island M^ch 21. 1876
Crew of 8 . white and
negro. and 1 stowaway.
Near this stone lie six
bodies never claimed

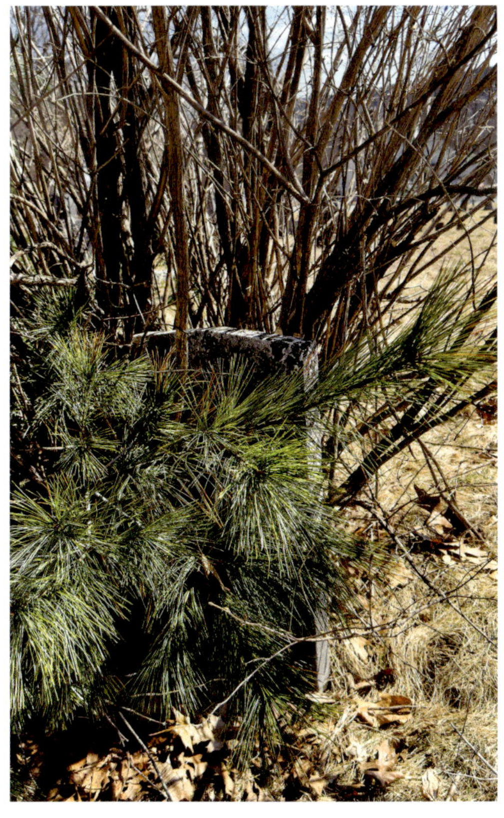

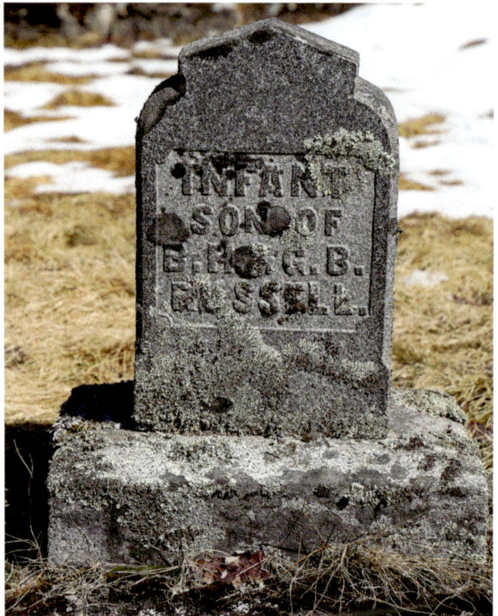

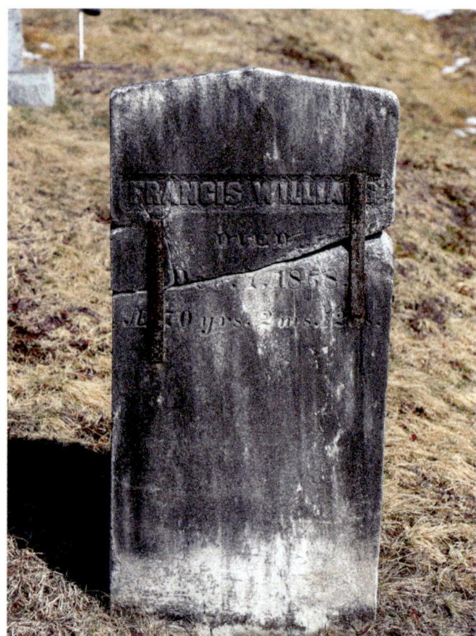

Above right: Caratunk, Maine's climate is one that is not meant for the weak. Considering this it is no surprise that seventy-year-old Francis' 1868 gravestone has needed intervention to survive to today.

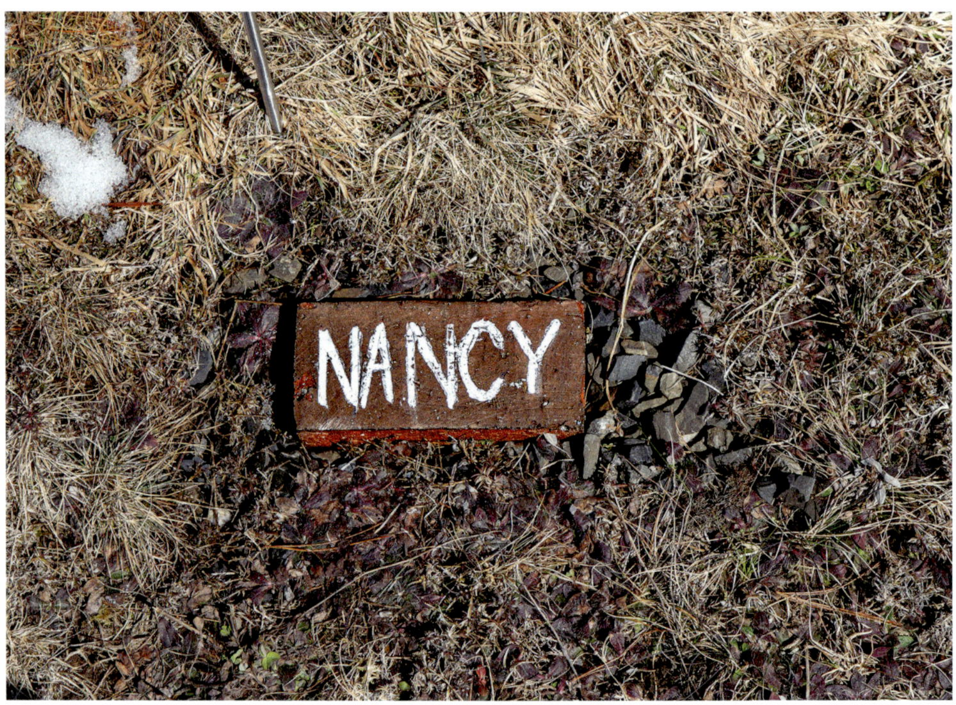

In central Maine, the climate rules the day leaving burials and headstone installations frequently at the whim of the ground.

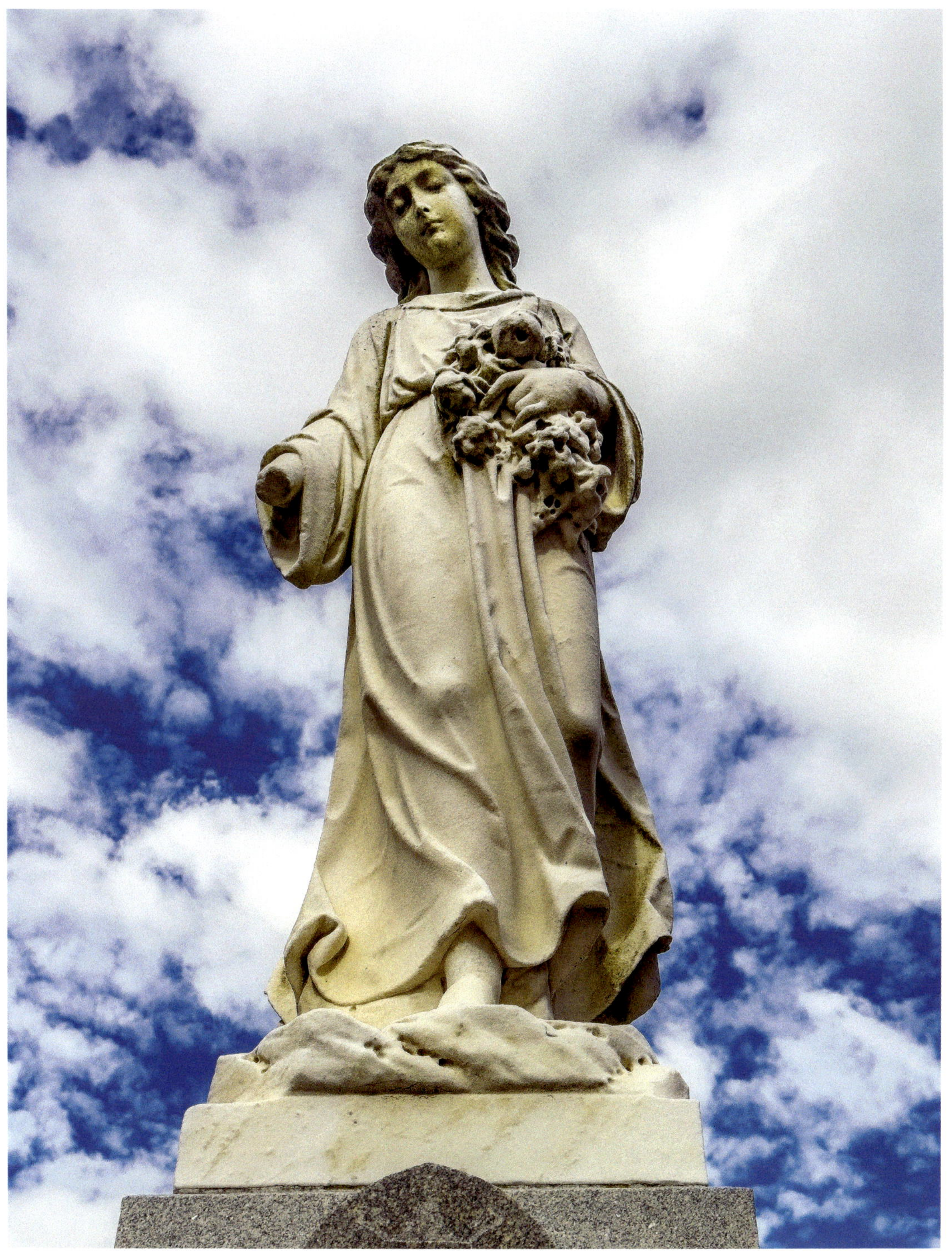

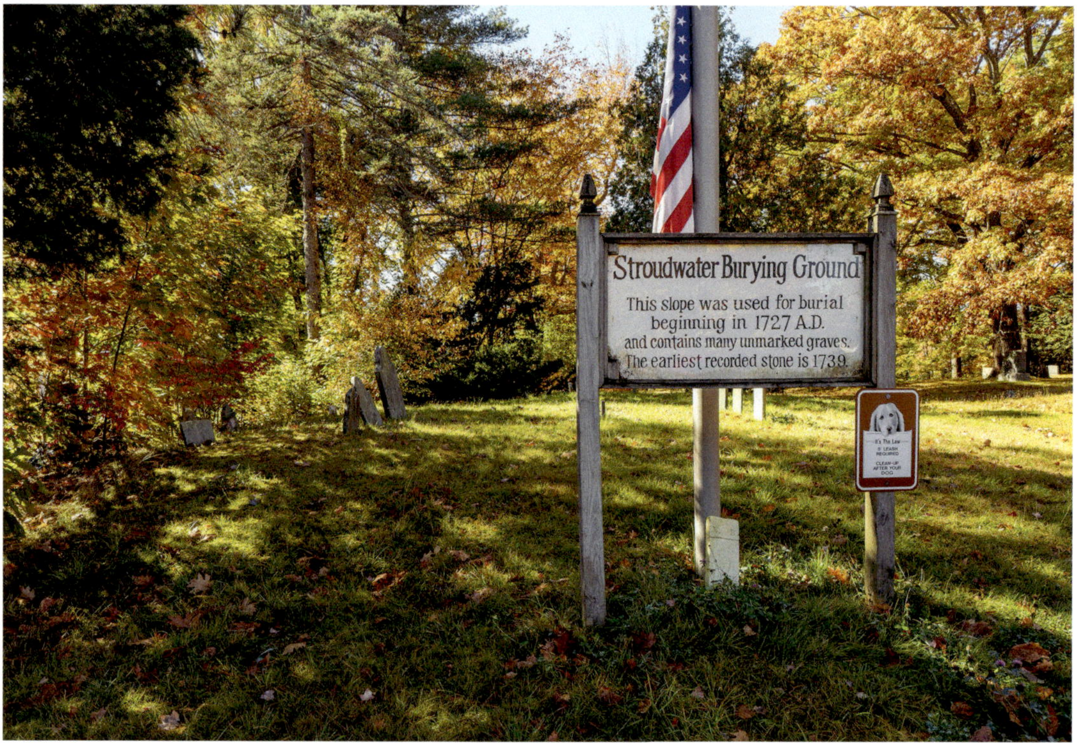

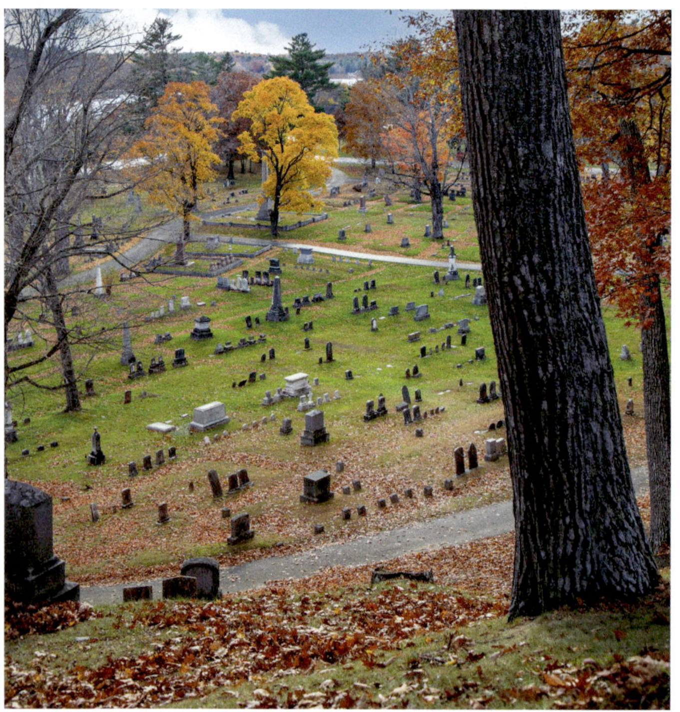

Above: Stroudwater Burying Ground, in addition to the marked gravesites, also contains many unmarked graves.

Left: Fans of Stephen King may be familiar with this shot which is featured in the 1989 film adaptation of one of King's many works.

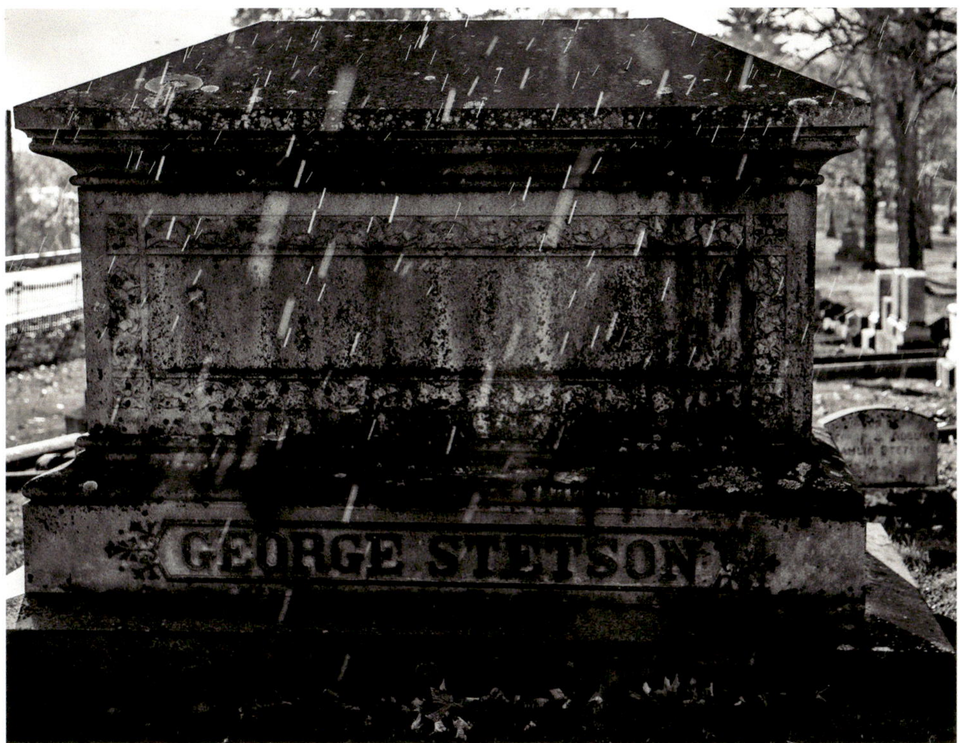

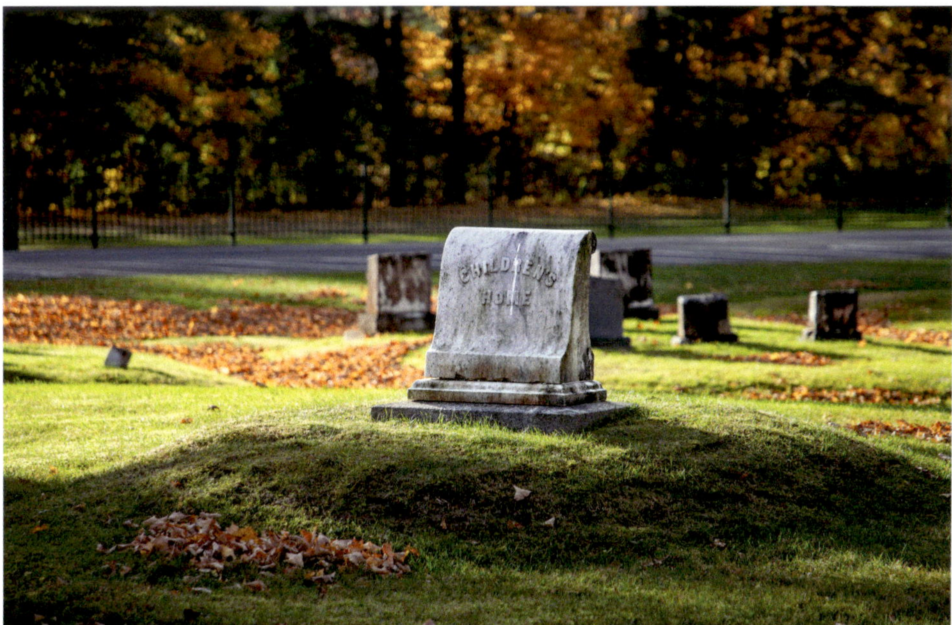

The Children's Home burial site inside Mount Hope Cemetery in Bangor is one of several burial spaces offered by the cemetery for charitable purposes.

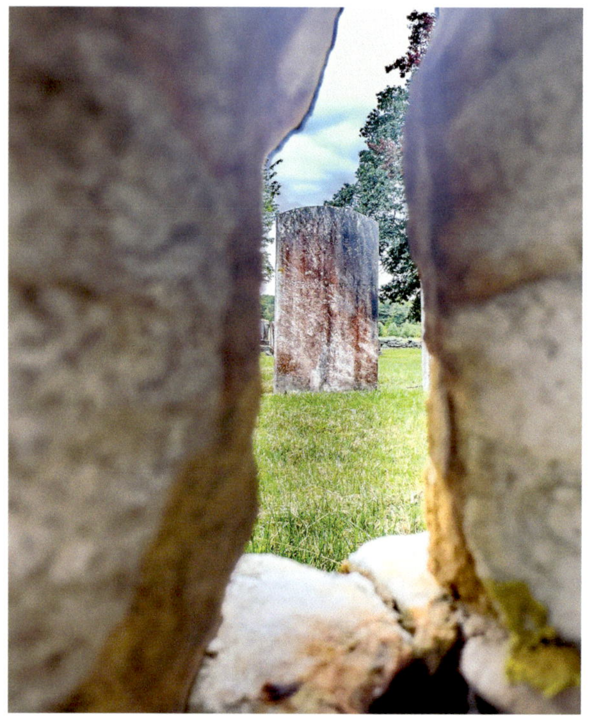

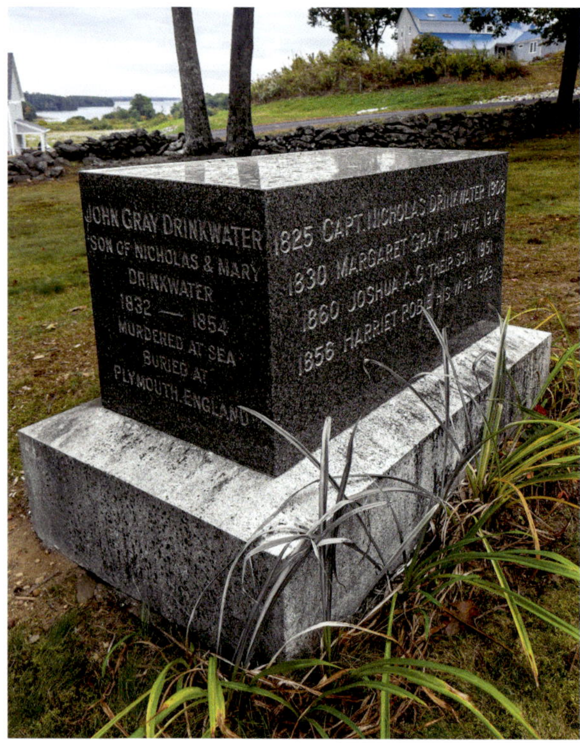

J.G. Drinkwater. Murdered at sea, buried in England.

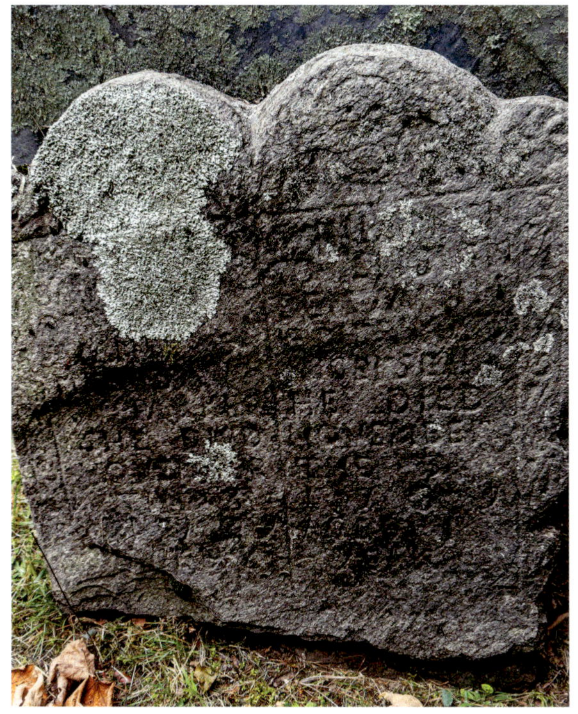

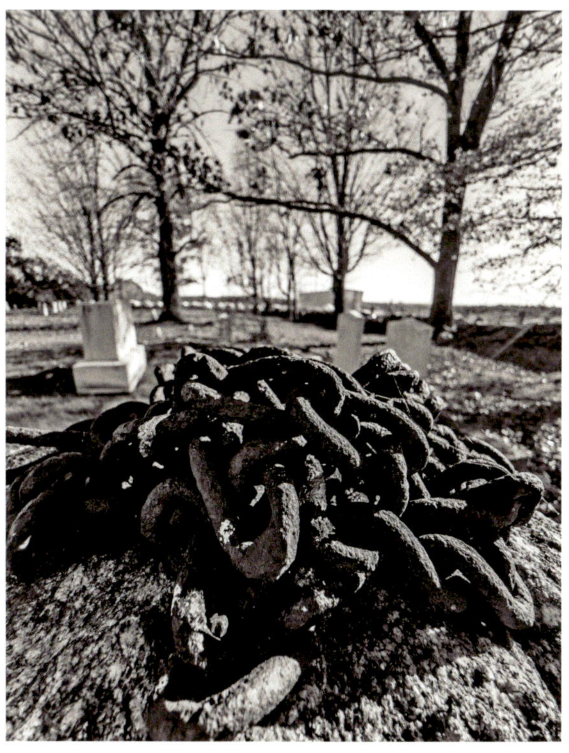

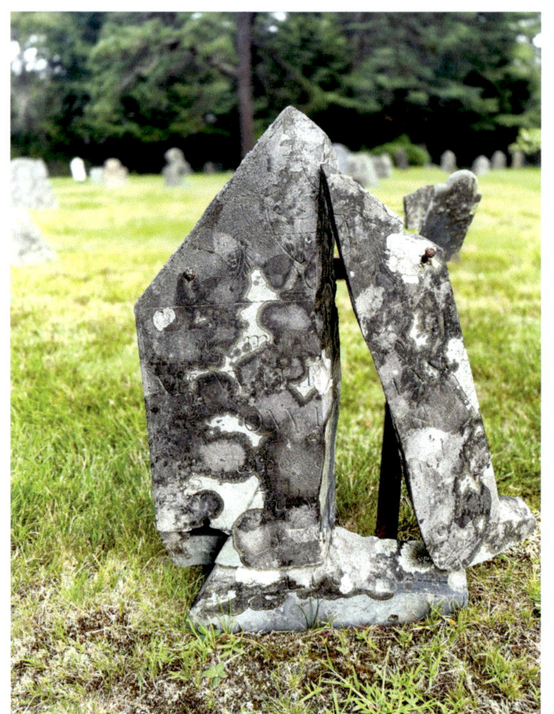

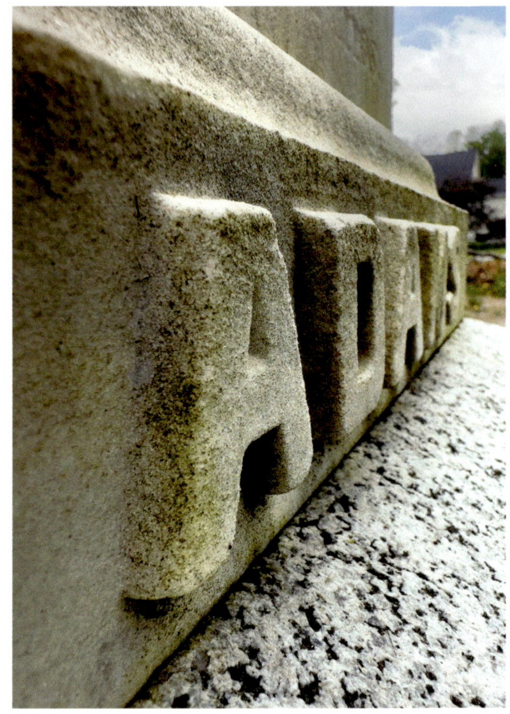

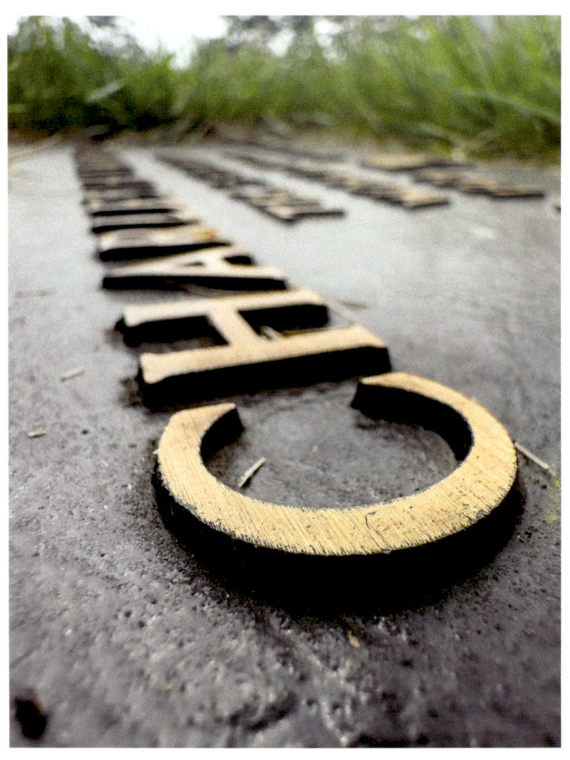

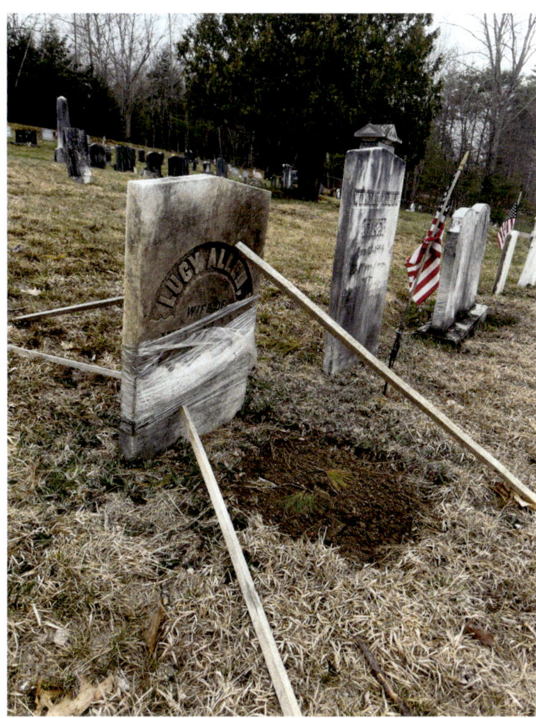

Plastic wrap and garden stakes as a means of preservation.

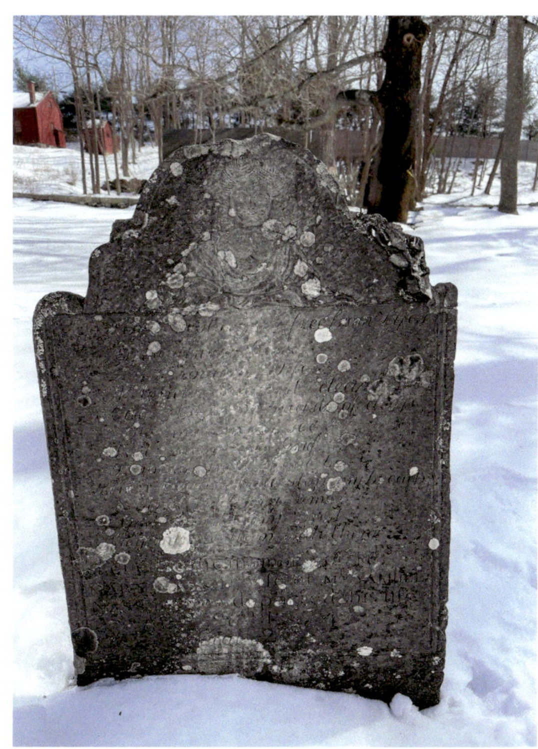

Mary Nasson died in 1774, however, her story continues to this day. Mrs. Nasson, years after her death and burial, would come to be called a witch.

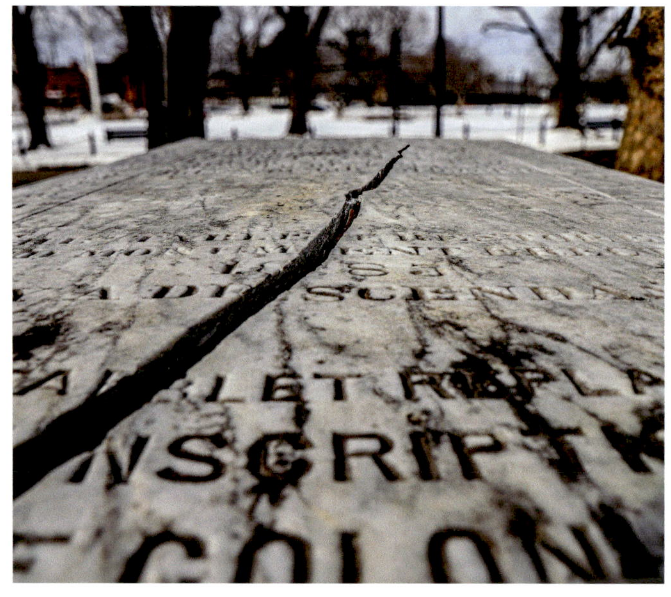

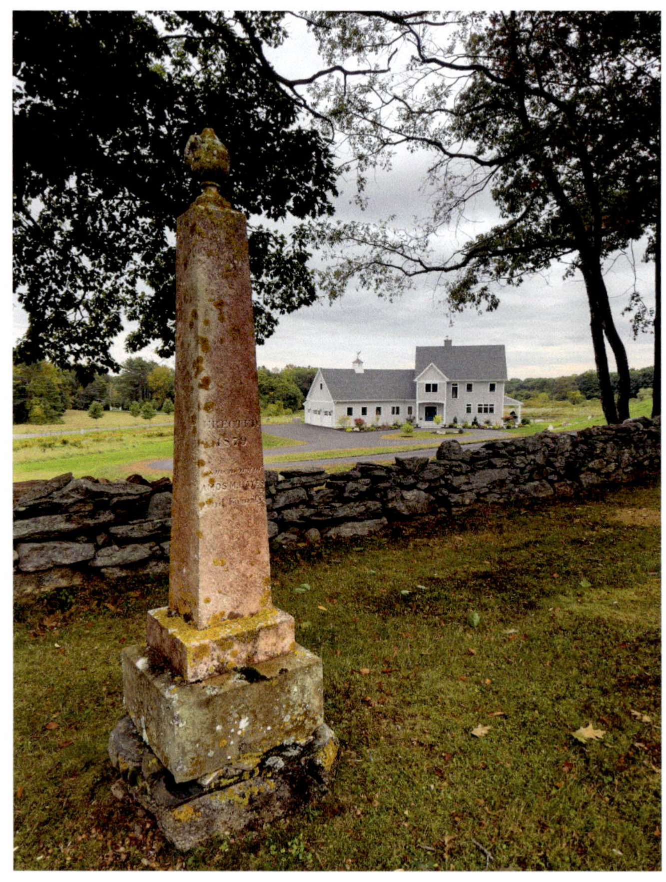

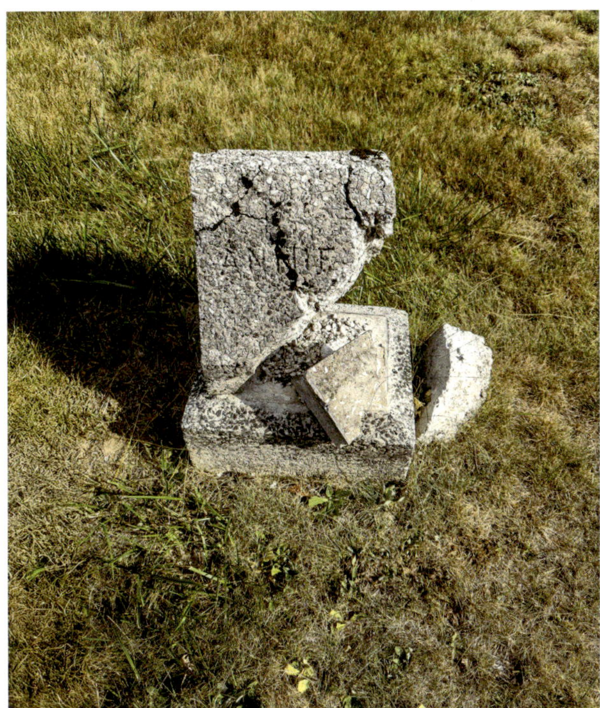

Right: Granite stones, while popular for a time, in the end proved too fragile to be tombstones.

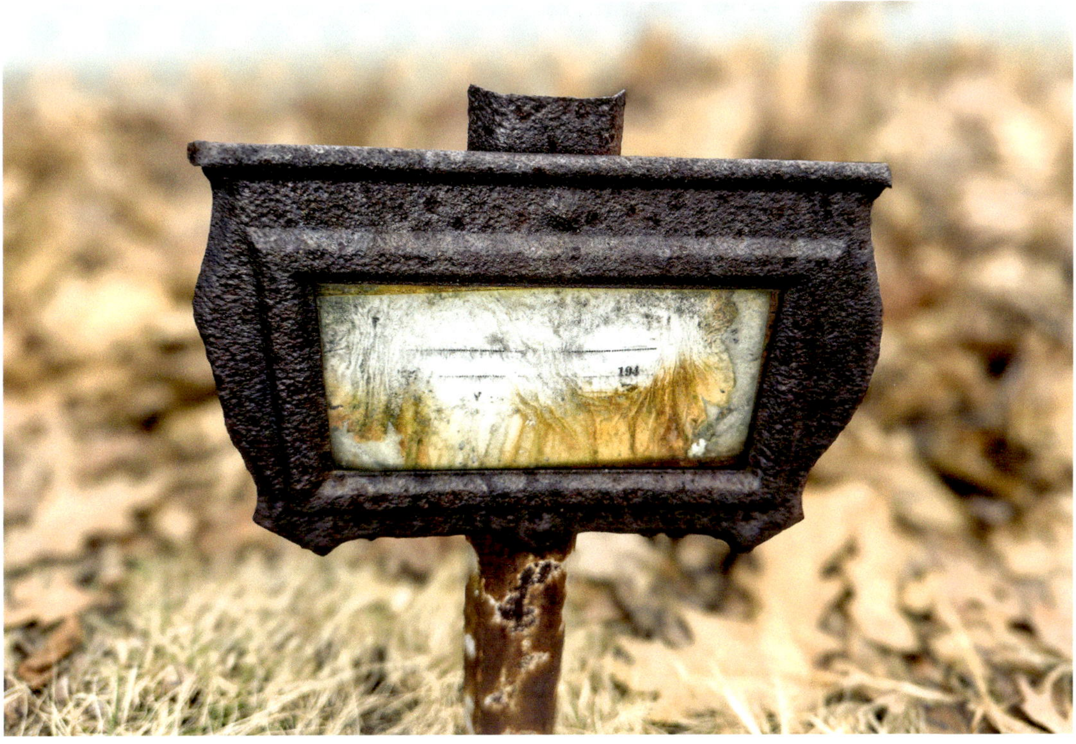

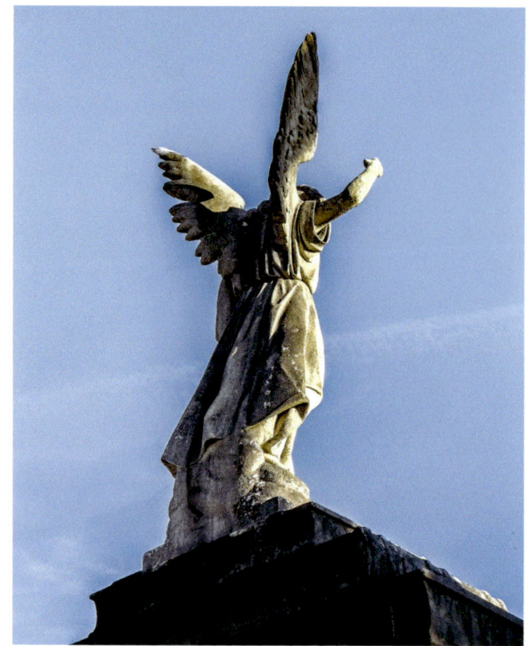

With an arm raised, this southern Maine grave topper sits high above the cemetery.

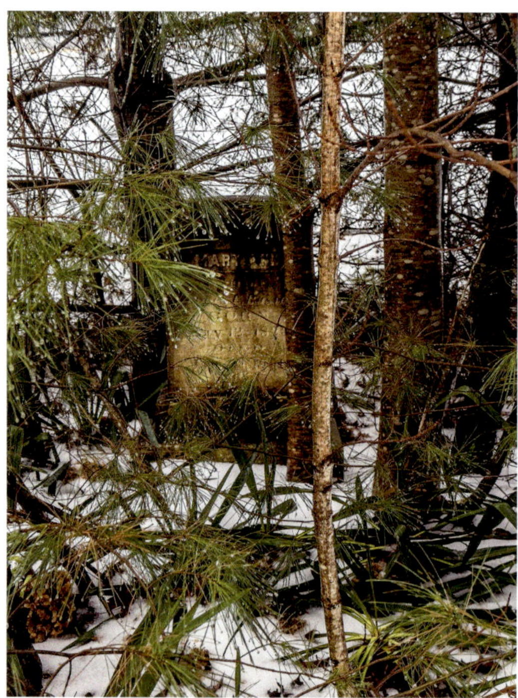

Lost in plain sight.